HAUNTED HOUSES
OF BRITAIN AND IRELAND

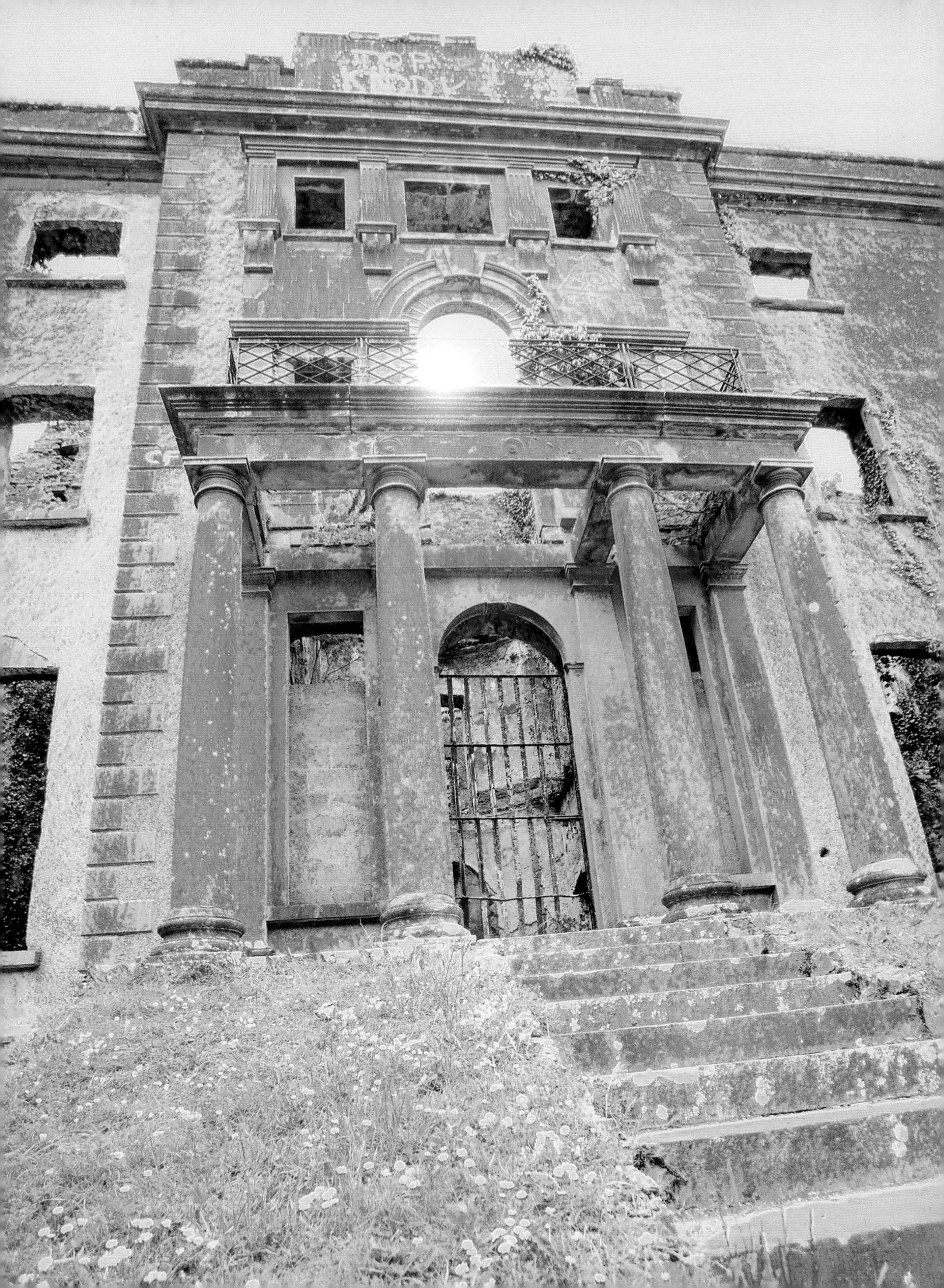

HAUNTED HOUSES
OF BRITAIN AND IRELAND

RICHARD JONES
Photography by JOHN MASON

NEW HOLLAND

First published in 2005 by
New Holland Publishers (UK) Ltd
London • Cape Town • Sydney • Auckland

www.newhollandpublishers.com

Garfield House, 86–88 Edgware Road,
London W2 2EA, United Kingdom

80 McKenzie Street, Cape Town 8001, South Africa

14 Aquatic Drive, Frenchs Forest,
NSW 2086, Australia

218 Lake Road, Northcote, Auckland, New Zealand

10 9 8 7 6 5 4 3 2 1

ISBN 1 84330 973 4

Publishing Manager: Jo Hemmings
Senior Editor: Charlotte Judet
Design: Alan Marshall
Cover Design: Adam Morris
Maps: William Smuts
Production: Joan Woodroffe

Reproduction by Pica Digital Pte Ltd, Singapore
Printed and bound by Kyodo Printing Co (Singapore) Pte Ltd

Page 1: Melford Hall, Suffolk
Page 2: Moore Hall, Ireland
Page 3: Harlaxton Manor, Lincolnshire
Opposite: Doddington Hall, Lincolnshire
Page 157: Woodstock House, Kilkenny, Ireland
Page 160: Little Moreton Hall, Cheshire

Contents

INTRODUCTION

In 1970 my parents took my sister and I on a weekend break to Buxton and in the course of that break I purchased from the hotel's bookshop a copy of Andrew Green's ***Our Haunted Kingdom***. For the remainder of that weekend I sat engrossed in that little paperback and by the time we left Buxton I was absolutely hooked on real-life ghost stories. That fascination has remained with me ever since – as indeed has Andrew's book which, although somewhat tattered from constant usage, still takes pride of place in my library.

Over the years since I first read that book I have come into contact with many people who have seen and experienced ghosts, and have listened to their recollections with the same intensity of fascination that I first felt 34 years ago. I have watched other people's reactions when I have shared my ghostly tales and am always amazed that, whether a person is an avowed sceptic or an affirmed believer, the telling of ghost stories can tweak the interest of both parties in equal measure.

Whilst researching this book I paid a visit to Hellens, the wonderfully eccentric and historic manor house in the equally eccentric-sounding village of Much Marcle in Herefordshire. A group of about ten of us were taken round and each of us kept to ourselves, listening to the guide's commentary, admiring the history and furnishings, but all the while maintaining that dignified detachment from our fellow visitors that seems to mark every historic house tour I've ever taken. But when we got to the haunted 'Queen Mary's Bedroom' something changed. The guide had just finished telling us about the room's resident ghost when an elderly gentleman, who seemed to me to have the bearing and tone of a magistrate, proceeded to regale us with the tale of how he had once seen a ghost. Suddenly everyone began swapping ghost stories and for the rest of the tour we were all chatting amicably about our surroundings, suggesting other haunted places that were worth a visit and genuinely enjoying each others' company. All because one of our group had felt compelled to tell us about the day he had visited a haunted house.

In the pages that follow you will find tales of the ghosts that haunt over 100 such houses throughout Britain and Ireland. There are grand palaces and stately homes, smaller family properties, and a fair number of houses that have long since fallen into ruin and which now stand as melancholic reminders of their days of glory. The one thing they all share in common, aside from being haunted, is that they are all open to the public. Some as historic houses, others as

RIGHT: *Little Moreton Hall was built on land that the Moreton family have owned for 700 years. The house was built by three generations over a period of some 120 years, beginning in the mid 15th century.*

ABOVE: *Chambercombe Manor has been lovingly restored from its time as a lowly farmhouse.*
OPPOSITE: *Paranormal Investigator Phil Wyman considers Llancaiach Fawr Manor to be one of the spookiest places he's ever visited.*

museums, and a number of them as hotels that offer the prospect of a decent night's unrest in their haunted bedroom!

Ghost stories are growing more and more popular with each year that passes. One of the most successful recent shows on British digital television is Living TV's *Most Haunted*, in which a team of paranormal investigators opt to spend a night at a haunted location. It has achieved cult status in Britain and has truly seized the public's imagination, whilst sparking an interest in the paranormal with people from all walks of life. As a result, one thing that has become noticeable to me as I have been going about my researches is the huge increase in the number of investigative groups that have come together to follow in the programme's footsteps and likewise spend a night at a haunted property in an attempt to make contact with its spirits.

In addition, many venues have also wised up to the appeal of ghosts and it is now possible for the general public to spend a night searching for supernatural activity at places as diverse as the wonderful, and much haunted, Llancaiach Fawr Manor in Wales, or the far smaller, but equally haunted, Derby Gaol in the Midlands. The fact that these nights are always massively oversubscribed is testimony to just how popular interest in the supernatural has become. That so many people are eagerly seeking to actually see a ghost does, I think,

signify a change in popular attitudes, with spectres becoming more fascinating than fearful. Indeed, I have always believed that there is more to fear from the living than from the dead.

Personally speaking, I have always seen ghost stories as being an important part of our oral tradition and see myself as a collector of folklore rather than a paranormal investigator. In this, my seventh collection of supernatural tales, you will find a variety of such stories. Inevitably, since she is the most frequently seen type of phantom, the ubiquitous white, grey, green or blue lady is much in evidence. She is accompanied, however, by several other types of spectre that allow her to take a well-earned break for a few pages. I have also included opinions and reports from several paranormal research organizations who have graciously allowed me access to their files and furnished me with some insightful quotes. I have also featured my own experience at Moore Hall in Ireland, which though not particularly dramatic was, none the less, certainly affecting.

I hope that you will enjoy reading this book as much as I have enjoyed researching and writing it, and also I hope it will inspire you to visit some, if not all, of the properties featured. If you happen to be in the right place at the right time and a spectral presence should happen to materialize before you, I'd be delighted to hear the tale of the day you were fortunate (or unfortunate?) enough to see a ghost. Good Hauntings!

Richard Jones
South Woodford, 2004.
www.Haunted-Britain.com

GREY LADIES AND SECRET

BOUGHS

All houses wherein men have lived and died
Are haunted houses. Through the open doors
The harmless phantoms on their errands glide,
With feet that make no sound upon the floors.

We meet them at the door-way, on the stair,
Along the passages they come and go,
Impalpable impressions on the air,
A sense of something moving to and fro.

There are more guests at table than the hosts
Invited; the illuminated hall
Is thronged with quiet, inoffensive ghosts,
As silent as the pictures on the wall.

From 'Haunted Houses'
by Henry Wadsworth Longfellow (1807-1882)

CORNWALL, DEVON AND SOMERSET

Cornwall exerts a powerful and magical spell over those who roam its lanes and byways in search of its secret, sacred and haunted places. '...[It] is pre-eminently the region of dream and mystery' wrote Thomas Hardy in 1870, describing his first experience of Cornwall, and few who have stood on its windswept cliffs or strayed into its timeless towns and villages can disagree with his description. It is an otherworldly gateway to the haunted realm beyond which lie the counties of Devon and Somerset, both of which are steeped in history and mystery and have much to tempt the intrepid ghost-seeker. The haunted houses that dot the West Country's spectral landscape are both fascinating and varied. They include the beautiful Lanhydrock House in Cornwall, where much psychic activity has been reported in 2004, and the equally picturesque Lewtrenchard Manor in Devon, where visitors not only can hear in hushed whispers 'all abut the ghost', but can also enjoy a night's haunted hospitality at what is now a luxury hotel.

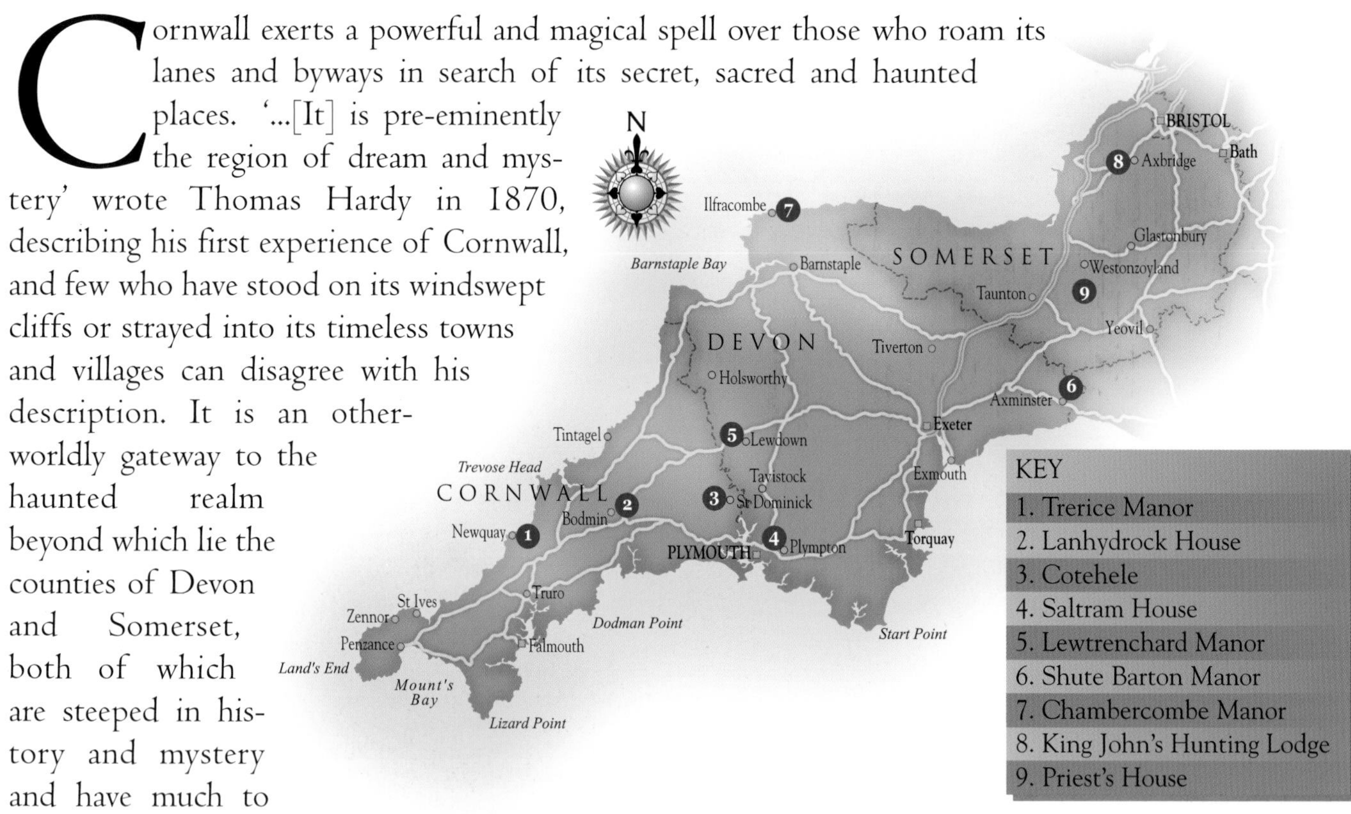

TRERICE MANOR

NEWQUAY, CORNWALL

The Ghostly Stable Boy

Built in 1573 by Sir John Arundell, Trerice Manor enjoys a secluded setting in a sheltered valley and nestles at the end of a winding, narrow lane. It gives the overall impression of being rooted firmly in a bygone age, its buff-coloured walls untouched by time. During the Civil War, the Arundells were staunch Royalists and as a result their fortunes suffered a downturn during Cromwell's Protectorship. This, however, proved little more than a blip in the family fortunes, for after the Restoration of the Monarchy in 1660 their estates were restored. In the 18th century they began spending less and less time at their Cornish retreat and in 1802 their 400-year occupancy ended and Trerice Manor passed to the Acland family. The Aclands set about restoring the property's great chamber and today this is undoubtedly its chief glory.

In 1915, after a residence of a mere 113 years, the family sold up and it was during this period that the first signs of otherworldly inhabitants became apparent. A guidebook from

PREVIOUS PAGES AND OPPOSITE: *An indignant stable boy is just one of several ghosts that haunt Cornwall's delightful Trerice Manor.*

this period describes Trerice as 'an ancient baronial mansion, which the country people still declare to be haunted...'. Tradition maintains that at some stage in the manor's long history 'wicked lord Arundell' seduced a young servant girl and cruelly discarded her when she became pregnant. The poor girl committed suicide and ever since her ghost has lingered. She is never seen, however, and the only way of knowing that her phantom is abroad is when the temperature drops suddenly and the delicate aroma of lilac fills the air. People have claimed that they have sensed her presence drifting past them and several have even reported hearing the rustle of her skirts as she goes by. She appears to have a fondness for the library, and many people have commented on the eerie ambience of that particular room - some visitors even pause on its threshold and refuse to enter. It is uncertain if she is the 'Grey Lady' whose solemn form is usually seen drifting around the house's gallery, or whether she is responsible for the inexplicable bumps and other noises that have been heard throughout the building at various times of the day and night.

Trerice Manor's other ghost is that of a stable-boy whose spectre appears in the vicinity of the courtyard and stables. It is said that he was killed when the horses bolted suddenly and trampled him to death. Perhaps the sheer terror of his final moments caused his spirit to become trapped at the place of his violent death? Or could it be a case of spectral indignation at the fact that his beloved stables now serve as the manor's public lavatories?

LANHYDROCK HOUSE

BODMIN, CORNWALL

Ghosts In Trust

One of the most fascinating late-19th-century houses in England, Lanhydrock is a place of rare beauty. Its 50 rooms are full of period atmosphere and are crammed with the trappings of a high Victorian country house. From the simplicity of the maids' bedrooms and the quaintness of the Nursery Wing, to the sheer breathtaking splendour of the Long Gallery with its beautifully worked plaster ceiling depicting biblical scenes, this is a house that warrants much more than a cursory visit.

The house was built in 1630 by the immensely wealthy Robartes family and successive generations of the family lived there for the next 300 years. The grandiose residence that greets visitors today, however, is the result of a 19th-century rebuilding, following a disastrous fire in 1881 that left only the north wing, entrance porch and gatehouse standing. Sixty-eight year old Lady Robartes was rescued by ladder from an upstairs window, but found her ordeal so distressing that she died of shock a few days later. Lord Robartes was so distraught at the loss of both his wife and the family home that he died the following year and it was their son, Thomas Charles Robartes, who undertook the rebuilding and also restored the adjoining church in memory of his parents.

In 1953, the property was taken over by the National Trust who, along with the usual fixtures, fittings and furnishings, also acquired several resident ghosts into the bargain. There is the little old lady dressed in grey who has been seen in the Long Gallery and the Drawing Room. Witnesses are never aware that she is anything other than flesh and blood until they approach her, whereupon she vanishes into thin air. The distinct aroma of

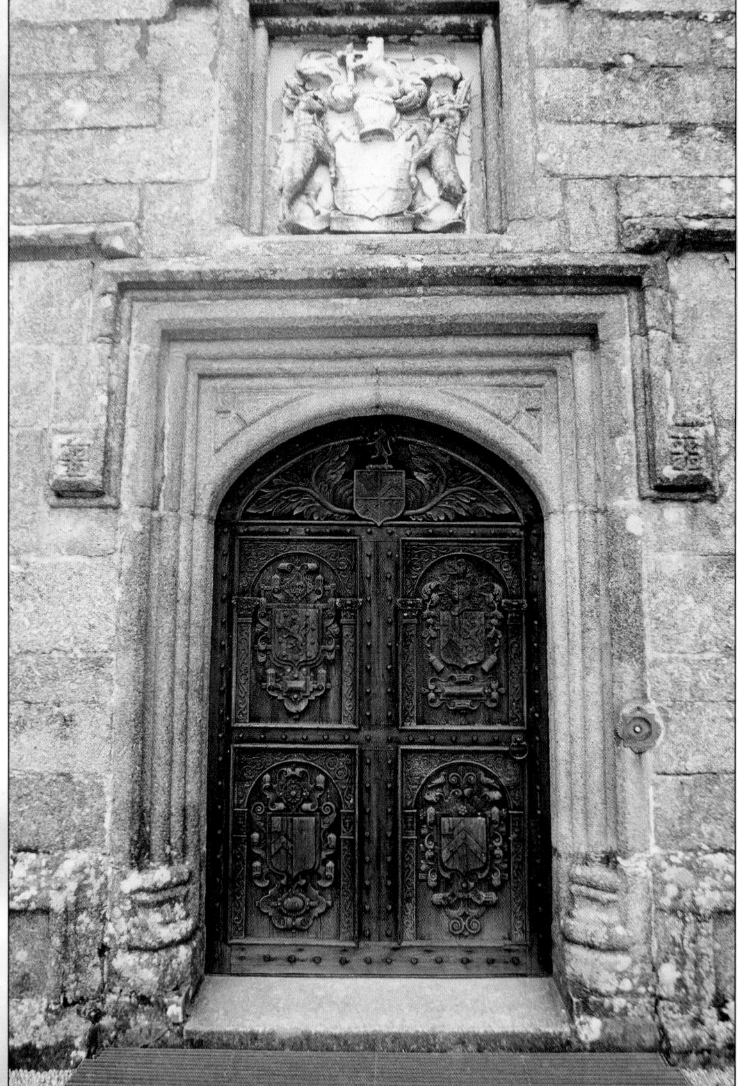

RIGHT: *Lanhydrock Manor is a place of rare beauty where many a ghost is known to wander.*

ABOVE: *A fragrant ghostly aroma is just one of the unexplained phenomena experienced at Cotehele.*

cigar smoke is another of the unexplained phenomena to be experienced at Lanhydrock House. In addition, several staff and visitors have over the years reported seeing or feeling various presences about the property, especially in the Long Gallery, the Nursery Suite, the male and female Servants' Quarters, the Prayer Room and the Prayer Room Corridor.

On 2nd July 2004 a team of investigators from the Cornwall-based Paranormal Research Organisation were invited to conduct a night-time vigil at the house to see if they could discover whether or not the property was haunted and if so, by who. Their President, Ian Addicoat, later reported that the group had achieved some remarkable results during their investigation and enthused about the 'sheer amount of activity' they had witnessed.

Several members heard the sound of a young girl giggling in the Nursery Suite, whilst others, including a journalist from the ***Cornish Guardian***, heard a sound that resembled 'a heavy table or chair being dragged along the wooden floor' of the Long Gallery. It occurred during a séance and appeared to be in response to investigator Mike Tomlinson asking any spirit present to make itself known in some way. It lasted for around five seconds, was quite loud and appeared to come from the dark recesses at the far end of the Gallery from where the group was sitting. Elsewhere, the Paranormal Research Organisation's 'biggest self-proclaimed sceptic' was somewhat taken aback when he witnessed a figure in the grounds where a male ghost is believed to walk. By the time the group came to leave the house all of them had witnessed some form of supernatural activity or inexplicable occurrences, and all agreed that the evening had been extremely worthwhile.

COTEHELE
ST DOMINICK, CORNWALL
The Girl In the White Dress

Constructed between 1485 and 1687 and little changed by the passage of time, Cotehele is blessed with a wonderfully intimate atmosphere. For centuries it was the home of the Edgcumbe family. Its solid, stone-built rooms contain rich tapestries, works of art and four-poster beds. Once you have walked the timeworn corridors throughout the property and feasted your eyes on the house's many treasures, let your imagination run riot and attune yourself to the many mysteries that crackle within its ancient walls.

ABOVE: *Plympton's Saltram House might look peaceful, but a long-ago act of infamy has left an indelible stain on its psychic fabric.*

SALTRAM HOUSE
PLYMPTON, DEVON
Murder on the Menu

Incorporating parts of a Tudor building that formerly stood on its site, Saltram House is a magnificent Georgian mansion that overlooks the Plym estuary. It is set in beautiful gardens, surrounded by 500 glorious acres of landscaped parkland. It was recently used as the location for Norland Park in the film adaptation of Jane Austen's ***Sense and Sensibility***, starring Emma Thompson, Kate Winslet, Hugh Grant and Alan Rickman. Its grandiose interior boasts ornate plasterwork, exquisite hand-painted Chinese wallpaper and several portraits by Joshua Reynolds - who was a friend of the Parker family whose house this was. If none of these are sufficient reasons to pay a visit, then there is always the chance of an encounter with several ghosts that can chill the marrow and perplex the mind in equal proportion.

Legend has it that at some stage in the distant past a kitchen maid was murdered in the house. The reason for her death and the identity of the murderer are now just two of the house's forgotten secrets. What is certain, however, is that her ghost still roams the property. A hooded figure in a dark cloak she glides across a corridor and melts through the door that leads into the dining room, although she never reappears on the other side. Another mysterious visitor to Saltram House is the ghostly child whose apparition a resident once woke to find sitting at the foot of her bed. The child said nothing, sat motionless for a few moments and then melted away into thin air.

Many visitors have commented upon the distinctive herbal fragrance that has been smelt all over the building. It is often accompanied by the sound of plaintive music, and occasionally hazy and indistinct figures are seen gliding about the house. In the past, servants used to talk of a girl in a white dress who was repeatedly seen in certain rooms, although her identity remains a mystery to this day. Visitors who have no prior knowledge of the ghostly girl have also encountered her and have remained unaware that she is a ghost. Only when they ask the staff about the young girl with the 'long hair' in the 'white, flimsy dress', do they realize that she is anything other than flesh and blood. Staff at the hall have been known to answer such enquiries with a brief shrug of the shoulders and the reassuring reply, 'Oh don't worry, You must have seen the ghost.'

LEWTRENCHARD MANOR
LEWDOWN, DEVON
Old Madame's Nebulous Wanders

Lewtrenchard Manor dates largely from the early 17th century. In 1626 its then owner, Sir Thomas Monk, found himself in prison for debt. In order to ease his financial predicament he sold the house to Henry Gould, and it is with his descendants that the history of the property is most inextricably linked.

On 19th March 1729, following her wedding at the nearby church, Susannah Gould was heading back up the drive of the house, when she suddenly let out a gasp and dropped dead from heart failure. Such a tragic end to so happy a day has inevitably left its mark upon the surroundings, and her forlorn phantom is said to drift sadly along the drive where the tragedy occurred - still dressed in her wedding gown.

In the 18th century, Captain Edward Gould made a valiant attempt to squander the family fortune at the gaming tables. Nicknamed 'The Scamp' by his family, Edward was not beyond resorting to desperate measures to recoup his losses. On one occasion, having suffered heavily during a game of cards, he dressed up as a highwayman and ambushed his gambling partner as he rode home. Unfortunately, the man resisted and the sadistic Edward shot him dead. 'The Scamp' was defended at his trial by John Dunning, a member of the family who was a brilliant and ambitious young lawyer. When the prosecution unveiled their sole witness, a man who claimed to have seen Edward commit the murder, and said that he had recognized his face by moonlight, Dunning produced an almanac showing that there had been no moon on the night of the murder, and so the witness must either be lying or mistaken. As a result, Edward was acquitted. Only later was it discovered that Dunning himself had had the favourable almanac specially printed! However, the trial left Edward penniless and he died in poverty in 1777.

Edward's mother, Margaret, then took over the property, and with dedicated astuteness set about rescuing the family finances. She was so successful that by the time of her death in 1794 the losses had been reversed and the house considerably improved. All who had dealings with her seem to have developed a genuine fondness and deep respect for this spirited matriarch and they gave her the affectionate nickname 'Old Madame'. She, for her part, had a great love for Lewtrenchard, and since her death has returned to the house many times to wander the Long Gallery, keeping a watchful eye on the comings and goings at her home.

Her daughter, Margaret, married Charles Baring, who was a member of the Baring's banking dynasty, and subsequent generations opted for the double-barrelled Baring-Gould. The most famous of these descendants was the Rev. Sabine Baring-Gould (1834-1924), a prolific writer and composer of such stirring anthems as 'Onward Christian Soldiers'.

Sabine Baring-Gould took Holy Orders in 1864 and was sent as curate to Horbury Bridge in Yorkshire. It was here that he met and fell in love with a 16-year-old mill girl named Grace Taylor. Having seen to it that she received an education, he married her in 1868 and in 1881 they moved to Lewtrenchard Manor, where he settled into his role of being both local squire and local vicar. Their marriage lasted for 48 happy years and produced 15 children. Their story is reputed to have provided the inspiration for George Bernard Shaw's *Pygmalion*. The size of his family appears to have caused Sabine Baring-Gould more than a little confusion. On one occasion, at a children's party, he is said to have called out to a young

BELOW: *Haunted Hospitality is just one of the luxuries on offer at Lewtrenchard Manor Hotel.*

ABOVE: *The tragic Lady Jane Grey may walk the corridors of Devon's Shute Barton Manor.*

child, 'And whose little girl are you?' The child promptly burst into tears and cried, 'I'm yours Daddy!'

Like 'Old Madame' before him, Sabine Baring-Gould lavished attention on Lewtrenchard Manor, and it is largely thanks to his efforts that it is in such good condition today. His portrait hangs in the front hall, whilst Grace's hangs in the back hall, and the whole house seems imbued with his spirit. It is, indeed, a little piece of secret England, lost in a sylvan landscape on the very brink of the bleak desolation of Dartmoor.

SHUTE BARTON MANOR
NR. AXMINSTER, DEVON
The Ghost of Lady's Walk

Shute Barton is one of the most important non-fortified medieval manor houses in England. It is entered through an imposing gatehouse, which is the earliest part of the property and dates back to 1380. The Grey family, who owned it throughout the 15th and early 16th centuries, were busily extending their property when, in 1554, they made the disastrous mistake of supporting the attempt to place Lady Jane Grey on the throne. Their properties were forfeited and the house was leased to the de la Pole family, who later purchased it outright. It is still the home of their descendants, the Pole-Carews, although it is actually run by the National Trust.

The house possesses a relaxed ambience, and although great changes have been made to the property, its ancient origins are still clearly visible, most notably in the Solar where there are two garderobes and exposed roof timbers. The house's entrance hall boasts the largest fireplace in England, which at 22 feet (6.5 metres) in width takes up the entire end wall of the room.

With such an impressive pedigree it would come as a great surprise if Shute Barton Manor House ***wasn't*** haunted. Fortunately, at least one former resident has chosen to remain behind as a grey lady. Her identity is uncertain, although some claim that it is the ghost of Lady Jane Grey, the so-called 'Nine-Day Queen'. Others, however, maintain that she was a member of the de la Pole family who is thought to have lived at the property during the Civil War. The de la Poles were staunch Royalists, and one day legend holds that a group of Parliamentarians ambushed this unfortunate lady as she walked through a grove near to the house. Placing a rope around her neck, they threw it over the branch of a tree and hanged her. A group of nearby trees is still known as 'Lady's Walk' in commemoration of this act of infamy. Her revenant is said to put

ABOVE: *Many people detect cold spots on the staircases at the lovely old Chambercombe Manor and some who have spent the night there have had their rest interrupted by its ghosts.*

in regular appearances near to the place where she was so brutally killed. Witnesses have described her as having a determined face, and an air of familiarity about her. Indeed, several have mentioned that she walks about 'as if she owns the place', which at one time she might well of done. She doesn't take kindly to being approached and should anyone attempt to do so she will fix them with an admonishing stare and a moment later vanish into thin air.

CHAMBERCOMBE MANOR
ILFRACOMBE, DEVON
He Robbed His Own Daughter

Chambercombe Manor is thought to date back to the 12th century. Although it most certainly saw days of glory (including a visit from Lady Jane Grey, herself a descendant of the house's original owners the Champernons), at some stage in its history it fell from its lofty pedestal and for much of its recent past was used as a farmhouse.

Yet it was as if during those lowly days the house was just biding its time, waiting for the dawn of a new era when it would awaken from its long slumber and bask once more in the grandeur of its surroundings. Thankfully, many of the original fixtures and fittings survived and today, thanks to the efforts of a dedicated Trust, the house and its grounds have been beautifully restored, and visitors can soak up its atmosphere, while keeping a keen eye peeled for its otherworldly inhabitants.

The origins of the house's most famous ghost go back to 1865 when the then tenant carried out repairs to the roof and came upon the outline of a window for which he could find no matching room. Mystified, he began a search of the interior and realized that there must be a hidden room between what is now Lady Jane Grey's Room and the one it adjoins. He and his wife broke through the wall and, poking a candle through the hole, gazed into the gloom of a secret chamber at the centre of which stood a four-poster bed surrounded by a musty curtain. Scrambling into the room, they pulled the bed curtain aside and found a gleaming white skeleton.

Although it was later ascertained that the skeleton was that of a young woman, subsequent enquiries failed to shed any light on either her identity or the cause of her death. A tradition grew up that the events which led to the woman's incarceration date back to the 18th century when the tenant of the house was a William Oatway. His father, Alexander, had been a notorious local 'wrecker'. Wreckers were villains who would wave lights from the shore during storms at night hoping to lure ships onto the treacherous coastal rocks, so that they could plunder the wrecks and murder any survivors.

William, however, was of an altogether more law-abiding disposition than his father. He married a beautiful Spanish woman, whom he had saved from one of his father's 'wrecking' expeditions, and leased Chambercombe Manor. He and his wife were extremely happy and their joy intensified when they had a baby daughter, who they christened Kate and who grew into a beautiful and spirited young woman. William's only regret was that he didn't have the money to purchase the house outright.

In time, Kate met and fell in love with an Irishman named Wallace, who was the Captain of a pirate ship. The two were married and decided to settle in Dublin. Tearfully, Kate bade her parents farewell but promised them faithfully that she would one day return for a visit. William and his wife settled down into a house that now seemed so empty without the presence of their vivacious daughter. But eventually they grew used to her absence and eagerly looked forward to the day when they would see her again.

One day a ferocious storm blew up along the Devon coast and William went down to the beach to see if any ships were in distress. As he stood gazing out to sea, bracing himself against the lashing rain and the howling wind, he heard a faint murmur from the nearby rocks. Clambering over them he found a badly injured young woman, whose bloodied face had been rendered unrecognizable by being smashed against the rocks. Lifting her up, William carried her to the manor house where he and his wife tried desperately to save her life. Her injuries, however, proved too serious and later that night she died without regaining consciousness.

As they searched her body for some clue to her identity they found a money belt around her waist. Opening it, William discovered that it contained enough gold coins and jewels to enable him to achieve his cherished ambition of owning Chambercombe Manor. The temptation proved too great – he reached out and relieved the dead woman of her valuables.

Next morning, a shipping agent came by to enquire if they had any knowledge of a woman passenger who was missing off a wrecked ship. Realizing that if he admitted to having found the woman he would probably be forced to return the valuables, William denied all knowledge of her. As

ABOVE: *No one had ever solved the mystery of why a ghostly cat should haunt King John's Hunting Lodge in Axbridge.*

the agent was leaving he asked William to keep an eye on the coastline should the body of the woman, Mrs Katherine Wallace, be washed up. William, realising that he had robbed the dead body of his own daughter, was horrified and reacted by walling her body up in a secret chamber and then he and his wife left Chambercombe Manor, never to return.

So runs one of several legends that attempt to explain the mysterious skeletal remains at Chambercombe Manor. Thus has Kate Wallace's ghost written itself into the history of this lovely old house, her spectral footsteps walking along its corridors, whilst a low moaning has been heard emanating from the former secret room where her remains were found.

But the ghost of Kate Wallace is not the only ghost to haunt Chambercombe Manor. Two spectral little girls have been seen in the upstairs rooms, whilst a phantom lady in a long white dress has been seen in the vicinity of the pond behind the café. Mediums visiting the house have picked up on several spirits including that of a rather friendly man, who once tried to possess a woman during a séance held in the Tudor Room. In addition to ghostly appearances, the house also has several cold spots and there is a staircase from the Dining Room to the Tudor Room that has a decidedly unnerving atmosphere and which few people like to go up!

King John's Hunting Lodge

Axbridge, Somerset

The Phantom Feline Moves Around

King John's Hunting Lodge is a much restored early Tudor merchant's house. Its name commemorates the time when Axbridge was a favoured base for royal hunting parties. It is a small, timber-framed structure that occupies a corner of the market square and which gives the impression of leaning wearily against its neighbours for support. Several visitors have reported sightings of a beautiful Elizabethan lady garbed in a shimmering white dress inside the house. Nobody knows who she was, or why she chooses to wander the old building in spirit form. The staff are somewhat dubious about her existence and dismiss her as little more than a product of overactive imaginations.

However, the other ghost that haunts the property is less easily doubted because it has been sighted by a number of local residents, who have been only too happy to talk of what they saw. It is the spectral form of a tabby cat which has been seen in the vicinity of the doorway to the panelled room on the building's first floor. Some witnesses have been honoured with a full manifestation of the phantom feline, whilst others have simply caught brief glimpses of its tail. But whenever a search is carried out in the wake of a sighting there is never any trace of the mysterious ghostly cat.

Priest's House

Nr. Langport, Somerset

They Should Never Have Married

This late medieval hall house was once the residence of the priests who served the parish church on the opposite side of the road. It has large gothic windows and a long tradition of being haunted. The legend centres on a nun and a priest who, at some unspecified date, fell in love with each other and were secretly married. The couple settled down to a furtive life of marital bliss and the girl was hidden away in a secret room known only to her spouse. But one day the priest was called away on some parish duty and when he returned he found his lover dead in their secret hideaway. Since then there have been several reports of strange happenings at the old house. A ghostly monk was seen by a former tenant on a regular basis and this man also heard doors banging in the dead of night, although whether these were anything to do with the mysterious death of the nun has never been ascertained.

BELOW: *A priest and nun's tragic love story appears to have left a ghostly monk to roam the night hours at the Priest's House.*

BATTLESCARRED ROAMING

WALLS AND REVENANTS

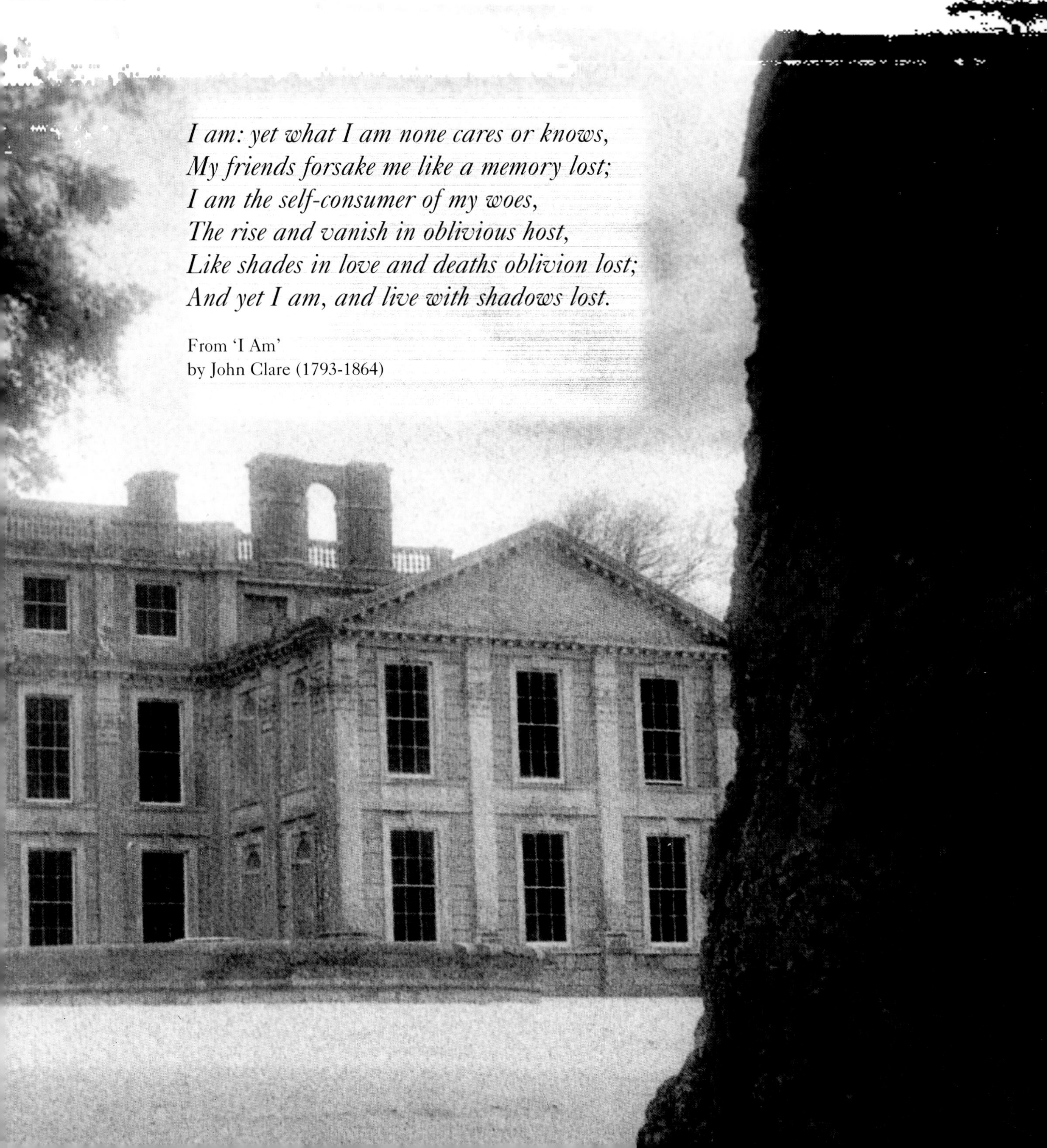

I am: yet what I am none cares or knows,
My friends forsake me like a memory lost;
I am the self-consumer of my woes,
The rise and vanish in oblivious host,
Like shades in love and deaths oblivion lost;
And yet I am, and live with shadows lost.

From 'I Am'
by John Clare (1793-1864)

DORSET, HAMPSHIRE AND WILTSHIRE

Once the core of the Saxon kingdom of Wessex, the legend-steeped landscapes of Dorset, Wiltshire and Hampshire are home to numerous haunted houses. This region is also the location of the prehistoric stone circle at Avebury, which is both larger and older than Stonehenge to the south. Many of its stones were incorporated into the lovely Avebury Manor, and perhaps some lingering vestige of these stones' power is responsible for the ghosts that haunt that delightful building. The area also contains the stunningly impressive Longleat, home to the Marquess of Bath, where in addition to hunting for ghosts, visitors can seek out the famous Lions of Longleat. Finally, it is worth taking the opportunity to journey to the Isle of Wight, which, despite being hardly any distance offshore, is a world removed from the mainland and possesses a magical aura where you just know that anything is possible.

KEY

1. Sandford Orcas Manor
2. Purse Caundle Manor
3. Athelhampton Hall
4. Longleat
5. Avebury Manor
6. Hinton Ampner Garden
7. Basing House
8. Appledurcombe Manor
9. Arreton Manor

SANDFORD ORCAS MANOR
SHERBORNE, DORSET
England's Most Haunted House

Only two families, the Knoyles and the Medlycotts, have actually occupied Sandford Orcas Manor since it was built in the early 1530s. It is an eerie-looking building the grey stone walls of which give the appearance of being every inch the traditional haunted house. Indeed, so many ghostly tales swirl around it that many people consider it the most haunted house in England. Intrepid ghost hunters really have their work cut out with the 14 ghosts that are said to reside here.

Colonel Francis Claridge, who leased the manor between 1965 and 1979, grew used to sharing his home with the ghosts of numerous former residents, but then his family motto was 'Fear nought but God'. One evening when he was closing the house to visitors he caught sight of an unkempt-looking lady who proceeded to walk through the gate and onto the grass. She seemed oblivious to his presence and so the Colonel went over to confront her. But no sooner had he walked onto the grass himself, than the woman suddenly melted away into thin air.

ABOVE: *Paraphysical researchers have decided there is a 'prima facia' case for Sandford Orcas Manor being haunted.*

PREVIOUS PAGES: *A tale of debauchery is just one of the many intrigues to ponder upon at the Isle of Wight's eerie Appuldurcombe Manor.*

It is believed that in the 18th century a farmer committed suicide by hanging himself from a trapdoor inside the house. Quite what tragic circumstances caused him to take his own life are now long forgotten, but his ghostly form has been seen roaming around the building. His nebulous ramblings received considerable publicity in the mid-1960s when a member of a BBC production team caught a glimpse of a man dressed in what she described as an old-fashioned farmer's hat and smock. She became ill with fright when it was explained to her that she had in fact seen the ghostly farmer.

More disturbing is the ghost of a former footman who, when alive, used to while away his spare time molesting the maids. Death has, apparently, done little to discourage his wickedness, as Colonel Claridge's daughter found out shortly after the family took up residence. Determined to see for herself whether there was any substance to the rumours of a mysterious tapping being heard in one particular room, she opted to spend a night there. No sooner had she fallen asleep than she was rudely awoken by a supernatural force which threw her to the floor. Suddenly, she was grabbed round the throat by icy, invisible fingers, but fortunately was able to fight her way free and flee the room. She refused to enter the house again after nightfall.

A lady in a beautiful red silk, Georgian dress; a little girl in black who is seen at the foot of the stairs; a wicked priest, whom guests have awoken to find bending over their beds holding a black cape with which he appears to be about to smother them; and a sinister man who walks from the gatehouse to the staff quarters, leaving the stench of decaying flesh in his wake, are just some of the other ghosts that haunt Sandford Orcas Manor. If an encounter with any of these is insufficient to cause cold shivers, there is always the ghost of the young man who, having grown up in the house, set off to join the navy. No sooner had he enrolled at Dartmouth College than he killed another cadet, was judged insane and sent back to Sandford Orcas Manor, where he was locked in a room at the back of the house, which he was never allowed to leave. He is said to have died at the age of twenty-seven and to have been buried in a secret passageway behind the Great Chamber. On certain nights when the moon is full, his ghostly cries are said to echo throughout the property and he is heard banging on the door of the room screaming to be released.

There are some who suggest that the ghosts of Sandford Orcas Manor are little more than the products of overactive imaginations, although those who have experienced them will testify to the fear they can inspire. So perhaps the last word on this most haunted of haunted houses should go to the group of fearless investigators from the Paraphysical Laboratory at Downton who, having carried out a detailed investigation of the house's ghosts, concluded that 'a reasonable prima facia case had been made out for the hauntings.'

PURSE CAUNDLE MANOR
SHERBORNE, DORSET
The Hounds Depart

Purse Caundle is a delightful little village at the centre of which stands a fine 15th-century church and an enchanting manor house, dating from 1470. The manor is haunted by several ghosts, the oldest of which belong to a previous house on the site, which was a hunting lodge owned by the Crown. This was the residence of one John Aleyn, whose duties included tending to King John's sick and injured hounds. Quite what long-ago event has caused these creatures to return to the manor in phantom form is unknown, but legend maintains that they come baying their ghostly way onto the bowling green on New Year's Eve and Midsummer's Eve. Their yapping and howling will last for a little time until they are brought to heel by a blast from a phantom horn blown by a ghostly huntsman. Thereupon they will dutifully disappear, returning once more into the past.

In 1874 the then owners of the manor took the drastic measure of removing the newel staircase, because a ghostly apparition that was often seen on it was causing consternation amongst the ladies of the house. Its removal appears to have had the desired effect and now, spectral hounds aside, the only regular haunting to occur at Purse Caundle Manor is the chilling sound of plainsong that has been heard drifting around the house and grounds. No one knows quite what lies behind this phenomenon because, as far as anyone knows, the house has never had any religious or monastic associations.

ATHELHAMPTON HALL
NR. PUDDLETOWN, DORSET
The Possessive Ape

A legion of ghostly tales come marching out of the mist-shrouded past of Athelhampton Hall, which is one of the most beautiful and historic houses in the west of England. Phantom duellists have been known to re-enact their conflicts in the Great Hall, whilst a 'grey lady' of unknown identity chills the blood of those who encounter her in the Tudor Room. On one occasion a maidservant saw her sitting in a high-backed chair and mistook her for a visitor who had stayed beyond the house's official closing time. She asked if she would mind leaving, whereupon the obliging revenant stood up, walked to the panelling and promptly disappeared into it. Another spectral visitor is that of a priest garbed in a black cassock who has appeared at sundry locations.

The most famous, and decidedly unusual, phantom to plod its weary way around the old house however is the spectral ape that was the adored pet of one of the daughters of the house. Jilted by a feckless lover, the heartbroken girl decided to take her own life and made her way to a secret chamber above the Great Hall where she could do the deed uninterrupted. Unfortunately, she failed to notice that her pet ape had followed her through the hidden doorway and when she

closed the door of the secret chamber, the poor creature became trapped on the stairway where it slowly starved to death. Now, when the shadows of night fall and the old hall settles from the activity of the daylight hours, the ghostly ape can be heard scratching upon the panelling, desperate for someone to release its spirit from its eternal prison.

LONGLEAT
WARMINSTER, WILTSHIRE
Her Ladyship's still searching

Sir John Thynne was a remarkable man who over a 40-year period worked his way up from a clerk of the kitchens to Henry VII, to a position of social power and great wealth. In 1541, during Henry VIII's Dissolution of the Monasteries, he paid the princely sum of £53 to acquire the former priory of the Black Canons of the Order of St Augustine, and he set about building a magnificent country pile that would reflect his wealth and status. When his first house was destroyed by fire, Thynne purchased a quarry of Bath stone and rebuilt it, although the property was unfinished when he died in 1580. The house has remained in the possession of his descendants ever since and subsequent generations of the family have left their mark on their magnificent house. In 1949 Longleat became the first of Britain's stately homes to be opened to the public.

ABOVE: *There are many reasons to visit Athelhampton Hall but a chance encounter with its spectral ape might not be to everyone's taste!*

ABOVE: *Lady Louisa still searches the rooms and corridors of Longleat hoping to be reunited with her faithful retainer.*

The house has proved an irresistible draw to visitors from all over the world, and so welcoming are its elegant corridors and sumptuous rooms that otherworldly visitors are also wont to put in occasional appearances. The most famous is the 'green lady' (some accounts maintain that she is a 'grey lady'), whose living self is said to have been Lady Louisa Carteret, the beautiful and saintly wife of Thomas Thynne, 2nd Viscount Weymouth. Thomas was reputedly an arrogant and thoroughly unpleasant individual and when he and Louisa married on 3rd July 1733, more than a few aristocratic eyebrows were raised at the thought of such an angelic lady marrying such an unpopular man. On 13th September 1734, Louisa gave birth to a son who was christened Thomas and who would become the 1st Marquess of Bath. A little over a year later she gave birth to a second son, by which time the marriage, if legend is to be believed, had hit a decidedly sticky patch.

Louisa had brought a footman to Longleat and the favouritism she bestowed upon him rankled with other servants. Some versions of the story maintain that the footman and Louisa were embroiled in an affair, others that he simply provided her with a shoulder for her to cry on as her marital problems increased. Either way, the other servants saw to it that word of her Ladyship's fondness for her footman reached his Lordship. Thomas wasted no time in punishing the unfortunate man. He ambushed him one day as he left the Old Library and threw him down the spiral staircase, breaking his neck.

The footman's corpse was carried downstairs and buried beneath the flagstones in the basement. Thynne then spread the rumour that the man had decided to leave on a sudden impulse and had been in such a hurry that he hadn't even bothered to say goodbye to his doting mistress. Louisa, however, was unconvinced and she took to searching the top floor rooms in the hope that she would find her faithful retainer, whom she was convinced had been imprisoned by her husband.

Shortly afterwards she became ill and died at their house in Mayfair on Christmas Day 1736. Thomas, overcome with remorse at the part his actions must have played in her demise, left Longleat and moved to nearby Horningsham where he died in 1751. However, there were whispers that the real reason he removed himself from the house was that he was terrified of being confronted by Louisa's ghost, which was known to walk the top corridor searching, ever searching for her footman.

In the early 20th century, when central heating was being installed at Longleat, workmen had to lower the floor in the basement in order to fit the new boiler. When they lifted the flagstones and began digging up the earth beneath, they found the body of a young man, which instantly crumbled to dust on being exposed to the air. All that remained was a skeleton and a pair of boots that dated from the early 18th century. It is widely accepted that the workmen had discovered the remains of the unfortunate footman and they were laid to rest in the same cemetery where, by an odd coincidence, the remains of his supposed murderer, Thomas Thynne, also lie buried. For the saintly Louisa there can be no rest and her ghost continues to walk its timeworn path along the upper floor corridor, desperate to be reunited with her loyal servant.

Avebury Manor

Nr. Marlborough, Wiltshire

The Stones are the Key

The mysterious ancient stones of the megalithic monuments for which the village of Avebury is famous, make intriguing neighbours to this splendid Tudor mansion, which has monastic origins, beautiful gardens and at least two resident ghosts.

ABOVE: *Broken up boulders from Avebury stone circle were used in the construction of Avebury Manor. Is it any wonder that strange things happen there?*

The first phantom to appear out of the past is that of a ghostly Cavalier whose spectral wanderings are presaged by a sudden drop in temperature, followed by the strong smell of roses. He is believed to be the ghost of Sir John Stawell, a staunch Royalist who was stripped of his possessions in the aftermath of the Civil War. His devastation at losing his beloved Avebury Manor appears to have proved eternal.

The house's second ghost belongs to that same conflict, although this one takes the form of a traditional 'white lady' who glides sadly around the house and grounds, much to the consternation of some who chance upon her. She is said to have been a girl of the household who flung herself from one of the building's upper windows in despair when her Cavalier lover was killed in a battle.

There can be no doubt that the village of Avebury is one of the most supernaturally charged locations in the whole of the British Isles, and to wander the gardens and corridors of its exquisite manor house is as rewarding as it is intriguing. Should you, in a quiet moment, be overwhelmed by the aroma of rose petals, or shiver at the eerie rustle of ancient skirts, comfort yourself in the knowledge that you have encountered ghosts at one of Britain's most mystical places.

HINTON AMPNER GARDEN

BRAMDEAN, HAMPSHIRE

Driven Out By The Ghosts

Designed by Ralph Dutton, 9th and last Lord Sherborne, Hinton Ampner Garden is regarded as one of the great 20th-century gardens. Although the house is worthy of a visit, it is to a previous property, which stood some 50 yards from the current building, that the ghostly occurrences belong. The Stewkelay family had owned the house since the end of the 16th century, and by the mid-18th century it was in the possession of Edward, Lord Stawel who had married Mary Stewkelay, a woman ten years his senior. When Mary died in 1740 Edward took up with her much younger sister Honoria, and local gossip was rife that he had had a child by her, although the infant mysteriously disappeared soon after birth. Whatever the child's fate, Lord Stawel was widely regarded in the district as a 'notorious evil liver', and when his mistress died in 1754 the gossips considered her death retribution for the wicked and debauched goings-on to which she had been privy. There suspicions seemed well founded when a year later Lord Stawel himself died from a sudden fit of apoplexy in the parlour of Hinton Ampner House.

Over the next ten years the house acquired a sinister reputation. Locals whispered in hushed tones of strange sounds heard echoing from within its walls in the dead of night, and of the figure of a gentleman in a drab-coloured coat who was seen standing in the moonlight, holding his hands behind him in the manner favoured by the late Lord Stawell. By the end of the decade it was well known that the house was haunted and locals avoided it at night, whilst servants would never stay for very long, giving the ghostly goings-on as their reason for leaving.

BELOW: *Although the Garden of Hinton Ampner Manor is worth a visit, it is to a previous building on the site that the ghostly tales belong.*

Unperturbed by its reputation Mr and Mrs Ricketts rented the house in 1764 and set about turning it into a respectable family home. No sooner had they moved in, however, than the supernatural occurrences increased dramatically. Doors were slammed violently in the early hours of the morning and agitated footsteps were heard stomping through rooms. Convinced that some of the villagers had acquired spare keys to the house, Mr Ricketts changed all the locks, but to no avail. The strange events continued and the family came to accept that they were living in a haunted house.

In 1769 Mr Ricketts was called away to his estates in Jamaica and his wife and children were left to face whatever entities were on the prowl alone. No sooner had he left than the ghostly phenomena became far worse and one by one the servants left. Mrs Ricketts herself frequently heard the rustling of a woman's skirts and on one occasion was woken by the distinct sound of a man's heavy footsteps approaching her bed. In addition she would often hear a disembodied shrill female voice that would be joined by two equally nebulous male voices, yet despite the fact the spectral conversation was going on right next to her, she could never catch a word of what was being said.

Shortly afterwards Mrs Ricketts was visited by a close friend Mrs Gwynne and she, too, became familiar with the ghosts. One night Mrs Ricketts was scared half out of her wits by 'a most deep, tremendous noise, as if something was falling with great velocity and force' onto the lobby floor adjoining her room, followed by 'three dreadful shrieks that grew fainter and fainter as they appeared to sink into the floor'. It was decided that something must be done and Mrs Ricketts enlisted the assistance of her brother, Captain John Jervis, who together with his friend, a Captain Luttrell, set out one night to confront whatever entities were roaming the house. Having explored every room and examined every possible hiding place, the two men armed themselves with pistols and

'THREE DREADFUL SHRIEKS THAT GREW FAINTER AND FAINTER AS THEY APPEARED TO SINK INTO THE FLOOR'.

HINTON AMPNER MANOR

ABOVE: *Basing House was once the largest private residence in England. Its ghosts don't seem to mind that it has been a ruin for over three hundred years.*

settled down to watch and wait. Moments later they heard the sound of dreadful groans, and Captain Jervis felt something flit past him. The sounds continued and appeared to be coming from the floor directly above them, so the two men rushed upstairs and commenced a vigorous search of the premises, but nothing was discovered.

The next morning Captain Jervis declared that the house was an unfit residence for any human being and shortly afterwards Mrs Ricketts and her children moved out. A Mr Lawrence took over the tenancy but he suddenly left and the house remained empty until it was pulled down in 1797. No sooner had workmen commenced the demolition than under the floor of the lobby they uncovered a box containing a pile of bones and what, according to some witnesses, appeared to be the skull of a baby. Unfortunately, no professional opinions were sought as to whether or not these could be the remains of the infant whom the local gossips had long maintained was the child of Lord Stawell's relationship with his sister-in-law, Honoria.

Basing House

Basingstoke, Hampshire

Battered But Not Broken

Basing House once enjoyed the notable distinction of being the largest private residence in England. It was built for William Paulet, 1st Marquis of Winchester, a rich and influential servant of the Tudor monarchs whose climb up the greasy and precarious pole of courtly politics began in the reign of Henry VIII. In 1531 Paulet was created 'Surveyor of the King's Widows and Governor of All Idiots and Naturals in the King's Hands', and a year later, in May 1532, he was made Comptroller of the Royal Household. Paulet continued to serve the Crown loyally throughout the reigns of Henry's children, assuming greater heights of office when he became Lord Treasurer of England in the reign of Elizabeth I. When the Queen visited him at Basing House she was so pleased with the hospitality afforded her that she playfully lamented his great age, declaring, 'for, by my troth, if my lord treasurer were but a young man, I could find it in my heart to have him for a husband before any man in England.' Paulet was still very much in harness when he died at Basing House on 10th March 1572, at the ripe old age of almost ninety. He had served throughout the tempestuous reigns of four Tudor monarchs, had managed to avoid the pitfalls and fates of many of his contemporary statesmen, and had lived to see 103 of his own descendants. He instilled a deep sense of loyalty to the Crown into all the members of the Paulet family, a loyalty that would ultimately result in the destruction of Basing House.

During the Civil War John Paulet, 5th Marquis of Winchester, had fortified his palatial mansion against Parliamentary attack, and is said to have used his diamond ring to scratch the family motto, 'Love Loyalty', onto every window-pane in the house. Thereafter he successfully withstood a series of prolonged sieges and by 1644 Basing House was the last Royalist garrison on the route between London and Bath. On 8th October 1645 Oliver Cromwell himself arrived with a brigade of the New Model Army and six days later 3,000 Ironsides attacked the house, while a further 4,000 ringed it to ensure that no one escaped. The defenders fought gallantly but they were no match against their highly trained adversaries. When the fortress fell, the looting began. All the women and most of the men suffered the indignity of being stripped of their clothing. The Roundhead soldiers carted away any of the treasures that took their fancy, with Cromwell collecting a £250,000 worth of loot which, he declared, was 'good encouragement'.

The pillaging ended, most of the surviving male defenders were hanged, including four Catholic priests who had taken refuge at the house. John Paulet was taken prisoner and removed to the Tower of London, although Cromwell spared his life and allowed him to escape to France. Finally, his house was set on fire and around 74 of the captive garrison were simply left to perish in the flames. The local people were then allowed to cart away the stone and bricks in order to rebuild their own houses, and Basing House became little more than a melancholic ruin.

It is not surprising that with such a dramatic history the ruins of Basing House are thoroughly haunted. No less a personage than Oliver Cromwell is just one of the spectres that are said to wander the ruins. There is also the shadow of a giant man that has been seen flickering across the grounds, leaving sensations of terrible coldness in its wake. Ghostly footsteps have been heard walking up and down stairs in the visitors display area, and several visitors have even smelt the overwhelming odour of thick smoke, which is perhaps a lingering psychic impression of that long ago day when the gallantry of the defending garrison ended in terrible conflagration.

BELOW: *The sobbing cries of a distressed infant have echoed around the eerie shell of Appuldurcombe Manor.*

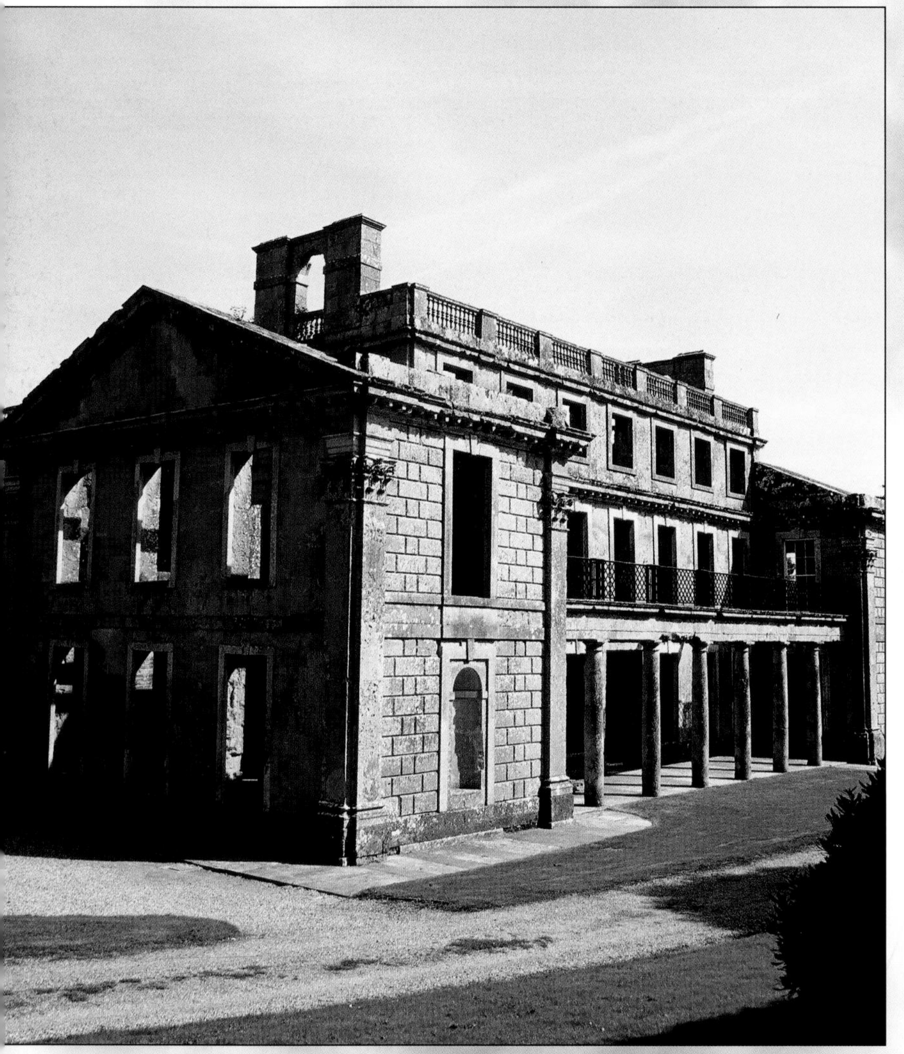

Appuldurcombe Manor

Wroxall, Isle of Wight

A Dream Home With Ghostly Residents

The building of the present Appuldurcombe Manor was begun in the early 1700s on the site of a former Tudor mansion house. It was begun by Sir Robert Worsley, extended by his great nephew, Sir Richard Worsley, and by the time it was finished it boasted 52 rooms (one for each week of the year), 365 windows (one for each day) and was considered one of the grandest houses on the Isle of Wight. Unfortunately, no sooner had Sir Richard completed his dream home than his wife, Lady Seymour, ran off with Captain Maurice George Bisset. Sir Richard sued Bisset for £20,000, but at the subsequent court case his wife admitted that Bisset was just one of 27 lovers and that her husband had not only condoned her infidelities but had positively encouraged them! Sir Richard was awarded just one shilling in damages and the resultant disgrace ruined him. His death in 1805 brought to an end the Worsley association with Appuldurcombe Manor, and thereafter the house passed through several ownerships and usages. It has been a hotel, a school for young gentlemen, a temporary home for the monks of Quarr Abbey and a billet for troops in both world wars.

Today, it is little more than a hollow shell, its floors and walls devastated by the combined effects of time, the elements and vandalism. Yet every so often some dormant vestige of its past stirs within its hollow bulk and ghosts of yesteryear walk once more through the places that they knew in life. Most disturbing of these lingering psychic imprints is the sound of a baby crying. This is most often heard in the vicinity of a hedge where the house's wash-house and laundry used to stand. It is so distinct that several people have been convinced that an infant has genuinely been abandoned, and it is only after a thorough search has revealed nothing that they accept the cries have a ghostly origin.

The house's most persistent ghost, however, is that of the 'mad' monk, described as being short in stature, dressed in a dark robe and carrying a lantern on a staff. This mysterious figure has been seen walking across a field directly in front of the house, although no one knows to which period or monastic order he belongs. The lands hereabouts were owned by the Church throughout the Middle Ages, and the house was occupied by the Benedictines from Quarr Abbey between 1901 and 1908, so the phantom friar could belong to either era. He is, however, a harmless wraith more inclined to incite curiosity than fear as he glides along his time-honoured path, intent on some duty that he may not have finished in life but which he appears determined to complete in death.

ARRETON MANOR

ARRETON, ISLE OF WIGHT

Bed, Breakfast and Bumps in the Night

Arreton Manor has a much more ancient pedigree than a cursory glance might suggest. Indeed, although the present building is Jacobean in origin, the manor itself goes back to at least 872. It was specifically mentioned in the will of Alfred the Great in 885, was later owned by Edward the Confessor, and then for over 400 years was in the possession of the abbots of Quarr Abbey until the Dissolution of the Monasteries (1536-1540), when their lands were forfeited to the Crown.

By the reign of Elizabeth I the Manor was owned by the immensely wealthy Barnaby Leigh. As Leigh languished upon his deathbed his son, John, became somewhat impatient with the amount of time it was taking for his father to die. Anxious to claim his inheritance sooner rather than later, John took a pillow from the bed, and pressing it hard over the old man's face, suffocated him. Setting down the pillow and rearranging the bed clothes, John turned to leave the room, eager to break the sad news of his father's demise to the rest of the family. But as he did so, he was horrified to discover his little sister, Annabelle, standing by the door watching him. Realizing that she had seen the whole incident, John rushed over, grabbed her by the arm and dragged the terrified child to an upstairs window from which he flung her to her death.

Needless to say, reverberations from those long-ago murders still echo within the history-steeped walls of this wonderful old property. Annabelle's restless shade is known to make regular returns to the house and grounds. Witnesses describe her as being aged about eight years old, with curly light blonde hair and wearing a long blue dress that reaches down to her ankles. Some don't actually see her but hear the sound of her childish, ghostly footfall as she walks invisibly along corridors and up staircases. The most disquieting aspect of her manifestations is the sorrowful little cry of 'Mamma, mamma', that her sad spectre has been heard to emit and which has moved witnesses to feelings of pity rather than of fear.

BELOW: *Two heartless murders have resulted in the distressed shade of a young girl being left earthbound at Arreton Manor.*

MIST-SHROUDED

Nor first, as I shut the door,
I was alone
In the new house; and the wind
Began to moan.

Old at once was the house,
And I was old;
My ears were teased with the dread
Of what was foretold.

'The New House'
by Edward Thomas (1878-1917)

Spectres of Bygone Days

Herefordshire, Gloucestershire, Worcestershire, Warwickshire and Oxfordshire

This region is rich in lore and legend and boasts an abundance of haunted houses to chill the blood of intrepid ghost-seekers. It was on this leg of my journey that I came across a house that I found truly enchanting, Woodchester Mansion. This unfinished 19th-century building is the house that time forgot, and its secret location – hidden within a steep, wooded valley - is truly heaven on earth. Whilst writing this book I was contracted to appear on Living TV's *Most Haunted Live* and witnessed possible poltergeist activity at Hall's Croft, Stratford-upon-Avon, the home of Shakespeare's daughter, Susanna, and her husband Dr John Hall. All in all this is a beautiful part of the country to explore and the chance of a ghostly encounter in its lovely old houses should more than reward a summer's or winter's afternoon of exploration.

Hergest Court

Kington, Herefordshire

The Faithful Hound

Hergest Court is now a shadow of its former glory. It is a sad-looking house of white walls and dark timbers that exudes a weary air of detached indifference. Yet, for longer than anyone can remember, it has held a reputation so sinister that, even today, there are people who will not walk past it during the hours of darkness for fear of encountering the frightful entity that haunts it.

Towards the end of the 15th century Sir Thomas Vaughan

resided at Hergest Court in the days when it was a grander and more heavily fortified property than the farmhouse that greets visitors today. Vaughan was the personification of the archetypal wicked squire, and was known in the district simply as 'Black Vaughan'. During the Wars of the Roses, he fought originally for the Lancastrians but switched his allegiance to the Yorkist cause and was killed at the Battle of Banbury in 1469. According to one version of events, he was decapitated, but no sooner had his head hit the ground than a fearsome howling echoed across the field of battle. Suddenly Vaughan's faithful, black bloodhound bounded across the blood-soaked ground, scooped up his master's head and set off at full pelt for Hergest Court with the gruesome relic jouncing in its jaws.

Thomas Vaughan's headless cadaver was subsequently buried in the rather eerie family vault in Kington church. But his ghost remained at large taking the form of a black bull that rampaged about the district accompanied by a fearsome black hound. So terrified did the inhabitants become that they refused to leave their homes to the detriment of the town's economy. It was therefore decided that an exorcism must be performed and 12 priests summoned forth Black Vaughan's evil spirit. It took a great deal of shouting, chanting and bible quoting, but eventually they reduced him to the size of a blowfly and confined him inside a snuff box which was then buried under a heavy stone slab on the bed of the lake at Hergest Court.

The spirit of their wicked Lord may have been laid, but ridding the district of his fearsome bloodhound proved an impossible task and during the centuries that followed it came bounding onto the pages of local folklore to strike terror into the hearts and minds of all who crossed its path. It was especially feared by the Vaughan family to whom it remained a harbinger of death until the immediate family became extinct in the 19th century.

According to a local tradition, Sir Arthur Conan Doyle viewed the Hound of the Vaughans as a source of inspiration rather than fear, and incorporated both it and the evil squire into ***The Hound of the Baskervilles***, transferring the action to the bleak desolation of Devon's Dartmoor.

RIGHT: *Did the Phantom Hound of Hergest Court inspire Sir Arthur Conan Doyle's* The Hound of the Baskervilles?

PREVIOUS PAGES: *Hellens is a secret place that rewards ghost seekers with a truly haunting ambience.*

HELLENS
MUCH MARCLE, NR. LEDBURY, HEREFORDSHIRE
Hetty's Long Imprisonment

During the Civil War, Fulke Walwyn rode out through the 17th-century wrought-iron gates of his family home, Hellens at Much Marcle, and headed off to lend his support to a besieged Charles I. Unfortunately, when Charles was routed by the Parliamentarians, Fulke was unable to return and chose instead to keep a low profile in nearby Hereford. The grand gates, which had been locked behind him, were never reopened and remain locked for almost 400 years – just one of the many curiosities at this truly curious house.

Its most famous ghost story is centred on the John Walwyn bedchamber named for the 17th-century owner of the house whose youngest daughter, Mehettabel, or Hetty, eloped with a man whom the family considered to be beneath her social class. By the time she was twenty her husband had died and Hetty returned home. Her unforgiving family locked her in the bedchamber for 30 years, because she had brought disgrace upon them and her indiscretion had rendered her unmarriageable. A length of rope connected to a bell in the roof still hangs through the ceiling into the room. This was her only means of letting the rest of the family know if she was in trouble. She whiled away her time gazing down onto the courtyard below and using her diamond ring to engrave upon a window-pane the poignant lament: 'It is a part of virtue to abstain from what we love if it should prove our bane.' Her words can still be read today and her ghost is the most prominent of several that wander during the night hours at Hellens. Curator Nicholas Stephens, who lives at the house with his family, told a local newspaper '... I did see Hetty myself a couple of years ago. I was sleeping in the room above hers when I saw her. It wasn't a fleeting glance, she stayed there for a sustained time.'

Hellens' other haunting centres on Queen Mary's Room, so-called because Mary Tudor is reputed to have stayed there.

ABOVE AND BELOW: *The Ghost of Hetty Walwyn joins with that of a murdered priest to make a visit to Hellens a memorable experience.*

The ghost belongs to the turbulent Cromwellian period when Catholicism was outlawed and an elderly Catholic priest was being sheltered at the house. One day a band of Parliamentarian soldiers launched a raid and caught the priest unawares in the hallway. Desperate to evade them he fled up the stairs in search of a suitable hiding place. The roundheads cornered him in Queen Mary's Room and cold-bloodedly hacked him to death.

The violent trauma of his death has left traces on the surroundings and several people who have stayed in the room have seen his ghost. On one occasion a naval lieutenant awoke to find a male figure, dressed in a long dark dressing-gown with a hood, frantically running backwards and forwards between the window and the door. So real did the figure appear that the lieutenant didn't even realize that it was a ghost and thought he was 'some dotty old member of the family who had escaped from his keeper!' It was only later that he learnt that he had in fact witnessed the revenant of the murdered priest.

Hellens is one of those special places where past and pre-

sent mingle and where the mark of history is imprinted on every inch of its ancient fabric. As you explore its atmospheric interior you get the very real sense that the eyes of past occupants are upon you. It would come as little surprise if a figure in period costume suddenly stepped from the shadows. It is a house that is well and truly timeless and there is a pervasive sense of it being both haunted and haunting.

ABOVE: *Woodchester Mansion sits lost at the end of a wooded valley and is the house that time forgot.*

Woodchester Mansion
Nympsfield, Gloucestershire
The House That Time Forgot

There is a sense of genuine enchantment about the sylvan landscape that cradles one of Britain's most enigmatic haunted houses. Woodchester Mansion is approached via a long and rutted track that meanders through a tranquil valley, where with every step you feel the modern age slip further behind you. Suddenly, you round a bend and there, huddled against a hillside, is a glorious vision in golden limestone. Turrets and towers loom over you, hollow windows gaze out and grotesques and gargoyles leer down from the soaring walls.

The valley now occupied by Woodchester Mansion was originally the estate of the Ducie family. Legend holds that when the 2nd Earl of Ducie threw a lavish dinner to celebrate his succession to the earldom in 1840, he was somewhat taken aback when his father's ghost interrupted the festivities by occupying the seat that he was intending to sit in at the head of the table. Indeed, it gave him such a fright that he left the place never to return.

In 1845 the northern part of his estate was purchased by William Leigh, an immensely wealthy gentleman and recent convert to Catholicism. Leigh set about planning a house that would stand as a lasting testimony to his Catholic leanings and approached Augustus Pugin, the master of Gothic Revival, whose designs included the Houses of Parliament. The two men, however, didn't exactly see eye to eye, especially where money was concerned, and by the 1850s the project was given to a much younger local architect, twenty-one-year-old Benjamin Bucknall.

Bucknall set about designing a truly grandiose house, and for 16 years craftsmen and builders laboured on its construction. Then suddenly in 1868, for reasons which have never been fully explained, the workers downed tools and left the site. Rumours persist that the workers left because of a murder on the site. It has even been suggested that supernatural activity may have been responsible. The likeliest explanation is that the project proved too costly, even for William Leigh's deep pockets, and the money

> 'So real did the figure appear that the lieutenant didn't even realize that it was a ghost'
>
> Woodchester Mansion

ABOVE: *A truly dramatic haunting used to be re-enacted at Chavenage whenever one of its owners died.*

simply ran out. Whatever the explanation, the result today is that on entering the mansion you step into a time warp and onto a mid-19th-century building site. Ladders remain propped where they were left against exposed walls, fireplaces hang suspended in mid-air, doors lead nowhere, and upstairs corridors end at precarious drops. The unfinished construction emphasizes the sheer magnitude of what this remarkable house would have looked like if completed.

Following William Leigh's death in 1873 his son, also William, asked Bucknall to supply him with two quotes, one for completion, the other for demolition. When both proved prohibitively expensive, the mansion was simply abandoned, although there was a sudden flurry of activity in 1894 when the drawing room was hurriedly completed for a visit by Cardinal Vaughan, Roman Catholic Archbishop of Westminster. This, however, was the only room ever to be finished and thereafter the house was neglected.

Without doubt one of the most curious parts of the house is the chapel. Some people have said that they have smelt freshly extinguished candles there, although no candles had been burning prior to the appearance of the mysterious aroma. Others have caught sight of a short man standing in one of the chapel doorways. He does nothing except gaze up at the ornate windows and gives the impression that he is somewhat concerned about them. It has been suggested that he may be the ghost of a stonemason and that he is anxious about the damage to the stonework caused by water penetration.

Woodchester Mansion is a truly unique place and a true aura of enchantment hangs over the whole edifice. I can honestly say that I found it one of the most moving properties I have ever visited. It was with some reluctance that I walked back along the rutted track and left the house to its memories, mysteries and shadows.

Chavenage
Tetbury, Gloucestershire
The King Came a-Calling

On a late December afternoon in 1648, a group of horsemen galloped along the rutted highways of Gloucestershire. Muffled against the bleak December weather they forced their mounts on until their hooves clattered along the approach to Chavenage, where Nathaniel Stephens, Knight of the Shire in Parliament, came out to greet the travel-weary band. Shaking their leader warmly by the hand, Stephens invited the group inside and closed the door against the winter's night.

Moments later frozen hands were cupped around warming tankards of hot spiced ale, and numbed limbs were thawing before a roaring log fire. It was then that the group's leader and Nathaniel Stephens left the rest of the company and settled down to discuss the matter that had brought Henry Ireton, son-in-law of Oliver Cromwell and a leading Parliamentarian, to Chavenage – the killing of King Charles I.

With the Civil War now over, and Charles Stuart a prisoner, it had become apparent to Cromwell that the King would have to be executed if Royalist uprisings were to be deterred. However, many baulked at the prospect of committing regicide. Amongst them was Colonel Nathaniel Stephens, a mild man who hesitated to support the decision to end the life of the King. As Ireton arrived at his door he had almost made up his mind against it. The two men are reputed to have sat up all night discussing and arguing the point and it was with great reluctance that the next morning Stephens finally agreed to give his acquiescence. Ireton returned to London and on 30th January 1649, Charles Stuart, King of England, was beheaded outside Whitehall Palace.

The fortunes of Nathaniel Stephens fared little better than those of the King. His daughter, Abigail, had been away at the time of Ireton's visit. She returned shortly after the New Year and was so furious at her father for bringing the family name into such disrepute, that she placed a curse upon him. Soon afterwards Colonel Stephens became terminally ill. Following his death, a hearse driven by a headless man is said to have pulled up at the manor house. Legend holds that Nathaniel Stephens rose from his coffin and, having knelt in reverence before the figure, was seen to climb into the hearse. As it sped away the headless coachman assumed the shape of Charles I, and this was seen as retribution for the Colonel's disloyalty to the rightful monarch. Thereafter, until the line became extinct in 1891, whenever a head of the family died the ghost of Charles I would reputedly appear in a spectral hearse to spirit him off to the great beyond.

Other spectres, however, have chosen to visit Chavenage in far less melodramatic fashion. Princess Marie Louise, a granddaughter of Queen Victoria, was a frequent visitor. Her lady-in-waiting, Mrs George Lowsley-Williams, wrote of her own ghostly experiences in her book, ***My Memories of Six Reigns***. On one occasion she was sitting sewing in an antechamber when a lady in an old-fashioned dress materialized before her and proceeded to drift into the adjoining bedroom where Princess Louise was resting. Mrs Lowsley-Williams watched the woman bend over the Princess, study her for a few moments and then back silently away, fading into nothingness as she did. The lady's identity was never discovered. Certainly no harm befell the Princess following the ghostly visitation. It might just have been that a long-dead resident was simply curious to get a closer look at such an illustrious visitor who just happened to be sleeping in ***her*** house.

Aston Hall

Trinity Road, Birmingham

His Lordship Was Not Impressed

Aston Hall was one of the last great homes to be built in the ostentatious Jacobean style. It was built for Sir Thomas Holte (1571-1654) who had previously resided at Duddeston Manor, where he was rumoured to have killed his cook in a fit of rage by splitting the poor unfortunate's head with a meat cleaver 'so that the left half of the skull fell onto his left shoulder and the right half fell onto his right shoulder'. However, the allegations proved unfounded and Sir Thomas subsequently won an action for slander against his accuser, William Ascrick.

In 1611, Sir Thomas purchased the title of baronet and, since he now outranked all the other local families, he decided that a grander home was necessary. He spared no expense in ensuring that it would reflect both his wealth and his new status. Aston Hall was completed in 1635 and seven years later, on 18th October 1642, Charles I came to stay, just before the Battle of Edgehill (the first major conflict of the English Civil War). In 1645 the house came under attack from the Parliamentarian forces and the damage inflicted by their cannon-shot is still clearly visible on the magnificent Great Staircase.

By all accounts Sir Thomas Holte was an arrogant, obstinate, mean-spirited bully. He was furious when his daughter refused to marry the husband he had chosen for her. Instead she attempted to elope with the man she truly loved, but was caught in the act and as punishment was locked in an upper room for 16 years until she eventually went mad and died. Her spirit, however, lingered on at Aston Hall as a ghostly white lady who still wanders the upper floor. She is seen at least twice a year by visitors who often assume that she is a member of staff in costume, only to discover that they have seen a ghost when they enquire after the lady in fancy dress. A medium once visited the house and succeeded in not only seeing the white lady's ghost but also talking with her. She learnt that her appearances are not motivated by regret at her incarceration but rather by a deep love and affection for the house itself.

Another ghost that is frequently seen at Aston Hall is that of a 'green lady', who it is thought may be the spirit of Mrs Walker, housekeeper to Sir Thomas Holte. In 1992 a boy on a school visit to the house saw her sitting in a shell-backed chair in the Great Hall. A woman who encountered her seated form in the armchair in the Housekeeper's Room mistook her for a guide and asked her a question. But no sooner had she done so than the mysterious figure vanished.

The roof of the house contains a long corridor that leads to the servants' quarters and the central tower. 'This gloomy spot ... is rendered still more dreary by the associations connected with it,' wrote Alfred Davidson in his 1854 history of

ABOVE: *Aston Hall stands as a lasting testimony to how important its first owner, Sir Thomas Holte, considered himself.*

the Holte family. 'It has long been known by the name of "Dick's Garret", being so denominated from a domestic who there hung himself from a low rafter in the roof.' Legend has it that Dick lived during the reign of James I and that he committed suicide when he was spurned by his lover. His dejected spectre was a common apparition in the 19th century, although in recent years his appearances have been few and far between.

Aston Hall stands as towering testimony to the ambition and wealth of its original owner, Sir Thomas Holte. Its ranks of chimneys, towers and gable ends stand firm against the modern structures - including Aston Villa Football Ground - that encroach upon it. It is a special place to which the ghosts of previous times seem drawn and from where they seem loathe to depart.

Hall's Croft

STRATFORD, WARWICKSHIRE

Flying spoons and Tumbling Ladies

Situated a stone's throw from Holy Trinity church where William Shakespeare is buried, Hall's Croft stands in Old Town Stratford and enjoys an idyllic almost rural setting. It is a fine, timber-framed house and is named for Dr John Hall, a highly successful 17th-century physician who was also the husband of William Shakespeare's eldest daughter, Susanna. The couple were married in June 1607 and purchased this desirable des res, which they extended to include an impressive consulting room and dispensary. Here Dr Hall dedicated himself to treating a whole gamut of human ailments and diligently recorded his efforts in a medical diary that was published posthumously in 1657 as Select Observations on English Bodies.

It is also probable that he tended to his father-in-law during his final illness in 1616. Certainly William seems to have placed a great deal of faith in his son-in-law's reputation and competence. He left the bulk of his estate to the Halls, evidently on the understanding that they would look after his widow, Anne Hathaway. The couple took up residence at Shakespeare's handsome town house, New Place, and ownership of Hall's Croft passed to a family of Stratford gentry. In the centuries that followed it served as a residence to professional classes such as doctors and lawyers, and then, in the mid-19th century, it was converted into a school, first for boys and then for girls. It reverted to a home in the 1880s when it became the residence of wealthy widow, Catherine Croker, who in 1899 let it for a few months to Queen Victoria's favourite

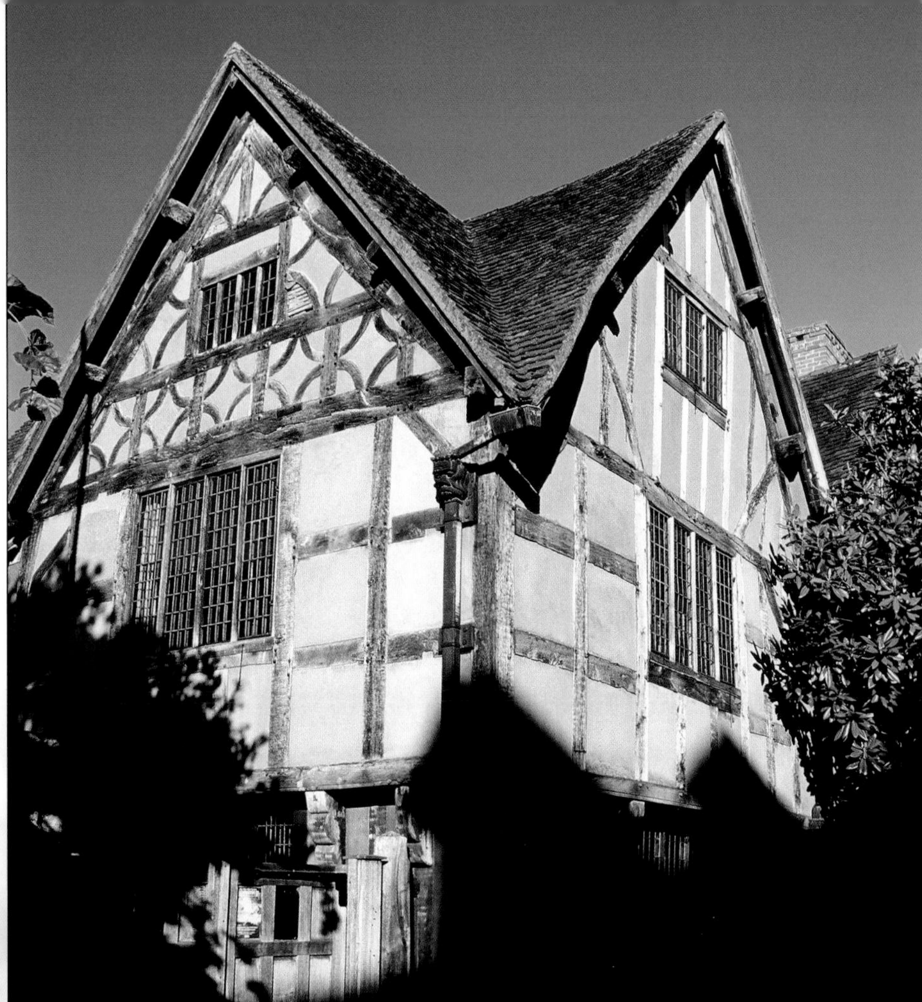

novelist, Marie Corelli (a woman whose social pretensions would later lead Mark Twain to dub her 'an offensive sham').

Following Catherine Croker's death in 1913 the house was purchased by an American, Josephine Macleod, who lived there with her sister, Betty Legett, the widow of a millionaire New York grocery tycoon. In 1931 Betty died following a fall down the stairs. Her body was laid out in the master bedroom for four days prior to her funeral, and some believe that her spirit has remained behind at Hall's Croft ever since. Some visitors have felt a push when standing in the vicinity of the stairs, whilst others have experienced a cold chill brushing past them. There have been reports of a ghostly lady in a blue dress seen standing in an upstairs corner, and one lady became quite hysterical when a red-haired woman she spied through the shop window suddenly vanished into thin air.

In February 2004 the team from Living TV's ***Most Haunted Live*** paid a visit to Hall's Croft. Two million television viewers watched in astonishment as an antique spoon, which was normally attached to an upstairs table by a wire, was hurled across the room at great speed, narrowly missing presenter Yvette Fielding's head. A rigorous investigation appeared to rule out any human involvement. The programme's regular historian, Richard Felix, declared it 'one of the most convincing pieces of paranormal activity in recent decades'. Many viewers were left convinced that they had witnessed genuine poltergeist activity.

ABOVE: *Once owned by Shakespeare's daughter Susanna, Hall's Croft was the scene of surpising poltergeist activity witnessed by millions of television viewers in 2004.*

Shrieves House
STRATFORD, WARWICKSHIRE
Ghosts Galore

Shrieves House is named for William Shrieve, a man about whom little is known, save that he was an archer during the reign of Henry VIII and between 1536 and 1542 he was the tenant of this house - No. 40 Sheep Street. The house is one of the oldest structures in Stratford and to step through its huge oak gates and walk (carefully) across the ancient cobbles of its courtyard is to step into a long past age. It has survived fire, plague and the Civil War, and may well have been visited by William Shakespeare. It now enjoys the reputation of being one of Stratford's most haunted properties.

The back of the house is a huge converted barn and it is here that visitors can wander through an eccentric little museum, where an eclectic mix of interesting articles are displayed. It is also here that many visitors have experienced the unnerving sensation of feeling breathless, as if 'something' is trying to smother them. Occasionally, the huge figure of a man,

ABOVE: *Shrieves House is widely regarded as Stratford's most haunted house, and visitors often have close encounters of an ethereal kind there.*

dressed in stockings with cross lacing, has been seen on the upstairs floor. Mediums visiting the property have also seen the form of a man whom they are convinced is William Shrieve. He appears holding a large axe, which he lets slide through his fingers onto the floor as he gazes at them with evil intent.

Elsewhere in the building an old lady holding a candle has been seen drifting slowly up the staircase. It is in this part of the house that a soldier is said to have hanged himself from a beam during the Civil War and was hastily buried under the floor. Many mediums arriving at the top of the stairs have been forced to back away, so overwhelming is the psychic energy, and many members of the public have spoken of feeling cold and uncomfortable at this particular spot.

All manner of inexplicable happenings and mysterious phenomena have been recorded at Shrieves House. People have been pushed in the back, patted on the head or stroked on the neck by unseen hands. Hazy figures have been seen in some of the rooms, whilst in certain areas visitors have complained of smelling the stench of rotting flesh. A group of paranormal investigators who spent a night at the property in January 2004, sprinkled flour over a section of the floor beneath which a child is reputed to be buried and were astonished when the letter T mysteriously appeared in the flour. That same night the team were sitting in one of the rooms when an icy mist suddenly began to swirl around them and proceeded to fill the room.

It is generally agreed that Shrieves House barn is one of the most psychically active buildings in Warwickshire. In February 2004 the viewers of Living TV's ***Most Haunted Live*** voted it the creepiest house in Stratford. 'I'm not surprised [that it has] been voted the most haunted building in Stratford,' Steve Devey, the house's owner, told the ***Stratford Herald***. 'We have always known that there have been strange goings-on in the Shrieves House barn. [This] proves that it is truly, a genuinely haunted museum.'

WHATELY HALL HOTEL

BANBURY, OXFORDSHIRE

A Priest Dying To Meet You

BELOW: *Once a safe haven for Catholic priests, Whately Hall is now the haunt of one unfortunate who died there.*

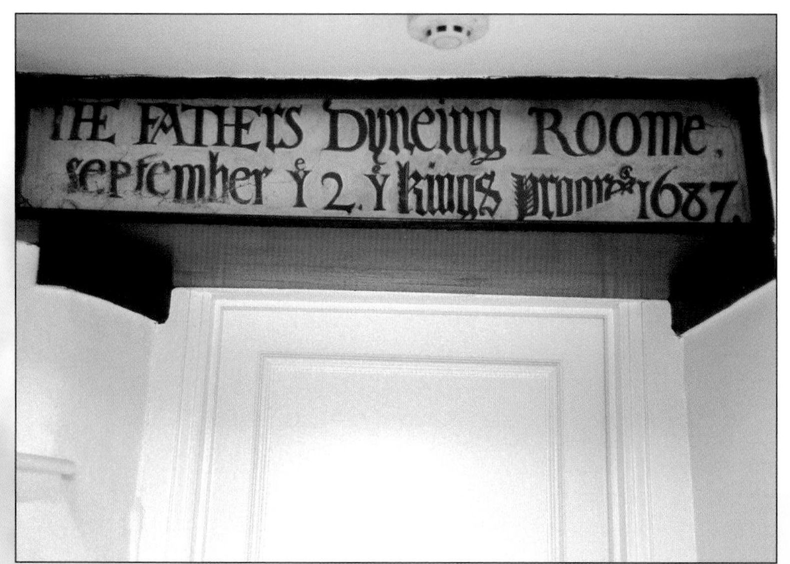

At first glance it seems hard to believe that this elegant hotel actually started life as a 17th-century coaching inn, for it has a frontage that would do any manor house proud. It also possesses a strangely mysterious air, perhaps due to the fact that during the Cromwellian persecutions of Catholics it was used as a haven for priests. Here they would conduct clandestine masses in a room specially set aside for the purpose, and could hide in secret staircases, hidden tunnels and priests holes should Cromwell's soldiers ever come looking for them. If this happened a special alarm bell would be rung as a warning to make for the nearest hiding place.

One night a servant decided to play a joke on a priest by the name of Father Bernard. He sounded the alarm when there was no approaching danger, and the unfortunate Father Bernard was so terrified that he dropped dead from a heart attack. His ghost has haunted Whately Hall ever since and has a particular fondness for suite 52, where his friendly spectre flits across the room and vanishes. More commonplace are the mysterious whisperings that often fill that particular room and which are frequently accompanied by the faint sound of chanting, as though Father Bernard, or one of his fellow priests, is conducting a service for an invisible and long-dead congregation.

WESTON MANOR HOTEL
OXFORDSHIRE
Mad Maude Checks In

The Weston Manor Hotel nestles at the end of a majestic tree-lined avenue and dates largely from the 14th and 16th centuries, although the frontage is a Victorian addition. Stepping into its magnificent hall you find yourself suddenly back in a bygone age. In winter months a fire crackles in the beautiful Tudor fireplace, its flickering glow casting shadows across a 15th-century refectory table that stands before it, a sturdy reminder that this ancient building was once owned by the abbot of Osney.

In 1535, at the time of the Dissolution of the Monasteries, the house was given to Lord Williams of Thame, and the family resided there until 1589. The Earl of Lincoln then decided that it would make a fine home, and took possession of it after a violent siege. Less than a hundred years later, in 1631, ownership changed again and the house passed into the possession of Sir Francis Norreys, a staunch Royalist who gave shelter to Prince Rupert following his defeat at the Battle of Islip. The Prince was somewhat unnerved when General Fairfax, the commander of the victorious Parliamentarian forces, also arrived to spend the night at the house. It is said that the General actually slept in the same room where Prince Rupert was hiding, inside the chimney. Early the next morning, as Fairfax lay sleeping, Rupert sneaked out from his hiding place, donned the clothes of a dairymaid and made good his escape.

Subsequently, the house remained in private ownership until the late 1940s when it was converted into an hotel. With such an eventful and fascinating history, it comes as little surprise to find that this property is haunted. Its most famous ghost is that of a nun who was reputedly burnt at the stake in the Manor's grounds 'about five centuries ago' for becoming involved with one of the monks, and committing the crime of being caught in his cell one night. Whether or not there is any historical truth in the tale she has become an established part of Weston Manor folklore, and has long been known by the rather unflattering nickname of 'Mad Maude'.

ABOVE: *Guests at the Weston Manor Hotel can look forward to making the acquaintance of its resident ghost, 'Mad Maude'.*

The site of the cramped and chilly cell where Mad Maude's indiscretion was discovered is now the hotel's finest bedroom, the Oak Room. Some of those who have spent the night in its ancient four-poster bed have been overcome by a feeling of dreadful foreboding. It has been suggested that they are picking up on faint traces of Maude's distress. In September 1975, a representative of the British Tourist Authority spent a night in the Oak Room and complained that his rest had been disturbed by an unusual sensation of heat. 'I cannot remember even in Africa such a close and oppressive atmosphere,' he later recalled. 'I was not only hot but unable to breathe properly.' However, come dawn the room's temperature began dropping and finally returned to normal.

CAPITAL HAUNTI

LUR

NGS AND
KING TERRORS

Come to me in the silence of the night;
Come in the speaking silence of a dream;
Come with soft rounded cheeks and eyes as bright
As sunlight on a stream;
Come back in tears,
O memory, hope, love of finished years.

From 'Echo'
by Christina Georgina Rossetti (1830-1894)

London, Berkshire, Buckinghamshire, Bedfordshire and Hertfordshire

The peaceful normality of the counties covered in this chapter belies their truly haunted heritage. Inevitably that heritage is dominated by London, which, despite claims made by Derby and York, is far and away the most haunted city in England. It is also home to a house that in the early 20th century acquired a chilling and sinister reputation and a ghost that seemed intent on inflicting harm and even death on the living (a very rare phenomenon in the annals of haunted history). Elsewhere I must confess to feeling somewhat sceptical about the legendary ghost that is reputed to haunt Hatfield House. However, given that ghostly horses and carriages were in the past a staple fixture on Britain's spectral landscape, I thought I should include at least one in this book, if only to provide a break from the ubiquitous ladies of different hues that make up the vast majority of ghosts. Despite its urban spread, it's surprising how close London is to beautiful and peaceful countryside. Consequently, many who worked or lived in the metropolis established rural retreats in the counties to the north and west, and several of them, such as Benjamin Disraeli, have found the allure of their country homes so irresistible that they feel compelled to return time and again in spirit form.

KEY

1. Handel House Museum
2. 50 Berkeley Square
3. Sutton House
4. Charlton House
5. The Berystede Hotel
6. Highenden Manor
7. Flitwick Manor Hotel
8. Hatfield House
9. Knebworth House

Handel House Museum

25 Brook Street, London

A Female Entity who Came to Stay

George Frideric Handel was thirty-eight years old when, in the summer of 1723, he moved into the newly built house at 25 Brook Street. He lived there for thirty-six years, and died in the upstairs bedroom in 1759. In 2000, the upper storeys of the building were leased to the Handel House Trust and on 8th November 2001 'Handel's spirit was brought back ... when the Handel House Museum opened to the public.'

However, during the restoration project it was reported that a spirit of a very ethereal kind was haunting the building. In July 2001, the Handel House Trust went as far as to call upon the services of a local priest, to see if he could lay the ghost that had been seen by at least two people. 'We weren't sure whether having a ghost would attract or deter customers,' commented Martin Egglestone, a trust fundraiser, who twice encountered the apparition in the room where Handel died. In June 2001, he was helping measure up for some curtains when 'suddenly the air got very thick'. The next moment a shape that resembled 'the imprint on the back of your retina when you close your eyes, having been looking at the sun for too long' appeared before him. Mr Egglestone described the apparition as being female and slightly higher than him. He observed how, 'There was no malevolent feeling. It felt like the pressure you get when you brush past someone in the Tube and they are too close to you.'

Staff also reported the strong, lingering scent of perfume hanging in the air of the bedroom. Although Handel lived alone, sharing his home only with his manservant, he was visited here by two sopranos, Faustina Bordoni and Francesca Cuzzoni. The singers vied with each other to perform in his operas, and Mr Egglestone raised the possibility that the ghost might be one of them. Interestingly, the upper floors of No. 23 next door, which are now part of the museum and used for changing exhibitions, were the home of rock legend Jimi Hendrix from 1968 to 1969 and he also claimed to have seen a ghost. Commenting on the most recent haunting a local priest told the Daily Telegraph, 'This is a soul who is restless and not at home. I don't see it as evil or horrible and one should help it to be at peace.'

ABOVE: *There are some very eerie sections of the house where Handel lived in Mayfair.*

PREVIOUS PAGES: *A spectral coach drawn by ghostly horses is said to race down the drive and up the staircase of Hatfield House, the splendid home of the Cecil family.*

50 BERKELEY SQUARE, LONDON

The Most Haunted London House

The plain Georgian exterior of 50 Berkeley Square contains an interior that still retains much of its 18th-century grandeur, whilst sweeping stairs, high plaster ceilings, over-mantel mirrors and marble floors and fireplaces lend the building a decidedly Dickensian air. For over 50 years it has been the premises of Maggs Bros, Antiquarian Booksellers, and the ceiling-high rows of heavy mahogany bookcases that line the walls are stacked with shelf after shelf of leather-bound tomes by long-dead men of letters - some famous, many forgotten. Yet there is nothing in the yellowed pages of the thousands of books on display that comes close to matching the sinister happenings that were once an everyday occurrence within these walls. Happenings so terrifying that for much of the 19th century 50 Berkeley Square was known simply as 'the most haunted house in London'.

Charles Harper in ***Haunted Houses***, published in 1907, stated that '... It seems that a Something or Other, very terrible indeed, haunts or did haunt a particular room. This unnamed Raw Head and Bloody Bones, or whatever it is, has been sufficiently awful to have caused the death, in convulsions, of at least two foolhardy persons who have dared to sleep in that chamber...'. One of them was a nobleman who, scoffing at tales that a hideous entity was residing within the haunted room, vowed to spend the night there. It was agreed, however, that should he require assistance he would ring the servants' bell to summon his friends. A little after midnight there was a faint ring, which was followed by a ferocious peeling of the bell. Rushing upstairs, the friends threw open the door and found their companion rigid with terror, his eyes bulging from their sockets. He was unable to tell them what he had seen, and such was the shock to his system that he died shortly afterwards.

As a result of its dreadful reputation, no tenant could be found who was willing to take on the lease of 'the house' in

ABOVE: *50 Berkeley Square was long considered the most haunted house in London. It is a little more settled nowadays, but it still has its ghostly moments!*

Berkeley Square, and for many years it remained empty. But its otherworldly inhabitants continued to be active. Strange lights that flashed in the windows would startle passers-by, disembodied screams were heard echoing from the depths of the building, and spookier still, the sound of a heavy body was heard being dragged down the staircase. One night, two sailors on shore leave in London were seeking a place to stay, and chanced upon the obviously empty house. Breaking in they made their way upstairs and inadvertently settled down to spend the night in the haunted room. They were woken by the sound of heavy, determined footsteps coming up the stairs. Suddenly the door banged open and a hideous, shapeless, oozing mass began to fill the room. One sailor managed to get past it and escape. Returning to the house with a policeman, he found his friend's corpse impaled on the railings outside, the twisted face and bulging eyes grim testimony to the terror that had caused him to jump to his death rather than confront the evil in the room above.

> '... IT SEEMS THAT A SOMETHING OR OTHER, VERY TERRIBLE INDEED, HAUNTS OR DID HAUNT A PARTICULAR ROOM'
>
> 50 BERKELEY SQUARE

Many theories have been put forward to account for the haunting of 50 Berkeley Square. Charles Harper reported that the house had once belonged to a Mr Du Pré of Wilton Park who locked his lunatic brother in one of the attics. The captive was so violent that he could only be fed through a hole, and his groans and cries could be heard in the neighbouring houses. When the brother died, his spectre remained behind to chill the blood and turn the mind of anyone unfortunate enough to encounter it. Another hypothesis holds that a Mr Myers, who was engaged to a society beauty, once owned the house. He had set about furnishing the building in preparation for their new life together when, on the day of the wedding, his fiancé jilted him. The disappointment undermined his reason, turning him into a bitter recluse. He locked himself away in the upstairs room and only came out at night to wander the house by flickering candlelight. It was these nocturnal ramblings that, so the theory goes, gave the house its haunted reputation.

Whatever the events, tragic or otherwise, that lie behind the haunting of 50 Berkeley Square, there is no doubt that the building has a definite atmosphere. It is said that the building is so charged with psychic energy that merely touching the external brickwork can give a mild shock to the psychically inclined. Nor are the ghosts, as is often claimed, consigned to the building's past. Julian Wilson, a bookseller with Maggs Brothers, was working alone in the accounts department, which now occupies the haunted room, one Saturday morning in 2001, when a column of brown mist moved quickly across the room and vanished. That same year a cleaner preparing the house for a party, felt the overwhelming sensation that someone, or something, was standing behind her. Turning round she found that that the room was empty. A man walking up the stairs was shocked when his glasses were snatched from his hand and flung to the ground. In October 2001 I was asked to appear in a BBC documentary on haunted London, and we were fortunate enough to film inside 50 Berkeley Square. Part of the programme entailed the soundman and myself having to stand in the dark in the haunted room for about five minutes, waiting for the signal to switch the lights on and off. Although nothing actually happened, I can honestly say that I found it a truly frightening experience, and we were both glad to be able to rejoin the rest of the crew in the street outside.

SUTTON HOUSE
HOMERTON, LONDON
Howling Hounds

The splendid red-brick Sutton House was built in 1535 by Sir Ralph Sadleir, who was one of Henry VIII's privy councillors. Since then it has been home to merchants, Huguenot silk-weavers, Victorian schoolmistresses and Edwardian clergy. By the 1980s, however, the building had fallen into disrepair, its decline aided by squatters and vandals. Thankfully, due largely to the efforts of the Sutton House Community Scheme, the building was restored in the early 1990s and is now open to the public under the auspices of the National Trust. Although it has, inevitably, been altered over the years, it still remains essentially a Tudor house, and has magnificent oak-panelled walls, a grand staircase and carved fireplaces.

Several ghosts wander its atmospheric interior. Dogs are heard wailing from the empty house in the dead of night. They are thought to be the dogs that belonged to a John Machell, a wealthy wool merchant who lived at Sutton House from 1550 to 1558. The dogs can still be seen in the coat of arms in the fireplace of the Little Chamber. Whenever dogs are brought into Sutton House they often stop rigid at the foot of the painted staircase, their hackles raised, apparently transfixed by something they can see on the stairs but which remains invisible to humans. Another ghost is that of the White Lady, thought to be Frances, the wife of John Machell the younger. She died giving birth to twins on 11th May 1574, and her shimmering shade has been seen gliding around the rooms. During the renovation in the 1990s, an architectural student, staying at the house, woke up in what is now the exhibition room to find a lady in a blue dress hovering over his bed. A house steward recently encountered this same spectre, when she rudely interrupted his slumbers by violently shaking his bed in the dead of night. Sudden drops in temperature, doors that open of their own volition and objects flung across rooms by unseen hands, are just some of the other phenomena to be regularly encountered.

ABOVE: *Sutton House is one of London's oldest manor houses and is also one of its most haunted.*

ABOVE: *A lustful phantom resides at Charlton House and seeks a lady to have his child.*

CHARLTON HOUSE
CHARLTON ROAD, LONDON
The Amorous Spectre

Charlton House was built between 1607 and 1612 for Sir Adam Newton, Dean of Durham and tutor to Prince Henry (1594-1612), son of James I. It is little short of a Jacobean statement in architecture and, as such, is one of the finest and best-preserved mansions of that era in London. When Newton died it passed to his son, Henry and then via successive owners until it came into the possession of a wealthy East India merchant, Sir William Langhorne. He may have been exceedingly rich, but Langhorne's fortune could do nothing to grant his dearest wish, that of begetting an heir. As he grew to old age he became increasingly distressed that he had no children. When his first wife died in 1715, undeterred by the fact that he was in his eighties, he took a second bride who was aged just seventeen. But when he died two months later, his young wife had not conceived, and thus the house passed through a number of different hands before coming into the possession of the Maryon-Wilson family who owned it from 1767 to 1923.

But Sir William Langhorne has proved both unable and unwilling to depart from the house, and his determination to beget an heir has continued beyond the grave. Thus his lustful ghost roams the corridors and passages of Charlton House in search of living ladies that take his fancy. Many was the time in the past that women staying over at the house would be awoken by the alarming sound of their bedroom-door handles turning in the dead of night. Those brave enough to investigate would throw open the door only to find the corridor outside dark and empty. Occasionally, women walking down the stairs have had their bottoms pinched by his invisible fingers.

During the First World War, Charlton House was converted into a military hospital and the owner, Lady Spencer

Maryon-Wilson, informed the nursing staff that they were on no account to put patients in a certain bedroom that had the reputation of being haunted. Unfortunately, as the number of patients increased her wishes had to be ignored and several of the wounded placed in the room claimed to have encountered its resident wraith.

In 1925 the house was purchased by the Metropolitan Borough of Greenwich and subsequently used as a community centre and library. In the Second World War the north wing was destroyed by bombing and, in the course of later restoration work, the mummified body of an infant was found concealed in one of its chimneys. Nobody could discover its identity, or the reason why it had been hidden there, but the grisly discovery may explain the sightings of a ghostly servant girl in old-fashioned clothing seen walking about the grounds with a dead baby cradled in her arms.

THE BERYSTEDE HOTEL
ASCOT, BERKSHIRE
You Can't Take it With You

In 1870 twenty-three-year old Henry Noailles Widdrington Standish married Helene de Perusse, daughter of the French Compte de Cars. He marked the occasion by having a grand country house constructed within easy reach of London and Windsor. Here they lived in Victorian opulence and frequently entertained their numerous high-class friends, including the Prince and Princess of Wales, the future Edward VII and Queen Alexandra.

On the 27th October 1886 a fire broke out in the early hours of the morning, forcing the household to flee the premises. They could do little but gaze helplessly on as the conflagration devoured the house. Suddenly one of their number, a French maid by the name of Eliza Kleininger, let out an anguished scream and rushed back into the burning building. The next day her charred remains were found at the foot of the servants staircase surrounded by a rich array of jewellery. Each of the trinkets had been gifted to her by either her mistress, Mrs Standish, or presented to her by unattended ladies who had been house guests. She kept the precious trinkets in a box in her room and had intended to use them to secure a comfortable retirement. Evidently the thought of her jewels being consumed by the flames had proved too much for Eliza and she was compelled to dash back into the blazing building.

The house remained derelict until 1903 when it was rebuilt as the grand hotel, which, apart from being requisitioned for use as law courts during the Second World War, it has remained ever since. However, the ghost of Eliza Kleininger remains at the hotel to wander its corridors and staircases in the guise of a blue lady. She particularly favours the area under the main gable on the north side where the staircase on which she met her tragic end was located. She is a harmless shade and few people find an encounter with her frightening. As far as many who work at the hotel are concerned she is just the oldest resident of this grand and atmospheric old house.

ABOVE: *A maid who tried to save her jewels from a fire now roams the cosy corridors of Ascot's Berysted Hotel.*

HUGHENDEN MANOR
HIGH WYCOMBE, BUCKINGHAMSHIRE
Mr Disraeli is Still At Home

In 1847 Benjamin Disraeli decided that he must acquire some landed property in order to enhance his status as a leading public figure. Not one to let a little thing like a lack of funds stand in the way of his ambition, he borrowed a considerable sum from Lord George Bentinck. He then set about purchasing Hughenden Manor, a modest Georgian estate which over the next few years he transformed into a substantial Victorian Gothicized red-brick house. It remained Disraeli's home for the rest of his life, providing him with a rural retreat away from the cut and thrust of London political life. Here he and his wife, Mary Ann, entertained the great and good of their age, including Queen Victoria.

Disraeli died in 1881 and the house underwent many internal changes. Following its acquisition by the National Trust in 1947, several of its rooms were restored more or less as Disraeli would have known them. Today, visitors can tour the rooms and corridors which display reminders of the Disraelis and their friends, and admire his upstairs study, which remains much as he left it. There is also the possibility of encountering the ghost of the man himself. Reports of spectral sightings of him are said to have been circulating shortly after his death and have continued into recent times. Although it must be said that the current staff are somewhat sceptical that the property is actually haunted by its most famous resident. The majority of sightings are in the region of the stairs and he has been seen several times standing near a portrait of himself. He is said to hold a bunch of papers in his hands. He was once seen by a lady visitor, and appeared to be totally unaware of her presence. He stood before her for a reasonable length of time, gazing ahead at nothing in particular, until the sound of approaching voices apparently caused him to melt slowly away into thin air.

FLITWICK MANOR HOTEL
FLITWICK, BEDFORDSHIRE
The Housekeeper's Roaming Reveneant

Flitwick Manor Hotel is a delightful Georgian house that was owned by the Brooks family from the end of the 18th century until 1934, when the last member of the family died. The first of the Brooks to live there were John Thomas Brooks and his wife Mary, who moved in following their marriage in 1816. They were blessed with three sons and a daughter, whom they christened Mary Ann, and on whom they both doted.

In March 1848 their beloved daughter became seriously ill with what appears to have been abdominal cancer, and having languished for several months, she died in the September of that year. The grieving parents were bereft at their loss, and John Thomas gathered the 'best and sweetest flowers' and having filled her coffin with them, placed a small nosegay in her hand. It has been suggested that the trauma of this sad event has left its mark upon the very fabric of Flitwick Manor, and that the female presence that is known to wander the hotel is that of Mary Brooks, the distraught mother. Others, however, dispute this and claim that it is just as likely to be the ghost of a female resident either prior to or subsequent to the Brooks's tenure. Interestingly, the ghost only began to appear after builders were carrying out renovations on the house and stumbled upon a little attic room, which apparently had not been used for some time and about which the hotel's staff knew nothing.

It would appear to be the discovery of this room that roused the ghostly lady from her slumber and caused her to become a truly active entity. Guests have been woken by the sensation of someone sitting down on the end of their beds. John Hinds, a purchasing director, was awoken by a shuffling sound coming from the bottom of the bed at around 1.15 a.m. Turning on the light he found the silhouette of a woman standing at the foot of his bed. She was gazing out of the window and remained visible for several minutes until he demanded to know who she was, whereupon his strange nocturnal visitor faded away.

Staff have heard footsteps plodding across bedrooms that they know to be empty and have grown used to their resident ghost switching the lights off at the most inopportune moments. A receptionist who once spent the night in room 7 suddenly awoke with a jolt to find an elderly woman, evidently in some distress, standing by her bed. The receptionist attempted to turn on the lights but was unable to find the switch. As she leapt from her bed and raced out into the corridor she seemed to be overcome with the woman's emotion. Moments later having composed herself, she nervously re-entered the bedroom to find the lights blazing. There was, however, no sign of the old woman.

According to Betty Puttick in her book ***Ghosts of Bedfordshire***, Sonia Banks, the general manager at the time of the discovery of the attic room, was convinced that since the

OPPOSITE AND ABOVE: *Benjamin Disraeli so loved Hugenden House that he is loathe to leave it even in death.*

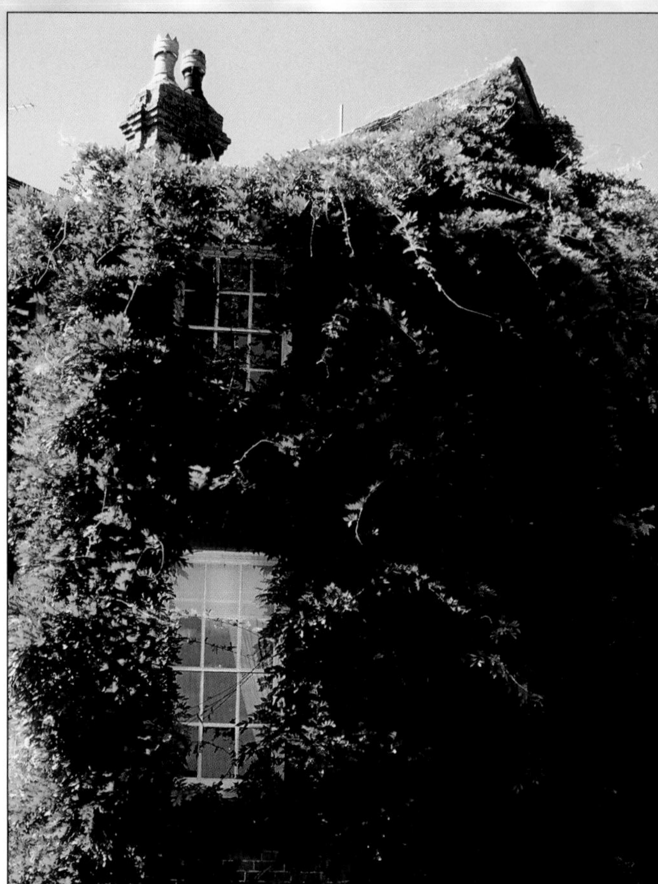

ABOVE: *When staff uncovered a hidden room at the Flitwick Manor Hotel they appear to have disturbed a long dead resident.*

servants used to live on the highest floor of the house, the mysterious room may well have belonged to a housekeeper who either didn't realize she had died, or else had remained earthbound at her place of service. 'When she started haunting the hotel, I wondered if it was because we had found her little room,' she said. 'So I wrote her a little note and said "Dear Housekeeper, I am sorry you are so upset, but please don't go away." I signed it and put it on the chair in the room where she mainly seems to be. I always know when she's there as the cushions in that chair show an impression, as if someone has been sitting there.'

HATFIELD HOUSE
HATFIELD, HERTFORDSHIRE
The Virgin Queen and the Ghostly Carriage

The old Palace at Hatfield was built in the 15th century for the Bishops of Ely, and it remained in their possession until 1553 when Henry VIII 'acquired' it and used it as a home for his children. Elizabeth I spent much of her childhood at Hatfield and it was here in 1558 that she learnt of the death of her half-sister, Mary I, and of her own accession to the throne. When her successor, James I, became King, Hatfield's days as a royal palace were numbered. James preferred Theobalds, which was a lavish property a little further to the south. In 1607 he persuaded its owner, Robert Cecil, to swap houses.

Cecil arrived at Hatfield determined to make his own mark on the surroundings and promptly had most of the old Palace pulled down. He used the stone to build a splendid new house, which today stands in its own magnificent 1,500-acre park, and is considered one of the finest Jacobean houses in England. It is still the home of the Cecil family and its state rooms contain world-famous paintings, exquisite furniture, tapestries and historic armour. Fine examples of Jacobean craftsmanship can be viewed throughout the house, amongst them the Grand Staircase, with its wealth of detailed carved wood and its ghostly apparition, which is, to say the least, somewhat dramatic.

The haunting (or bizarre legend to be taken with a hefty pinch of salt depending on how you view these things) takes the form of a spectral coach drawn by ghostly horses. It is said to materialize at the gates and to race at breakneck speed up the drive before passing straight through the door of the house and continuing up the staircase, where it fades away into nothingness.

KNEBWORTH HOUSE
KNEBWORTH, HERTFORDSHIRE
We Will, We Will Shock You

Although Knebworth House has been home to the Lytton family since 1490, the Gothic fantasy that greets visitors today was created in the 19th century by Sir Edward Bulwer-Lytton (a popular author and the man who coined the phrase 'the pen is mightier than the sword'). The house is a spectacular sight as it comes into view from the nearby A1. Its battlements, towers, turrets, onion-shaped domes and spiky pinnacles, resplendent with leering grotesques and gargoyles that watch your approach with unwavering attention, projects a chilling aura. The one thing you feel certain of as you approach this striking edifice is that without a doubt it must be a haunted house, and it comes as no surprise that one of its most active presences is that of Bulwer-Lytton himself.

Edward Bulwer-Lytton, in addition to being one of the most prolific writers of his age, was also a busy and active political reformist. One of his greatest passions, however, was the study of the occult and he conducted numerous experiments at Knebworth in which he hoped to make contact with the dead. He even invited one of the most popular mediums of the age, Daniel Dunglass Home, to conduct

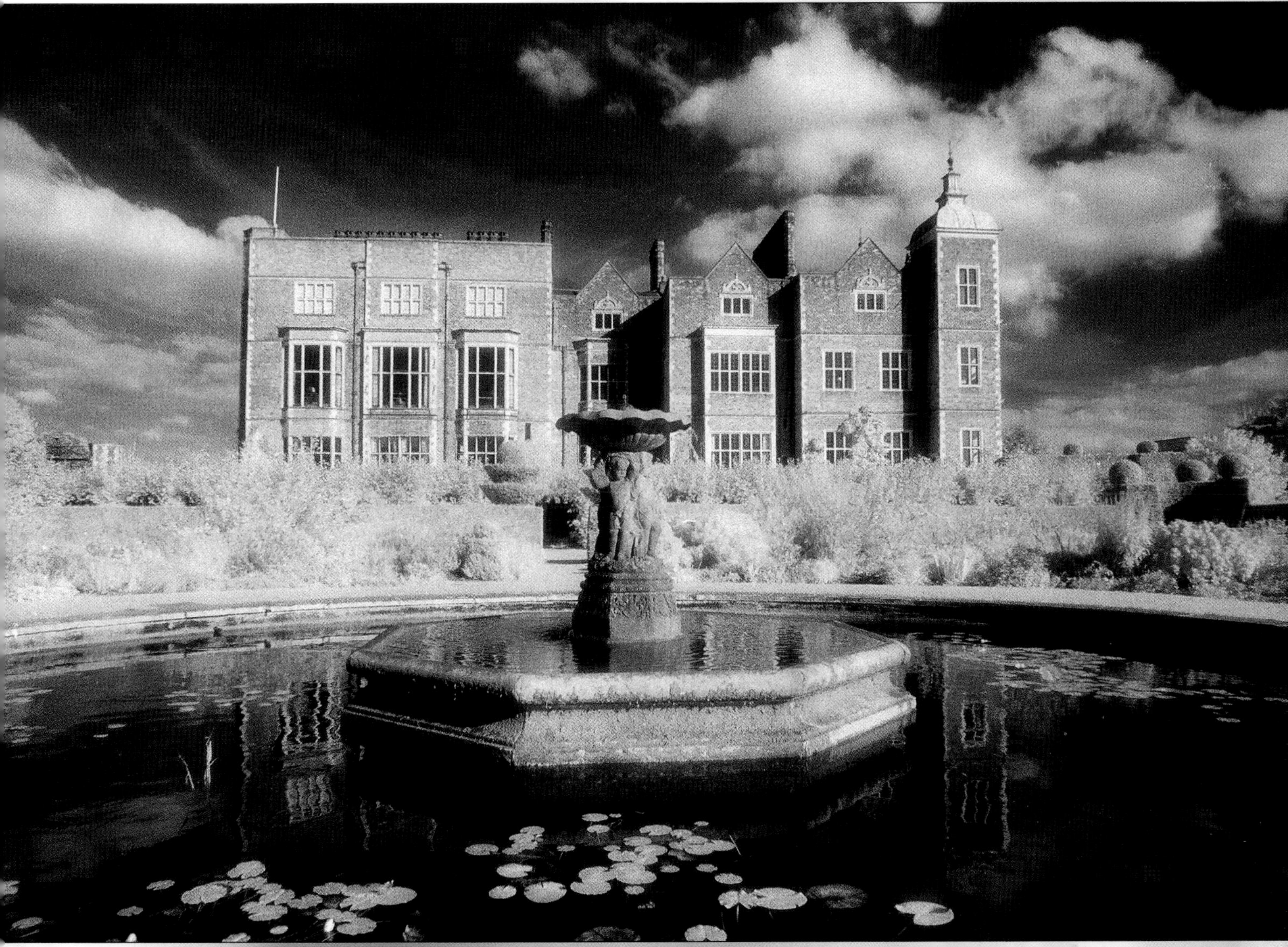

several séances for him. D. D. Home was the only major medium of the 19th century never to be caught out using fraudulent means to achieve his remarkable results. Some of his abilities included moving objects by simply staring at them, thrusting his head into a fire without burning himself, elongating and shrinking his body, and, most famous of all, levitating in front of astonished witnesses. Many of the greatest magicians of the age, Harry Houdini included, swore that they could duplicate Home's feats, though none ever did.

At his séances Home would produce spectral lights and ghostly hands that would shake hands with those present. Ghostly guitars would appear from nowhere and proceed to strum eerie music, and the spirits of the dead would spell out messages by pointing to letters of the alphabet printed on cards. Despite being unimpressed by Home himself, Bulwer-Lytton was nonetheless inspired by his remarkable achievements, and Home's wife would later complain that many of the paranormal depictions in Bulwer-Lytton's chilling short story, ***The Haunters and The Haunted*** , read like transcripts of a D.D. Home séance.

ABOVE: *Hatfield House – a former royal residence and haunted by horses.*

With such a long history and such a close association with the occult, it is inevitable that Knebworth House should have several ghosts. A female phantom is known to walk in the picture gallery. An American guest who was sleeping in the Queen Elizabeth Room, awoke one morning to find a young girl with long blonde hair leaning over her. It is, however, the spirit of Edward Bulwer-Lytton that is the most pervasive. His study remains more or less exactly as it was when he died in 1873 and some visitors have detected his presence in there. Others have spoken simply of a strange feeling in the vicinity and several cleaning staff have refused to enter the room on their own.

Knebworth today respects its past whilst at the same time enthusiastically embracing the modern age. It is famed for its rock festival which has taken place every June since the 1970s. It has been used as a location for numerous films and TV programmes, including, very aptly, the 1997 production of ***The Canterville Ghost.***

DECAYING AND

At the mid hour of night, when stars are weeping, I fly
To the lone vale we loved, when life shone warm in thine eye;
And I think that, if spirits can steal from the regions of the air
To revisit past scenes of delight, thou wilt come to meet me there,
And tell me our love is remembered even in the sky.

From 'At The Mid Hour of Night'
by Thomas Moore (1779-1852)

Spectres Lonely Ladies

Kent, Sussex and Surrey

The counties that lie to the south of London contain some beautiful and historic country houses which have the added attraction of being haunted. This is an area that has always been popular with royalty, and consequently some of its houses can boast several royal connections. The noble, the aristocratic or the just plain rich have also shown a fondness for the region and some wonderful family homes are scattered around the picturesque countryside. Many of them are now owned by the National Trust and offer visitors the opportunity to see how the other half lived in the days when the ruling classes enjoyed affluence beyond the dreams of avarice. Others have been converted into country house hotels and provide the chance to experience a little of that opulence at first hand.

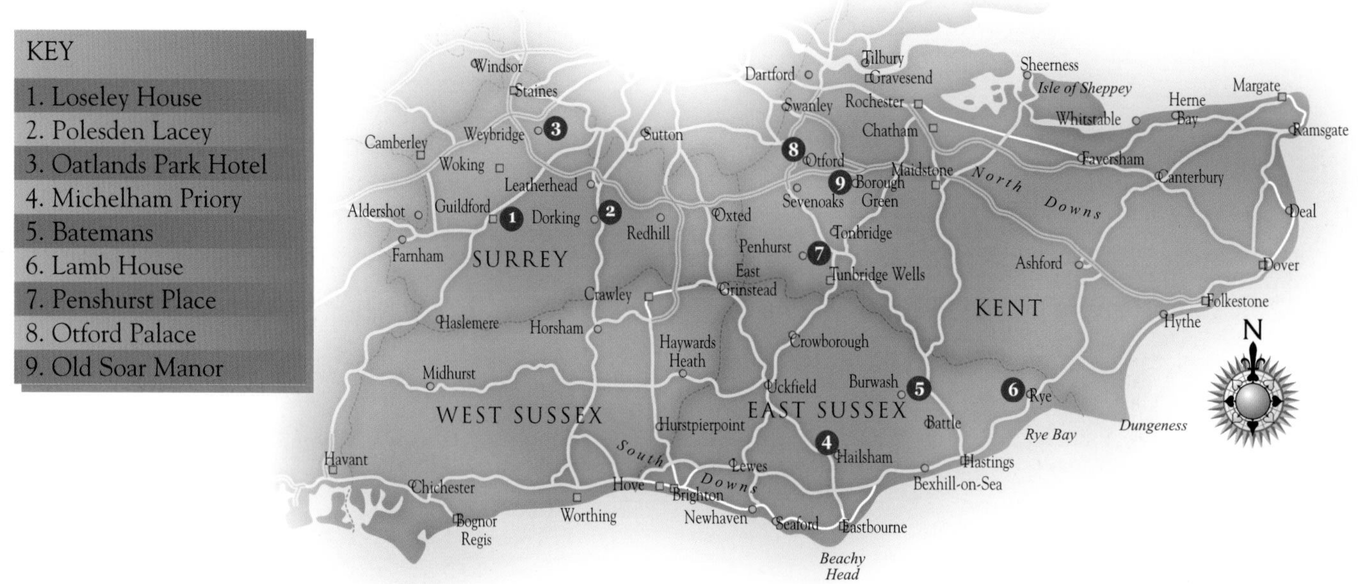

Loseley House

Nr. Guildford, Surrey

The Smiling Spectre

Built in 1562 for Sir William More, the beautiful and time-mellowed Loseley House is considered to be one of Surrey's finest Elizabethan dwellings. It even boasts panelling and tapestries that came from Henry VIII's Nonsuch Palace. It has been the home of the More-Molyneux family for almost 450 years and here they entertained Elizabeth I, James I, Queen Anne and Queen Mary II. In more recent times it has been much in demand as a stunning wedding venue and for filming television programmes as diverse as ***Blackadder, The Worst Witch, Spice World*** and ***Jonathan Creek.***

A smiling lady in Victorian dress, believed to be the wraith of a former resident, is just one of several ghosts to roam the property. There is also a spectral figure of a lady in a brown dress which has been seen by several visitors standing at the bottom of the stairs. Her appearances are frequently accompanied by a drop in temperature. The most prominent feature of this ghostly 'brown lady', which many witnesses have commented upon independently, is the fact that she fixes them with an intense and piercing stare. Legend has it that in the house's early years the second wife of the then owner murdered her stepson in order that her own son could inherit the estate. One version states that she did it by chopping off one of his legs and leaving him to bleed to death. Another account has her simply drowning the boy in the moat. Either way her husband was greatly displeased and locked her away in a small room in the upper part of the house, where she remained until her death many years later. Her ghost has haunted the house ever since, a trapped spirit doomed to wander the house in eternal remorse for her long-ago act of cruelty.

ABOVE: *For murdering her stepson, the brown lady of Loseley House has been condemned to wander the building in eternal remorse.*

PREVIOUS PAGES: *Penshurst Place is a lovely old house and few who visit fail to fall beneath its spell. Of course it helps that it's haunted.*

POLESDEN LACEY
NR. DORKING, SURREY
A Strange Whistling Noise

The ancient estate of Polesden Lacey sits high up on the North Downs and is dominated by an early 19th-century house. Prior to that the site was occupied by a 17th-century country mansion, the cherished home of theatrical impresario Richard Brinsley Sheridan who bought it in 1797. His plans to build a much grander residence were thwarted by financial difficulties and ill health, and gradually the house fell into ruin before being demolished in 1818, when Joseph Bosnor, a successful bookseller and stationer, acquired the estate. He commissioned Thomas Cubitt to rebuild Polesden Lacey in a neoclassical style. The rather dull and restrained house that resulted appears to have been sufficient for the tastes and needs of its 19th-century residents.

In 1906 the house was acquired by Mrs Ronald Greville, the daughter of William McEwan, founder of the famous Scottish Brewery. (I'd rather be a beeress than a peeress was one of her famous put-downs to a rather snooty aristocrat.) It was her father's fortune and influence that enabled her to make her way effortlessly into London society, where she met her husband, Captain Ronald Greville, a great friend of Edward VII. Over the next few years they began a restoration project that transformed the house into a place fit for hosting the highest in the land, and several members of the royal family were subsequently entertained there.

Following her husband's premature death in 1908, Margaret Greville established herself as both merry widow and leading society hostess. Numerous eminent guests, including writers, artists and politicians, came to Polesden Lacey to enjoy her hospitality, amongst them King George VI and Queen Elizabeth (the late Queen Mother) who spent part of their honeymoon there in 1923.

When she died in 1942 she bequeathed the house and its contents to the National Trust, on condition that it was open to the public at all times and that her treasures were placed on permanent display. Today its rooms are imbued with her spirit and provide an insight into the remarkable character of a woman who held such a sway over society. She was so determined to have a lasting presence at Polesden Lacey that she is buried at the back of the house, in front of the rose garden.

The ghosts that haunt the house certainly have their spectral work cut out keeping up with her larger-than-life

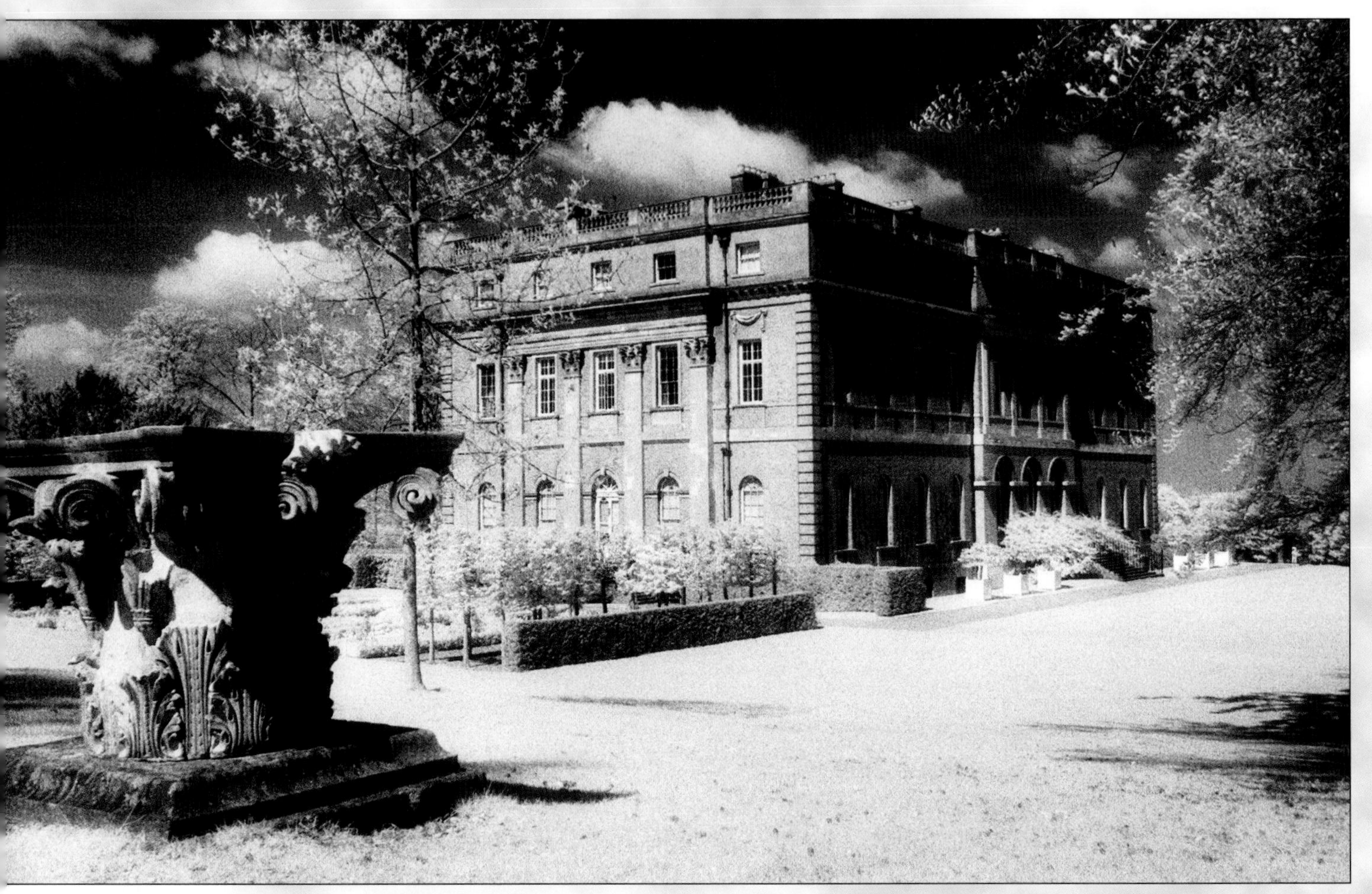

character, although this hasn't stopped them trying. Visitors enjoying the peace and tranquillity of the Nun's Walk, just inside the woods, have reported hearing a strange whistling noise which resembles a whirlwind. It isn't particularly loud and often continues unnoticed in the background for some time before anyone begins to pay it any attention. However, the moment they take note of it, it abruptly ceases. People have attempted to locate the source of the noise but no satisfactory explanation has ever been established.

To the west of the ornamental garden is a wooden bridge which crosses a sunken road and here a strange figure has been seen. It wears a long brown robe with the hood pulled over its head so as to obscure its face altogether. Nobody has ever been able to establish either its gender or identity, because whenever someone approaches for a closer look it fades quickly away.

Oatlands Park Hotel

Weybridge, Surrey

The Ghost in Room 1313

In 1538 Henry VIII forced John Rede to exchange Oatlands for the manor of Tandridge in Sussex, and then set about building

ABOVE: *In life the Merry Widow Margaret Greville lavished attention on Polesden Lacey and now lies buried in front of the rose garden at the back of the house.*

a magnificent palace for the reception of his new queen, Anne of Cleeves. As it transpired Anne never actually lived there and Henry himself was only a rare visitor, although there is evidence to suggest that he may have married Katherine Howard in its chapel. Both Edward VI and Mary I spent very little time at the palace. It wasn't until the reign of Elizabeth I that Oatlands truly came into its own because Elizabeth and her court paid frequent visits, often to escape epidemics in London.

Elizabeth made considerable additions to Oatlands, as did her successor James I who considered it one of his favourite royal residences. In 1649 the property was acquired by Robert Turbridge who promptly demolished it and built a more modest mansion on the site. That mansion burnt down in 1794, was rebuilt in the Gothic style, and over the next 60 years was renovated and modified until, following a major remodelling in 1856, it became the Oatlands Park Hotel.

Today it is a luxurious haven just a short distance from London, where guests can enjoy a relaxing break from the stresses and strains of everyday life. If you seek a little haunted hospitality, then you can look forward to a chance encounter with one of the hotel's 'friendly' ghosts. The first of

these is a 'grey lady' in a crinoline dress who sweeps regally across the floor of the restaurant and then disappears into the wall on the west side of the hotel. She is most often seen in the evening near to where there were once bay windows that led out into the garden. Over the years the restaurant has been partitioned off, forcing her to walk her path through the wall and into the less idyllic surroundings of the accounts department.

The most haunted room at the hotel is room 1313, situated on the third floor of the Tudor wing, just below the bell tower. Guests staying in the room have complained of feeling a 'presence' and of experiencing extreme temperature changes. It is believed that the paranormal activity there is the result of the suicide of a maid in the 19th century. According to tradition, she and her fiancée had a blazing row and the distraught girl rushed to the bell tower, barricaded the door, and jumped to her death. Ever since, her ghostly presence has remained in room 1313 and although she is never seen she is both sensed and heard. Drawers have been opened, the television has been moved, and on more than one occasion guests in neighbouring rooms have phoned reception to complain about the noisy residents of room 1313, only to be told that the room was unoccupied. On another occasion a deputy manager who spent the night in the haunted room became suddenly paralysed and felt as though someone was pressing on his chest, preventing him from moving. The feeling lingered for a few minutes before suddenly lifting as though whatever entity was responsible had just moved away.

ABOVE: *Set on its moated medieval island Michelham Priory has many ghosts to tempt intrepid thrill seekers over its threshold.*

MICHELHAM PRIORY

HAILSHAM, SUSSEX

A Slice of Haunted History

Set on a medieval moated island and dating back to 1229, Michelham Priory is a beautiful and impressive place. No one who approaches it through the towering 14th-century gatehouse can fail to be moved by the sight that greets them. The priory was owned by the Augustinians until the Dissolution of the Monasteries (1536-1540), after which it passed through several different ownerships until being purchased by Thomas Sackville in 1599. The Sackvilles owned the freehold for the next 300 years, and let it to a succession of tenant farmers who proceeded to surround the main house with barns and farm buildings.

In 1896 James Eglington Gwynne bought the Priory and set about restoring the medieval buildings. His purchase provoked a great deal of animosity from the then tenants who, stung by their eviction, threatened to murder the new owners. However, the matter was soon smoothed over and life at the Priory remained settled for the next 50 or so years. In 1959 it was given to the Sussex Archaeological Trust and it is they who now run it as a lovely tourist attraction.

Over the years the Priory has attracted the reputation of being one of the South East's most actively haunted houses, and a plethora of phantoms are known to reside there. Strange noises have been heard echoing throughout the building in the dead of night. Apparitions have been known to suddenly manifest in front of startled visitors, and just as quickly vanish. A ghostly white horse has been seen galloping through the gatehouse, and a spectral 'grey lady' has been seen to pass through the doors of the gatehouse. In 1969 two visitors were reading one of the explanatory boards inside the house, when they turned to find a man in a black cloak slowly descending from the ceiling, walking diagonally across the air to the floor. They watched open-mouthed as the figure moved in front of the inglenook fireplace and then proceeded to pass straight through the door. Barely had they recovered from this bizarre encounter, than a second apparition, this time of a woman in a Tudor gown, also appeared from the ceiling of the room and proceeded to follow the exact route taken by the man. There have been suggestions that a staircase once existed in that particular room, and that the ghostly visitors were simply imprints of two former residents going about their everyday business, oblivious of their intrusion into the 20th century.

A team of paranormal investigators once recorded the sound of a harpsichord playing of its own accord in the Music Room, even though the room was definitely empty at the time. On one occasion a group of investigators asked for a sign that 'someone was there' and were rewarded with a distinctive metallic tap followed by a sudden drop in temperature. The Music Room has the reputation of being one of the most haunted rooms in the house and several visitors have complained of getting severe headaches while in there.

Other ghosts that seem reluctant to depart from the old building include a 'lady in a funny dress' who once startled a ten-year old girl and her grandmother in the upper room of the gatehouse, the same room from which strange noises are heard when it is known to be empty. Meanwhile the Priory's Chamber, situated on the first floor, is renowned for the feelings of extreme unease it frequently causes in those who visit it for the first time. Equally disturbing is a horrible smell 'like the stench of burning hair' that sometimes hangs around a particular spot in the undercroft. The strange thing is that if those who smell it step to one side the odour goes, but if they step back again it reappears.

OPPOSITE: *Rudyard Kipling found his house, Batemans, so spiritual that he wove a tale of enchantment around its surroundings.*

On 5th April 2003 Kate Gearing, a member of the Ghost Club, the world's oldest psychical research organization, undertook a night-time investigation at Michelham Priory. At one stage she took a photograph inside the Priory's Chamber and when she developed it she was surprised to see the bearded figure of a man standing in front of the window looking straight at her. Several members of the team had earlier spoken of hearing a creaking sound in the area where the figure in the picture was standing. 'I was positive that there was nobody standing in front of me,' Kate later reported, 'and the figure does not resemble anyone present, not least because no bearded men were in the group ... there does not appear to be any explanation for the appearance of the mystery man!'

There is little doubt that the ghosts at Michelham Priory are extremely active. Whether you visit in the hope of encountering its otherworldly inhabitants or simply to admire a truly impressive building, enclosed by one of the largest moats in the country, you are bound to be rewarded.

BATEMANS
BURWASH, EAST SUSSEX
The Ghost of Rudyard Kipling?

Rudyard Kipling purchased this mellow stone 17th-century manor house in 1902, and it remained his home until his death in 1936. 'Heaven looked after it in the dissolute times of mid-Victorian Restoration,' he wrote to a friend upon moving in, 'and caused the vicar to send his bailiff to live in it for 40 years, and he lived in peaceful filth and left everything as he found it!' Kipling loved the surrounding Sussex countryside and it was at Batemans that he wrote ***Puck of Pook's Hill***, which is an enchanting tale of how two children make a Puck appear in the meadow beside the garden at Batemans by acting out ***A Midsummer Night's Dream*** on midsummer's eve. In 1910 Kipling's ***Rewards and Fairies*** was published; it contains what are probably Kipling's best-known lines:

If you can fill the unforgiving minute
With sixty seconds' worth of distance run,
Yours is the earth and everything that's in it,
And – which is more – you'll be a man my son!

Kipling's widow, Caroline, bequeathed the house to the National Trust who took over its ownership in 1939. Visitors to the property today get the distinct impression that the great writer is still very much in residence. The table at which he worked for over 30 years still stands in front of the

window of his study and is laid out with his pens and paperweights. His chair, raised up on blocks to correct the height, stands beside it, whilst his oak day bed stands near the fire and his books line every wall.

Several guides at the property and a number of visitors have spoken of seeing Kipling's ghost standing by his study window gazing out onto his beautiful garden. Others, who have not been treated to a full-fledged manifestation, have sensed a strong feeling of enthusiasm and energy in the vicinity of the study window, whilst one former resident of the house complained of always feeling uneasy in the bedroom where Mr and Mrs Kipling used to enjoy an exceedingly good night's rest.

LAMB HOUSE
RYE, SUSSEX
Henry James's Ghost Writer

This delightful red-brick Queen Anne building was home to American-born writer Henry James from 1898 until his death in 1916. He claimed that he was frequently disturbed by poltergeist activity and that he was often visited by the ghost of an old lady, wearing a mantilla, who helped him with his writing. Although no one else ever saw this woman, an amateur photographer who visited the house was surprised by the appearance of this spectral lady on one of the pictures he had taken. Following James's death, the author E. F. Benson became the tenant of the house and he too was troubled by poltergeist activity. Sometime later Rumer Godden, author of ***Black Narcissus***, moved into the property. When the poltergeist activity started afresh, she called in a priest and had him 'bless everything including the fridge'.

BELOW: *A Priest once blessed 'everything including the fridge' in an attempt to rid Lamb House of its resident wraith.*

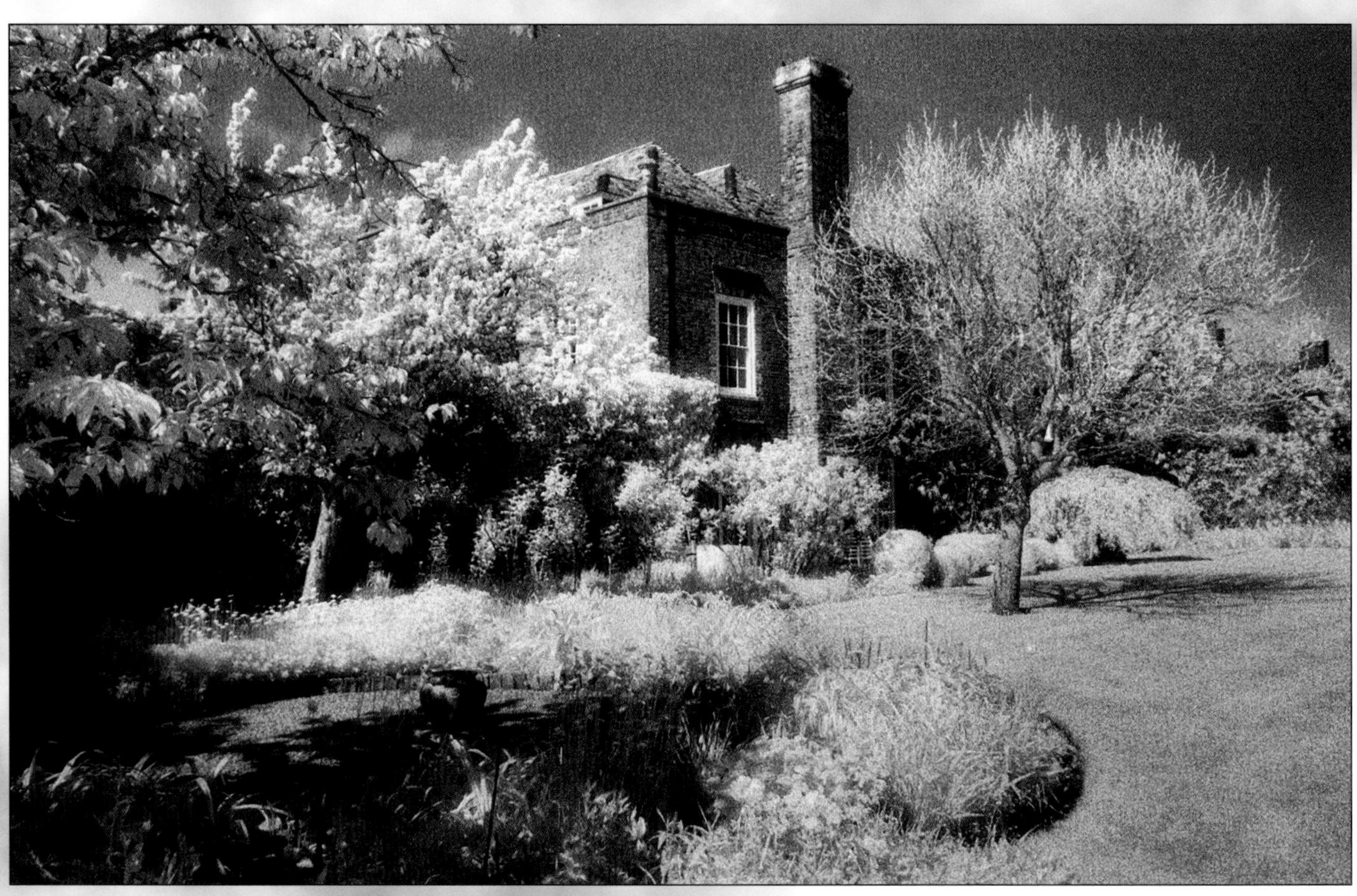

PENSHURST PLACE AND GARDENS
PENSHURST, KENT
Can I Come In?

Penshurst Place was begun in the 14th century by Sir John Pulteney, four times Lord Mayor of London. The Baron's Hall, the house's most remarkable feature, dates from this period. Its magnificent open-timbered roof, central hearth (from which the smoke escaped via a louvre in the roof) and minstrels' gallery evoke a sense of life in that slower-paced age. No one who ventures across its threshold can deny that the whole place exists in a time warp.

The house is predominantly Tudor in character, when Edward VI granted it to Sir William Sidney whose family have been in residence ever since. Sir Philip Sidney, the great Elizabethan courtier, poet and soldier was born at Penshurst on 30th November 1554, and later both Elizabeth I and James I came to visit. Following the execution of Charles I in 1649, Parliament placed two of his children, Princess Elizabeth and the Duke of Gloucester, in the care of Lady Leicester at Penshurst and instructed her to treat them as ordinary children of the nobility. Lady Leicester, however, had other ideas and curtly informed the Speaker of the House that she had too much respect to treat the children of her Sovereign as anything other than royal. Both children were heartbroken when they were removed from her custody and sent to Carisbrooke Castle on the Isle of White. Today, Penshurst Place retains the charm of a much-loved family home and Sir Philip Sidney, Viscount De Lisle, 'continues the family guardianship of this wonderful old house.'

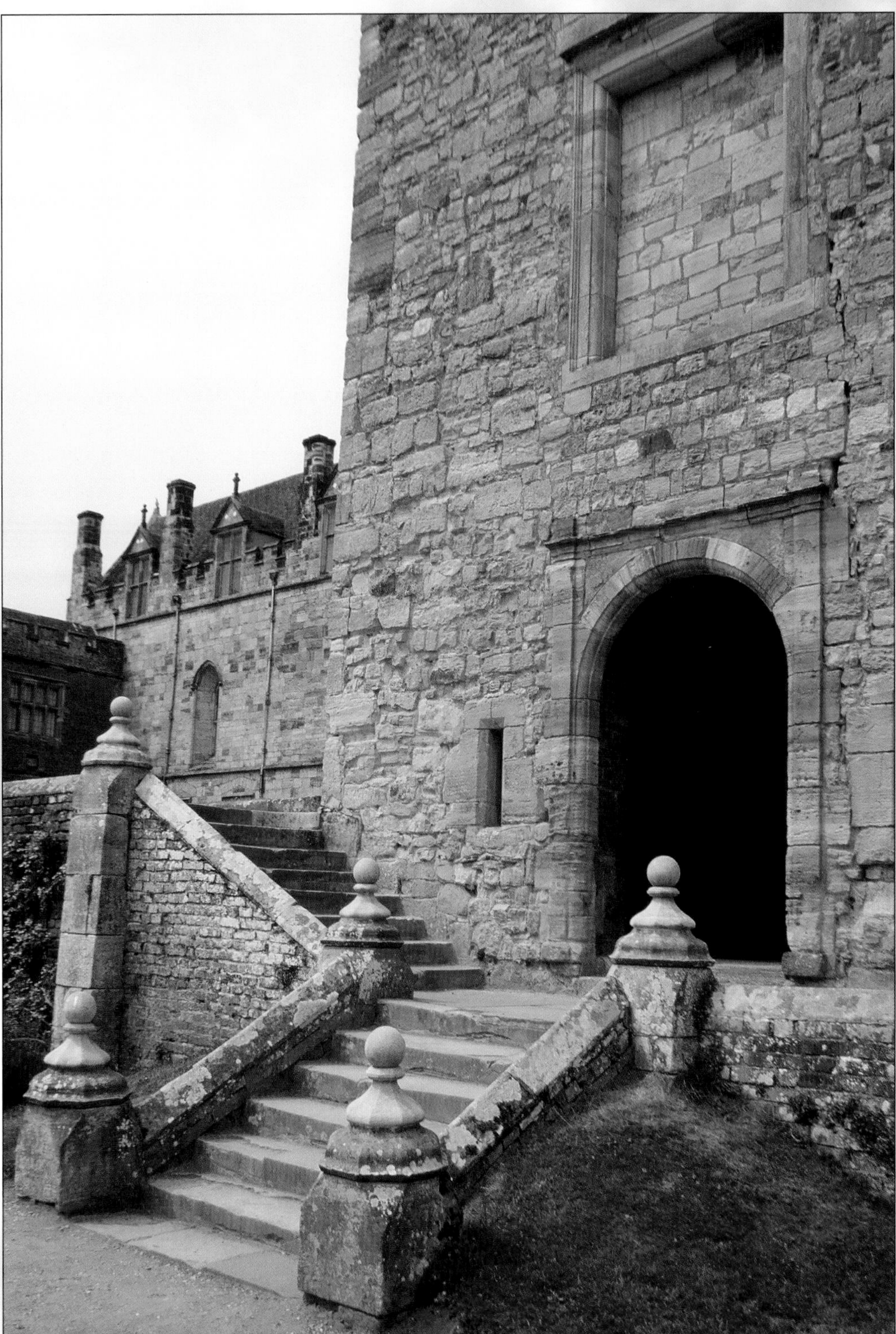

ABOVE: *Medium Judy Farncombe encountered several ghosts on an all-night vigil at the lovely Penshurst Place and declared it to be a truly beautiful location.*

On 16th November 2002 Judy Farncombe, medium and editor of the e-zine www.psychic-tymes.com, joined a group of paranormal investigators on a night-time vigil at Penshurst Place. At around 8 p.m. those present began easing themselves into the spirit of the place and the team that Judy was with began to investigate the Great Hall. Judy picked up on a medieval lady who goes up and down the spiral stairway to the Solar. Apparently she had died in childbirth and was sad because the 'children are buried in the Church'. According to Judy, 'she is one of those echo memories that hadn't grasped the idea she was dead ... I told her she was dead ... and thought I had got her to understand.' However, a little while later another medium also picked up on her, so apparently she wasn't quite ready to move on.

Judy then picked up on a far more unpleasant spirit on the same stairs up by the door. 'He was a horrible man. I got the

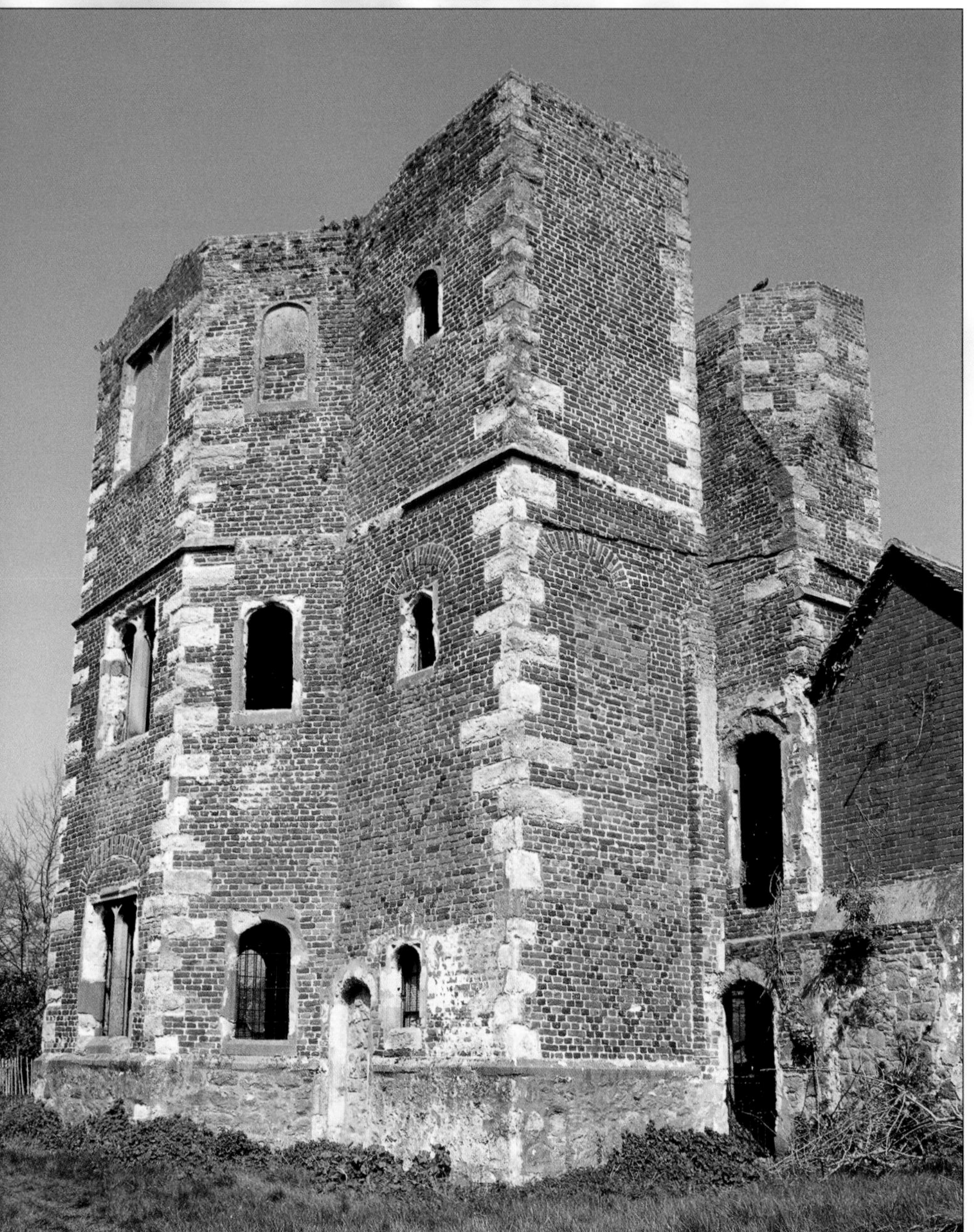

ABOVE: *You can gaze upon the remnants of Otford Palace and imagine yourself standing alongside Henry VIII.*

'I TOLD HER SHE WAS DEAD ... AND THOUGHT I HAD GOT HER TO UNDERSTAND.'

PENSHURST PLACE AND GARDENS

impression that he was a servant of the family, he smelt of wood smoke. He did not want to talk to us, just wanted us to be gone and said that we would not pass [through the door]; he was guarding it for his Lord.' She was aware of a dark cloud either crouching or moving around at the top of the stairs by the door. After an unsuccessful attempt to calm the man down and persuade him to depart, Judy felt quite drained and decided to leave him to his anger and go and sit down in the hall.

It was here that another member of the group was poked in the side by an unseen hand, which she was convinced was that of a child. Later on, in the course of a séance, Judy herself picked up on the ghost of a fair-haired boy in his early teens who was very mischievous and liked to play tricks on people. Another member of the group picked up on a man in armour that Judy felt was the 'grumpy man' whose presence she had noticed earlier. Although she could see his face she couldn't see what he was wearing, so was unable to be absolutely sure that the two impressions were of the same entity.

Interestingly, at the later debriefing session Judy learnt that the ghosts of a knight and a child had been seen in the Baron's Hall, the knight on the stairs and the child in the hall. Earlier Judy had also gone upstairs to a third room and as she approached it was overcome by a feeling of dread. 'I opened the door and peeked in ... I said out loud, "Can I come in?" There was a palpable feeling of being pushed away. As if there was a real barrier to entering.' During the debriefing session she learnt that that particular room has something of a reputation and 'even workmen [are] afraid of going into it'.

Despite her experiences Judy, like many visitors before and after her, came away enchanted by the lovely old building. 'Penshurst Place is a beautiful location,' she told me, 'and I was honoured to get the chance to attend the ghost hunt there. I would love to go back and try to talk to the ghosts again.'

OTFORD PALACE
OTFORD, KENT
She Bows Her Head, But Why?

Otford Palace was one of the residences of the archbishops of Canterbury. It was virtually rebuilt between 1514 and 1518 by Archbishop Wareham, who created a huge Renaissance palace which in turn provided the inspiration for Cardinal Wolsey's magnificent Hampton Court. Having 'acquired' the latter Henry VIII also cast covetous eyes over Otford Palace, and in

1537 he forced Archbishop Cranmer to hand it over to the Crown. Today, very little remains of what one Elizabethan historian described as a 'gorgeous place' that cost a remarkable £33,000 to build. It does, however, still inspire flights of fancy to gaze upon the remaining red-brick façade and imagine Henry VIII doing likewise.

Nobody knows for certain the identity of the mysterious young woman whose wraith has been seen gliding around the site. She is said to wear a long gown, which is described as being either blue or grey, and drifts nonchalantly around with her head bowed. She has a melancholic demeanour and the startling habit of vanishing into thin air should anyone pay her too much attention.

Old Soar Manor
BOROUGH GREEN, KENT
Jenny's Fall From Grace

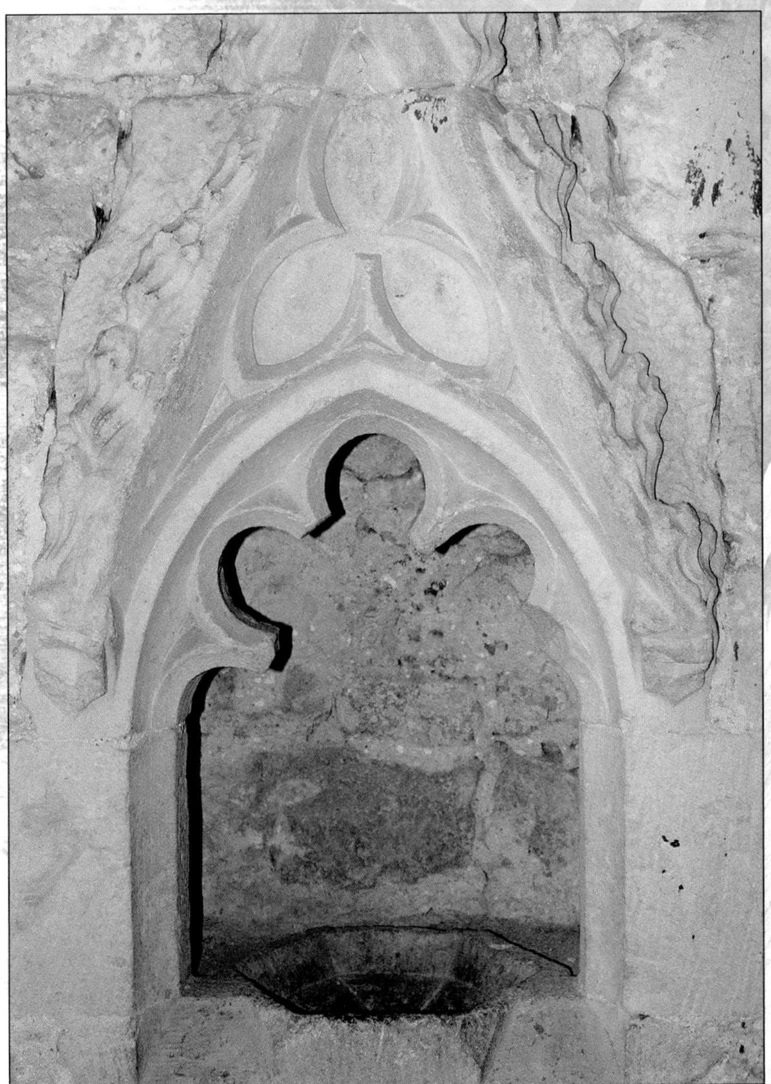

ABOVE: *Several accounts exist to explain how a servant named Jenny came to hit her head on the font at Old Soar Manor, but all agree a roguish priest was behind her death.*

Old Soar (Norman for 'grief') Manor was built in the 13th century and possibly for the Culpepper family, once the largest landowners in Kent and Sussex, who acquired their holdings, so tradition maintains, by kidnapping wealthy heiresses and forcing them to marry a son of the family. Although the medieval hall was demolished in the 18th century, the solar chamber, which stands over a barrel-vaulted undercroft, and which was once the living quarters of the lord of the manor, survives. Also still standing is the chapel where 'Jenny', the resident wraith, makes frequent appearances.

Jenny is said to have once been a servant girl who at Christmas 1775 was seduced by a drunken priest and left pregnant. Unsure what to do about her situation she asked the priest for his advice. According to some accounts he told her to marry her boyfriend, a prospect that, for some reason, caused the poor girl to faint and hit her head on the font. Other versions of the story maintain that the priest had little sympathy for her plight and following a violent altercation, he left her lying in the chapel face down in the font, where she drowned in just a few inches of water. The Geary family, who then owned the manor assumed that she had committed suicide and buried her at midnight in unconsecrated ground.

Ever since, her ghost has made frequent returns to the chapel determined to make known the truth behind the circumstances of her death. A seemingly pointless and unnecessary task because her story is a well-known piece of local folklore. She also wishes for her mortal remains to be given a Christian burial in order that her spirit might finally pass over and find rest. Sadly, since no one knows for certain exactly where those remains lie, the poor girl might also be disappointed in even this minor goal.

Many visitors to the property have spoken of ghostly encounters in the chapel, and June seems to be the month when paranormal happenings reach their zenith. Sudden and inexplicable drops in temperature can occur even on the warmest of days. Ghostly, agitated footsteps have been heard pacing backwards and forwards across empty rooms and strange lights have been seen moving around inside the empty building at night. Feelings of desperate anxiety and unhappiness have been experienced at certain spots in the chapel. Some people have even reported catching ethereal glimpses of the unfortunate Jenny, as she returns in spectral form to the very spot where in dramatically taking leave of the building she left her mark on it forever.

Watchful Queen and Headless

Dark house, by which once more I stand
Here in the long unlovely street,
Doors, where my heart was used to beat
So quickly waiting for a hand.

A hand that can be clasped no more -
Behold me, for I cannot sleep,
And like a guilty thing I creep
At earliest morning to the door.

From 'In Memoriam'
by Lord Alfred Tennyson (1809-1892)

S

Horsemen

Essex, Cambridgeshire, Suffolk and Norfolk

The counties that reach eastwards from London once formed the ancient kingdom of East Anglia, whose inhabitants included the North Folk (Norfolk) and the South Folk (Suffolk). Bounded to the west by the swamps of the Fens, buffered to the east and north by the sea, and hemmed in at the south by the thick woodlands of Saxon Essex, it was always a distant and mysterious region, and even today parts of it can appear centuries removed from the rest of Britain. Some of its countryside can be extremely eerie, especially when thick mists cover its marshes, fields and woodlands with a dense blanket, causing a strange aura of chilling silence to hang heavy over the landscape. These are the times when you just know that phantoms walk the earth, and that the nights are a time to pull close to a roaring log fire and tell tales of ghosts. Then can you believe implicitly that the headless body of Anne Boleyn is carried across the grounds of Blickling Hall in a carriage pulled by horses all of which are similarly deficient in the cranium region. Then can you begin to understand that, despite the evidence sceptical scientists uncover to 'prove' that ghosts don't exist, there will always be things that cannot be explained, as the mysterious places of haunted Britain continue to exert a powerful hold on our imagination.

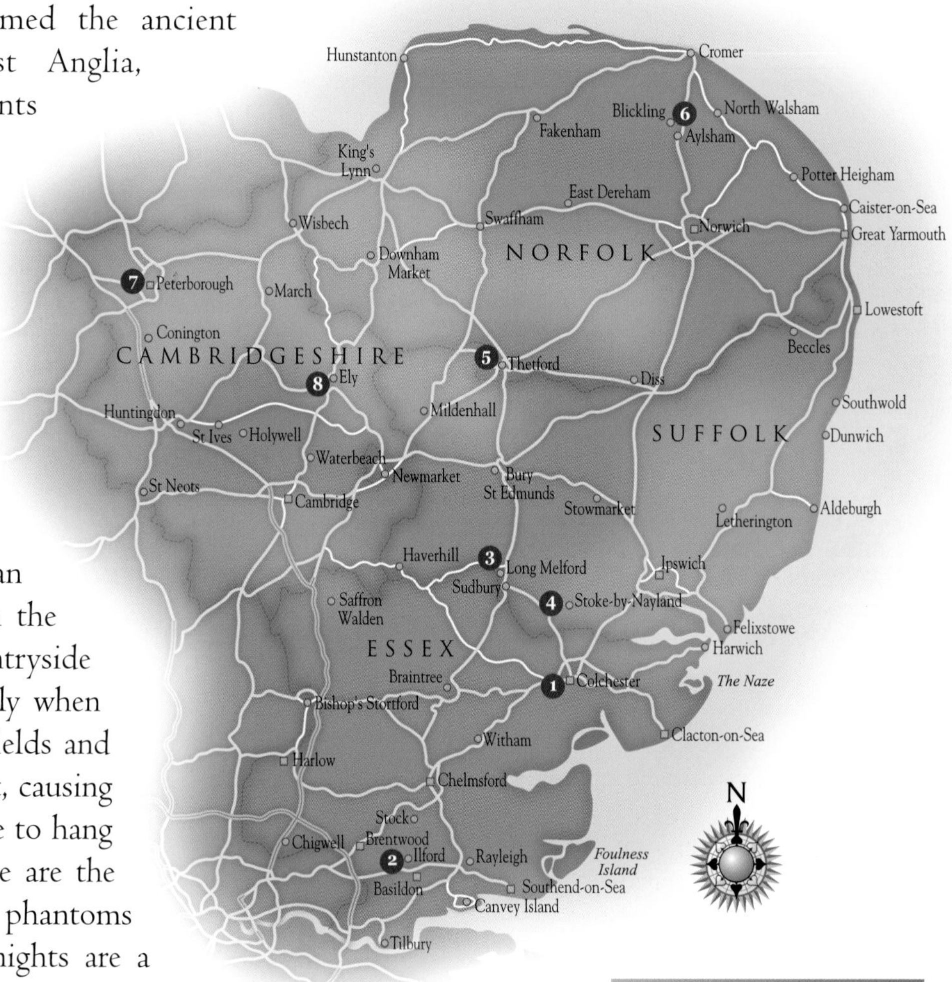

KEY

1. Layer Marney Tower
2. Rainham Hall
3. Melford Hall
4. Thorington Hall
5. Thetford Warren Lodge
6. Blickling Hall
7. Peterborough Museum
8. Cromwell's House

ABOVE: *The ghost of the first Lord Marney is said to ride his horse dramatically down 96 stairs at Layer Maney Tower.*

PREVIOUS PAGES: *Although the Countess of Rivers was forced to flee Melford Hall in life, in death cannot resist its allure and returns as a ghost to haunt it.*

LAYER MARNEY TOWER
NR. COLCHESTER, ESSEX
The Handsome Phantom

Layer Marney Tower was begun by Henry, the first Lord Marney, during the reign of Henry VIII. Henry died in 1523 and the construction was continued by his son, John, who followed his father to the grave just two years later, leaving the house unfinished and the family without a male heir to continue the line. This tragic state of affairs appears to have proved too much for Henry, and his ghost has returned to the house many times to chill the blood of unwitting visitors.

In the early 1800s two workmen who were undertaking repairs in the top room of one of the towers, were somewhat irritated by the sound of a door that kept slamming. Eventually, they went to find which door it was with the intention of locking it to prevent its disturbing them any further. However, their search unearthed only one door that it could possibly have been, and not only was it firmly locked, but its lock and hinges were so rusted away that it was impossible to open it, let alone slam it. They were even more surprised when a cloaked figure, holding what appeared to be a large seal in its hand, appeared by that very door, and having stood glowering at them for a few moments, promptly vanished. Later, when shown the Marney family tombs in Layer Marney church, it is claimed that thay identified the recumbent figure on one of the tombs as being the mysterious apparition that they had seen in the tower.

Of course it is little more than convenient speculation to surmise that it was the ghost of the first Lord Marney that they encountered, but there is a long-held tradition that his is the spectre most associated with Layer Marney Tower. His haunting is, perhaps, one of the most dramatic in Essex, for he is said to appear resplendent in full armour, mounted on a trusty steed which he proceeds to ride down all 96 stairs of the spiral staircase.

LEFT: *Ghostly footsteps are often heard plodding along the corridors of Thorington, But whose are they?*

OPPOSITE: *The ghost of Colonel Mulliner is loathe to depart from the beautiful Rainham Hall in Essex.*

RAINHAM HALL
ILFORD, ESSEX
The Colonel's Return

Built in 1729 for merchant and shipowner John Harle, Rainham Hall is a magnificent Georgian mansion set back from the road behind beautiful wrought-iron gates. It is haunted by the ghost of a tall man, dressed in grey tweeds with a fine collar who has only ever been seen during the hours of daylight. No one is absolutely certain of his identity but the general consensus is that he is the spectre of Colonel Mulliner, a resident of the house in the early 20th century. It would seem that he so loved the impressive old building that he is loathe to leave it even in death.

MELFORD HALL
LONG MELFORD, SUFFOLK
Her Ladyship is No Longer With Us

The Manor of Melford was once owned by the great Benedictine Abbey at Bury St Edmunds. It was granted to Sir William Cordell during the Dissolution of the Monasteries (1536-1540), a shrewd local lawyer who rose to become both Speaker of the House of Commons and later Master of the Rolls. In 1554 he began work on a house that would befit his ambition and prominence, and upon its completion in 1578 he was able to entertain Queen Elizabeth I at his new home in lavish style. During the Civil War, the house was ransacked by 3,000 Parliamentarians who objected to the Countess of Rivers' support for the Royalist cause. This grand lady was forced to flee for her life as the family home was plundered by the 'scum of Colchester', and the memory of this indignity appears to have followed her beyond the grave as her ghost is said to make occasional returns to walk the rooms and corridors of this magnificent red-brick house.

THORINGTON HALL
STOKE BY NAYLAND, SUFFOLK
Plodding Footsteps and the Drifting Girl

This lovely gabled house is owned by the National Trust and is only open by written appointment. It was built in c. 1600, extended in 1700 and restored in 1937. Mysterious heavy footsteps have been heard plodding their way along the building's ancient corridors. Nobody knows who they belong to and in which era of the house's past they originate. They sound too heavy to be in anyway connected with the house's other ghost, that of a girl in a 'brownish dress', which is tied at the waist with a cord. She is a harmless apparition who drifts aimlessly along the upstairs passage. She bothers no one, her appearances are brief and the only truly noticeable feature of her presence is the faint chill that she leaves behind in her ghostly wake.

ABOVE: *Does a ghostly leper roam the ruins of Thetford Warren Lodge?*

THETFORD WARREN LODGE

THETFORD, NORFOLK

Lepers and Spooks

There is some debate over the history of Thetford Warren Lodge, which is an early 15th-century stone and flint structure built by the monks of a nearby Cluniac priory for the keeper of the large Westwick rabbit warren. History and legend are in agreement that it is a fine example of a fortified warrener's house, and that it dates from the days when rabbits were an important source of meat and fur. Where the two divide, however, is over its later use as a Lazar house, or lepers' retreat. Historically speaking there is little evidence that the building was ever used for such a purpose. But according to legend and paranormal tradition, it most certainly was and it is one of these unfortunate former residents who returns to the lodge in ghostly form. The gibbering figure with ravaged face and burning eyes is said to appear before startled witnesses and pace fitfully around the ruin before abruptly disappearing. Whether historically accurate or not, it is certainly a dramatic and disturbing manifestation. It also provides a stark contrast to the lodge's other more cuddly spectral resident, that of a white rabbit that hops around the site, a reminder of the building's original function.

BLICKLING HALL

BLICKLING, NORFOLK

The Headless Re-union

Blickling Hall was built in the early part of the 17th century for Sir Henry Hobart, although the ghosts that reputedly haunt it are those of the occupants of a previous building on the site. This earlier hall once belonged to Sir Thomas Boleyn, father of the ill-fated Anne Boleyn. It was she who having caught the eye of Henry VIII, became his mistress and ultimately his second Queen, before finding herself accused of treasonable adultery, sexual deviation (with among others her brother, Lord Rochford) and, worst of all, witchcraft. Sentenced to death by her own uncle, the Duke of Norfolk, she was beheaded on 19th May 1536 by a skilled swordsman specially imported from France for the occasion - her husband's one merciful concession.

Her ghost is now one of the busiest in England, but it is here at Blickling on the anniversary of her death that she makes her most dramatic appearance. Indeed, the auspicious date is something of a ghostly family reunion in these parts. Anne herself appears dressed all in white, seated in a ghostly carriage that is drawn by headless horses, spurred on by a headless coachman. Anne, too, is headless - her severed, dripping head held securely in her lap as the ghastly vision careers along the drive of Blickling Hall. Upon arrival at the door the coach and driver vanish leaving the headless Queen to glide alone into the house, where she roams the corridors and rooms until daybreak.

Her brother, Lord Rochford, appears on the same night. He is headless as well although he doesn't enjoy the comfort of a carriage, for he is dragged across the surrounding countryside by four headless horses. Not to be left out of this unearthly family get-together, her father, Sir Thomas Boleyn, has been given a dreadful penance to perform on the same night. Once a year for a thousand years from his death in 1539, he must attempt to drive his spectral coach and horses over 12 bridges that lie between Wroxham and Blickling. He is also headless and carries his head under his arm, which makes controlling the horses a difficult task indeed.

A final spirit to haunt Blickling Hall is thought to be that of Sir Henry Hobart, who died of his wounds in the house following a duel in 1698. It is reported that his dying groans still echo down the centuries from time to time, chilling the blood of all who hear them.

Peterborough Museum and Art Gallery, Priestgate, Peterborough, Cambridgeshire

He was Buried Far From Home

At around 10 p.m. on 8th August 2003, the Cambridge Paranormal Society began an investigation at Peterborough Museum and Art Gallery that over the next six hours provided some interesting results. Most of the team picked up on unusual feelings around the building and each one of them, at some point or other in the vigil, got the distinct impression that they were not alone. One of their number on walking into the lecture room was overcome by an 'overwhelming sense of emotion and feeling of confusion', which proved so strong that he had to leave the room and compose himself. At 4 a.m. they decided to hold a final vigil in the Geology Department, but as they settled into the room two of the group became convinced that there was somebody else on the landing outside who was about to come in. When no one appeared they did a head count to see if anyone was missing, and when they found that no one was, they conducted a thorough search of all the rooms on that floor but found no trace of anyone. They were sure that there wasn't anyone else in the museum at the time and concluded that 'there is a plethora of connections to possible spirit activity within the building and a good deal of further research will be required to uncover many of the hidden truths that lay [sic.] buried within its ethereal fabric.'

The Georgian building that Peterborough Museum now occupies was built in 1816 and was originally the town house of Thomas and Charlotte Coke. In 1856 it was sold to the 3rd Earl Fitzwilliam, and a year later became the city's first hospital and remained as such until 1928, after which it was

BELOW: *Anne Boleyn makes a dramatic return to Blickling Hall sans head on the anniversary of her death.*

MUSEUM
PRESENTED TO THE CITIZENS OF PETERBOROUGH
JUNE 22 1931
BY
PERCY MALCOLM STEWART ESQUIRE

ABOVE: *A ghostly soldier is just one of the revenants to haunt Peterborough's, in parts, very eerie museum.*

converted into a museum and opened to the public in 1931.

Initially, the only full-time member of staff was a caretaker by the name of Mr Yarrow, who lived on the premises with his wife and two children in a first-floor flat in what is today part of the Geology Gallery. One afternoon in September 1931, Mr Yarrow took their two sons out and left his wife to deal with the last few visitors and lock up. Having done so she went up to their flat and busied herself preparing supper. About half a minute later she heard someone ascending the main stairs and presuming her family had returned, went out to greet them. Instead she came face to face with a young man of around thirty years of age, who had brown hair and was wearing a green or grey suit.

Thinking that he was a visitor whom she had inadvertently locked in, she moved forward to escort him from the premises. Then she noticed two peculiar things about him. Firstly, his footsteps were unnaturally loud, and secondly he was actually floating as opposed to walking up the stairs. Open-mouthed, she watched as he drifted towards her, passed straight through the closed doors next to her, and continued along the corridor where he suddenly vanished. Mrs Yarrow hastily left the building.

In the years that followed there were regular reports of the ghostly young man being seen at the museum. Thanks to the researches of the museum's Events Co-ordinator, Stuart Orme, there is reasonable certainty as to the ghost's identity. He is thought to have been a First World War Australian soldier named Thomas Hunter, who in 1914 enlisted in the Australian Army, the ANZACS, and served at Gallipoli. Seriously wounded in January 1916, he was treated for a time at a field hospital before eventually being shipped back to Britain where he was put on a train and sent north for treatment. Unfortunately, his condition worsened on the journey and the train was forced to make an unscheduled stop at the first convenient station, which was Peterborough. He was taken to the nearest hospital, which the museum then was, but it was too late and he died on 31st July 1916. He is buried in Peterborough's Broadway Cemetery, although his ghost is thought to roam the museum lamenting the fact that he died so very far away from home.

His appearances have become decidedly irregular since the 1970s, but hopeful ghost hunters can be encouraged by the fact that as many as eight other ghosts are known to haunt Peterborough Museum. A cold feeling is known to descend over certain parts of the building without warning, furniture is regularly and mysteriously moved around overnight, and many visitors have felt the alarming sensation of being touched by ice-cold hands as they wander the museum's rooms and corridors.

All in all Peterborough Museum is, supernaturally speaking, extremely active and the Cambridge Paranormal Society conduct regular and on-going investigations at the premises, whilst the general public can explore the night hours during the Peterborough Ghost Walk tours that begin at the museum.

'THERE IS A PLETHORA OF CONNECTIONS TO POSSIBLE SPIRIT ACTIVITY WITHIN THE BUILDING'

PETERBOROUGH MUSEUM AND ART GALLERY

CROMWELL'S HOUSE
ELY, CAMBRIDGESHIRE
Oliver Cromwell is Still At Home

ABOVE: *Several people who have attempted to spend the night in Cromwell's old home in Ely have been forced to flee in terror, unable to complete their vigil.*

Oliver Cromwell inherited the modest 13th-century, black and white timber-framed building that now bears his name from a maternal uncle in 1636. He and his family lived there for around ten years before moving to London. Following the execution of Charles I in 1649, Cromwell eventually became the most powerful man in the country as Lord Protector of England. He would live in palatial splendour at several residences, including Hampton Court Palace, which were a sharp contrast to his Ely house which he had shared with his wife, their six children, his two unmarried sisters and his mother.

Since 1990 the building has been home to the Ely Tourist Information Centre and incorporates an interesting little museum that tells the story of Cromwell's life and times. The kitchen is dominated by a huge fireplace and affords a lovely view of nearby St Mary's Church from the window at which Cromwell himself may have once stood. Next door is the so-called 'Haunted Room', where Cromwell is depicted lying upon his deathbed. It is in this room that several people have encountered paranormal activity. A medium who visited the house with the Cambridge Paranormal Society in November 2003 complained that the energy there made her feel quite sick and she felt an urgent need to leave the room. Prior to this incident, two reporters who had also attempted a night-time vigil, in the hope of witnessing the house's supernatural phenomena, found their experience so unnerving that they fled the house before the night had ended.

In their book ***Haunted Ely***, Vivienne Doughty and Margaret Haynes tell of a disturbing occurrence experienced by a lady guest who was staying at the house in April 1979. At the time the building was a vicarage and the room above what is now the Tithe Office was used as a guest bedroom. In the early hours of one morning the lady, who was staying in the room with her husband, awoke to find herself standing in a corner of the room. Her arms were being held very tightly in front of her by an invisible male presence. She had the clear impression that he was a powerful and authoritative personality, yet she didn't feel in the least bit threatened by him. On the contrary she felt a distinct bond with him. Suddenly the man released his grip and the lady returned to bed where she slept until morning. When she awoke, her arms were very sore and on pulling back the bed clothes she discovered that red finger-marks were clearly visible on both her arms. Since the Tithe Office was once Oliver Cromwell's office it has been suggested that the lady may well have encountered the invisible entity of Cromwell himself.

A great deal of ghostly activity has been reported at Cromwell's House. Doors are slammed shut by unseen hands, and several visitors have experienced the alarming sensation of icy-cold fingers being run down the backs of their necks. It oozes character and atmosphere, all of which is enhanced by the chance of an encounter with one of England's most imposing historical figures.

Wicked Lord and Fo

My life closed twice before its close -
It yet remains to see
If Immortality unveil
A third Even to me

So huge, so hopeless to conceive
As these that twice befell.
Parting is all we know of heaven,
And all we need of hell.

My Life Closed Twice Before Its Close.
By Emily Dickinson (1830- 1886)

S

RLORN WALLS

Northamptonshire, Leicestershire, Nottinghamshire and Lincolnshire

The counties that stretch inland from the Lincolnshire coast are home to some of the best-known legends in English history, and I thoroughly enjoyed uncovering and researching the haunted histories of the houses in this region. Grace Dieu Priory affected me deeply and although I wasn't lucky enough to witness its famous 'white lady', the melancholic appeal of this ruin more than compensated. Harlaxton Manor in Lincolnshire looks just as a haunted house should and I felt more than a little envious of the American students from Evansville University, Indiana, whose British campus the house has now become. Nottingham's Wollaton Hall, now the city's Natural History Museum, demonstrated the unrivalled allure of a haunting when a survey revealed that visitors believed that its ghosts were its most interesting feature. Meanwhile, a ghost captured on CCTV at Belgrave Hall brought Dr Larry Muntz (the parapsycologist on whom the film *Ghostbusters* was based) hurrying across the Atlantic to conduct an investigation.

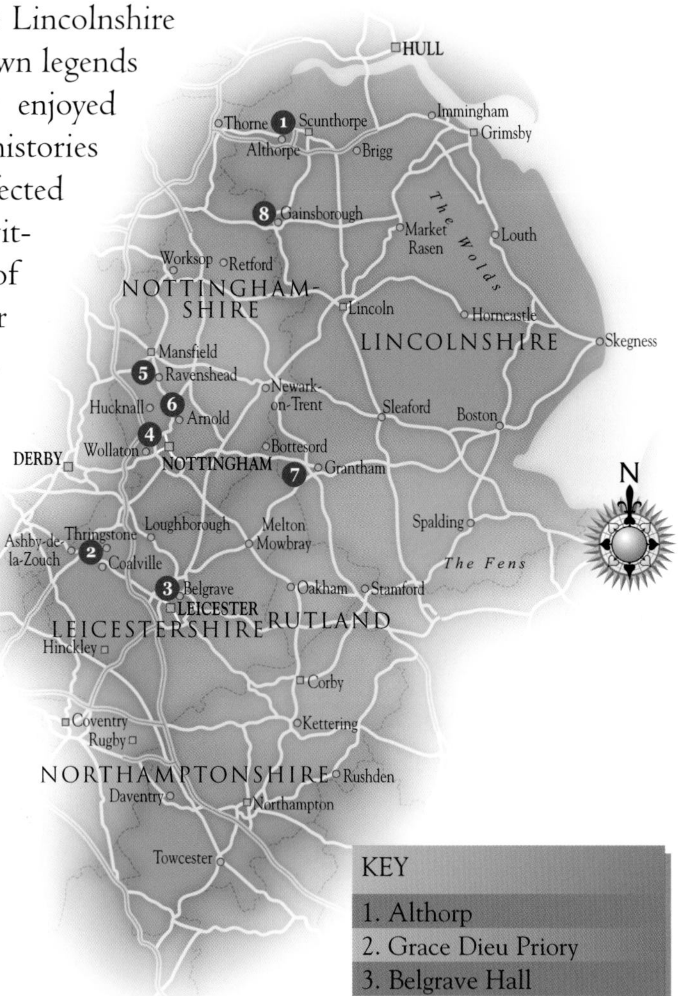

KEY

1. Althorp
2. Grace Dieu Priory
3. Belgrave Hall
4. Wollaton Hall
5. Newstead Abbey
6. Bestwood Lodge Hotel
7. Harlaxton Manor
8. Gainsborough Old Hall

Althorp
Northamptonshire
The Devoted Ghostly Servant

This magnificent mansion was constructed in 1508 by Sir John Spencer and remodelled in the 18th century. It has been the home to the Spencer family for almost 500 years and contains one of the finest private art collections in Britain. In recent years it has become most famous as the childhood home of Diana, Princess of Wales, and poignantly as her final resting place following her tragic death in August 1997.

Althorp's ghostly tale relates to a former servant of the house. One night a Mr Drury, later to become an archdeacon, was on a visit to the house and stayed up very late playing billiards with Lord Lyttleton. Their game over, the two men prepared to retire to their respective bedrooms, but as they did so a servant warned them to be sure that they extinguished their candles before going to sleep as his Lordship, Earl Spencer, was exceedingly nervous of fire.

As Mr Drury settled into his bed he ensured that he blew out his candle and, having done so, he sunk into a deep sleep. In the early hours he suddenly awoke with a start and found himself blinking at a bright light flickering across his face. As his eyes focused, he saw a man in a striped shirt and flat cap standing at the foot of his bed training the rays of a lantern upon him. His demand to know what the man wanted was met with a blank stare. Sitting upright he threatened to report this intrusion to Earl Spencer. The man's reaction was to turn and walk towards the dressing room. Mr Drury called after him telling him that there was no way out through there, but the man ignored him. Annoyed but evidently not overly concerned Mr Drury turned over and went back to sleep.

The next morning he was sitting at breakfast with his host's daughter, Lady Lyttleton, and proceeded to relate the story of his strange intruder, commenting that the man was probably drunk. Lady Lyttleton shook her head. 'He most certainly wasn't drunk', she told him, and went on to inform him that he was probably one of her father's favourite grooms who had died two weeks before. It had been his duty to go round the house at night and visit every room to ensure that none of the guests had fallen asleep without extinguishing their candles. Apparently, so devoted was this groom to his nocturnal duty that in death he continued his rounds keeping a concerned eye on the sleeping guests and their candles.

PREVIOUS PAGES: *Looking every inch the haunted house of tradition Harlaxton Manor has many a ghostly tale to chill the blood.*

Grace Dieu Priory

THRINGSTONE, LEICESTERSHIRE

Next Stop Eternity

Grace Dieu Priory is a rare example of an Augustinian nunnery and was founded in 1239/40 by Roesia de Verdun for 14 nuns and their prioress. In 1539, during the Dissolution of the Monasteries, the property was acquired by John Beaumont on extremely favourable terms and he set about converting it into a suitable family home. The Beaumonts sold the house to wealthy Leicestershire landowner Sir Ambrose Phillips in 1690. His short tenure saw the demolition of most of what remained of the nunnery church in 1696. Over the following years the property was abandoned and fell into such disrepair that by the time William Wordsworth paid a visit in 1811 he found little more than 'the ivied ruins of forlorn Grace Dieu.'

Today the Grace Dieu Trust is working hard to preserve the little that remains and hopes to eventually make it safe for public access. Meanwhile, the eerie ruins enjoy the

BELOW: *Risk assessments, especially where candles are concerned, are high on the priority list for Althorp's ghostly groom.*

reputation of being one of the most haunted locations in Leicestershire. There have been many reports of a phantom 'white lady' drifting around the site; the most infamous of these sightings occurred in 1954. The driver of a local bus stopped to pick up a woman in white who was waiting at the bus shelter opposite the ruins. Having opened the doors, the driver was somewhat mystified when nobody boarded the bus. Both he and the conductor searched the vicinity but the woman had, apparently, vanished without trace. Several passengers were later able to confirm the accounts given by the driver and conductor.

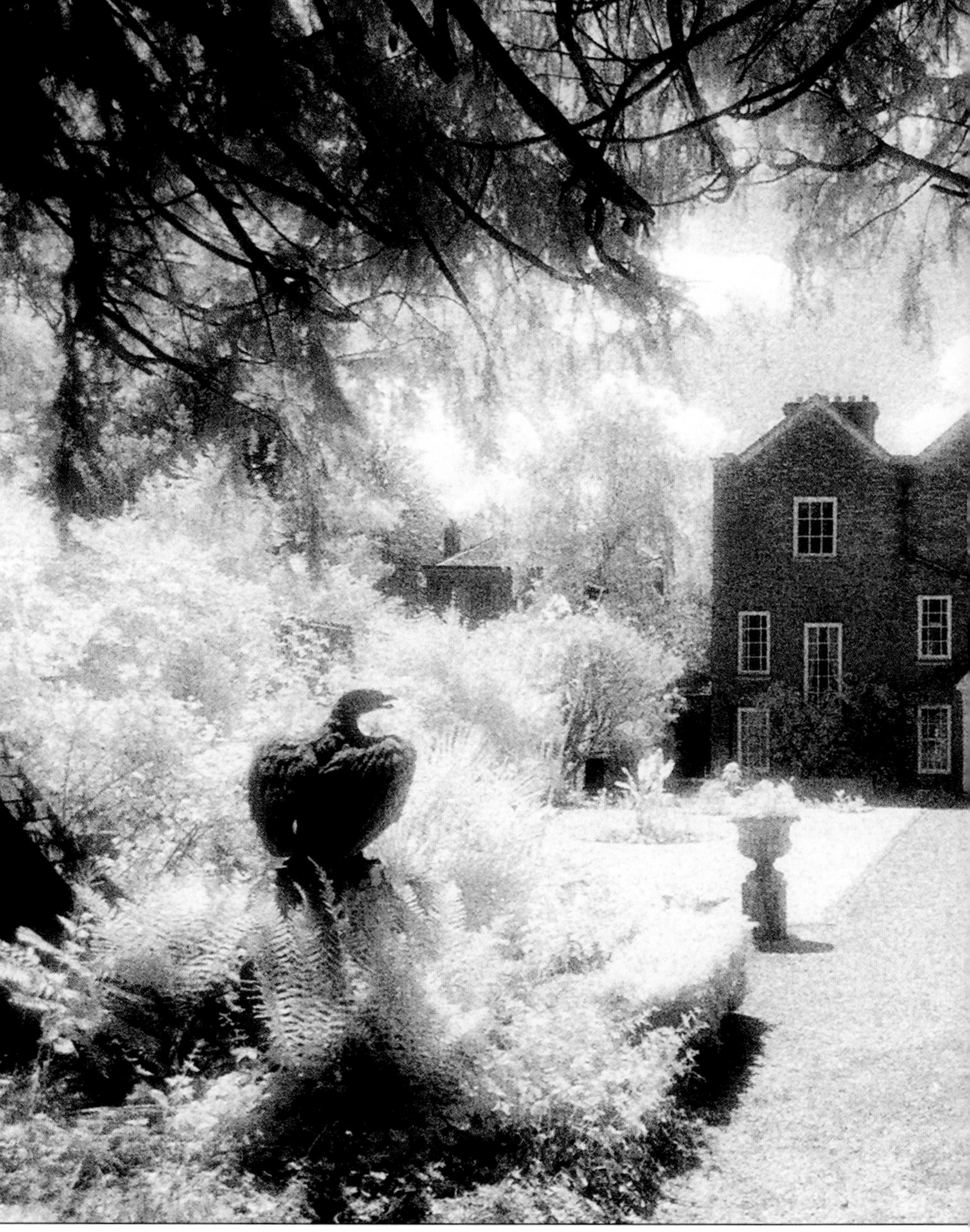

Although the 'lady at the bus stop' incident is now an established piece of local folklore, it is just one of a long list of similar happenings that, over the years, have appeared in the pages of local newspapers. In 1981 a local police officer was riding his motorbike past Grace Dieu. Suddenly the temperature dropped alarmingly and he was overcome by an intense cold. Moments later, a grey, hooded figure in a long gown proceeded to glide across the road and behind the bus shelter. Despite being 'absolutely petrified' the policeman stopped his bike and searched all around but found no trace of anyone or anything. In November 1997 a council warden involved in restoration work at the ruins was starting to pack up one night, when he looked up to find a lady standing there staring at him. He was pushed violently from behind, but when he turned around he found no one there.

The tradition of a mysterious figure drifting around the ruins of Grace Dieu is an old one, and there are witness accounts going as far back as the early 20th century. Many of the reports describe the apparition as being robed, having no hands or feet, and apparently gliding over the ground as opposed to walking on it. As to her identity there are several theories. One story tells how Agnes Litherland, the last Prioress of Grace Dieu in the 1530s, had an illegitimate child. The baby was cruelly drowned in the lake behind the Priory, whilst the mother was walled up alive as punishment for her indiscretion. Another legend, also featuring Agnes Litherland, holds that she managed to hide the Priory's treasures during the Dissolution of the Monasteries. She was captured by the King's men, but refused to disclose the hiding place and as a result was killed.

While theories as to the ghostly lady's origins are little more than speculation, what is certain is that there are numerous reports that attest to her existence and she is, without doubt, a firm fixture of Leicestershire's spectral landscape.

BELGRAVE HALL

BELGRAVE, LEICESTERSHIRE

Caught on Camera

When Belgrave Hall was built in the early 18th century, it stood at the heart of a tiny village, three miles from the centre of Leicester. Today, the surrounding countryside has disappeared

'BELGRAVE HALL IS ACTIVELY HAUNTED BY NUMEROUS DISCARNATE ENTITIES OF A BENIGN NATURE'

BELGRAVE HALL

ABOVE: *When there was something strange in their neighbourhood Belgrave Hall called in the original ghost-buster Dr Larry Muntz.*

beneath an advancing tide of urbanization and Belgrave Hall, which is now run as a museum by Leicester City Council, has become a tranquil oasis of memories and numerous ghosts.

In December 1998 the hall was catapulted into the international spotlight when the outside security cameras apparently captured footage of two ghosts. The museum's curator, Stuart Warburton, told how, 'The security cameras at the back of the hall triggered off one night at about 4.50 a.m., [and] two figures appear ... the camera freezes for about five seconds and then the figures disappear. And then we have a mist that swirls along the top of the wall, which we cannot explain.' Some of those who looked at the footage believed that one of the figures was wearing a long Victorian dress, although sceptics were quick to point out that the 'apparition' could just as easily have been a leaf, a moth or even an owl.

Ghost sightings at Belgrave Hall have been reported for years, and there are many witnesses to things going bump at all times of the day or night. Gardener Michael Snuggs once encountered a spectre in a red dress that walked down the stairs, paused to look out of a window, then turned, smiled and walked through to the kitchen, where she disappeared. Another ghost, known as the 'Victorian Lady' has often been heard by staff members as she walks around upstairs. The house is also honoured with occasional visits by both a 'Green Lady' and a 'Grey Lady'. A mysterious cooking odour sometimes permeates the hall, despite the fact that the kitchens are museum pieces and are never actually used.

Of course all these phenomena have been well known in the area for decades. Had it not been for the mysterious film footage this most recent event would probably have remained an intriguing bit of local folklore. However, news that a ghost may well have been captured on film attracted considerable international media interest. Eventually, Dr Larry Muntz, president of the International Society for Psychic research, and the inspiration for the film ***Ghostbusters***, travelled from California to join a team of internationally respected investigators in attempting to uncover the truth behind the haunting of Belgrave Hall. He dismissed the ghostly images on the CCTV footage as entirely natural phenomena 'created by atmospheric discharge'. It was pointed out that to be a ghostly apparition, the figure would in fact be over ten feet tall and it was more likely to have been a leaf or a moth.

However, the team, which included medium Derek Acorah, made some intriguing discoveries in the course of their all-night investigation. 'Belgrave Hall is actively haunted by numerous discarnate entities of a benign nature,' Dr Muntz later reported. 'They are former occupants ... who return there from the spirit world to visit the home in which they once lived happy ... lives.' One was a small child who had died of tuberculosis. Another was a man who had fallen and injured himself on the stairs. Only on the upstairs floor did they encounter an unfriendly spirit, when they came across a male energy that was so negative that they were forced to leave it in peace before it hurt someone or caused damage.

By the end of the night the team had put names to several of the spirits and Stuart Warburton was able to verify that three of them had indeed lived there in life. They were members of the Ellis family, who came to the hall in 1845 when John Ellis, a Leicester industrialist and Member of Parliament, bought the property. They included his daughters Charlotte and Margaret Ellis, both of whom died at the hall, and their stepbrother Edmund Shipley. 'It wouldn't surprise me if even death couldn't keep them from the hall,' observed Mrs June Stevens, who is a direct descendant of the family. 'They were Quakers and very spiritual people. Perhaps they've stuck around.'

BELOW: *When visitors were polled as to the most popular feature at Nottingham's Wollaton Hall they overwhelmingly voted for its ghost stories!*

WOLLATON HALL
WOLLATON, NOTTINGHAMSHIRE
Natural History with a Supernatural Twist

The magnificent Wollaton Hall is a pure expression of Elizabethan architecture. Built in 1588 by Robert Smythson for the hugely wealthy Sir Francis Willoughby, it sits proudly on the summit of a hill surveying its surroundings with an air of arrogant indifference. It's easy to understand how the cost of furnishing his splendid house plunged Sir Francis deeply into debt. He died in London in 1596 'unhappy and without an heir', and the house passed through successive generations of his family, one of whom was the naturalist Francis Willoughby (1635-72.) It was therefore more than apt that when Nottingham Corporation purchased the estate in 1925 they chose to locate the city's Natural History Museum there. Today, visitors can admire a startling array of minerals and other exhibits that include 'favourites like George the Gorilla and the impressive Giraffe upstairs'.

However, when Nottingham Council proposed a major redevelopment in March 2002 and began canvassing visitors' opinions on which aspect of their visit they found most interesting, it was supernatural rather than natural history that

topped the poll.'... Most people have voted for the ghost stories associated with the hall,' admitted general manager Phil Hackett, 'including tales of a tall dark figure and a white lady.'

Wollaton Hall has a long and well-attested tradition of paranormal occurrences and supernatural phenomena. Room 19 seems to be particularly rich in ghostly activity, and people walking through it have experienced sudden and violent drops in temperature as well as sensing a strong but hostile presence. On one occasion a lady visitor, who also happened to be a spiritualist medium, was overcome by an overwhelming sensation of grief. Sitting down, she began to speak of how the room had experienced both great happiness and great sadness. It was later discovered that room 19 had been used by the Middleton family (owners of the hall from the 18th century until its purchase by the council in 1925) as a maternity room and also the place where dead members of the family were laid out prior to their burial. The room is also prone to more traditional forms of supernatural activity, including doors being mysteriously slammed and lights being seen from outside after the hall has closed for the night.

Ghostly footsteps have been heard in both the Great Hall and the Minstrels' Gallery above. There are also several reports of a lengthy whispered conversation in a foreign language being overheard in the Great Hall, whilst a mysterious misty smoke has been known to drift from left to right across the Minstrels' Gallery. The inevitable 'white lady' has put in occasional appearances around the premises, and the figure of a uniformed German officer has been seen striding across the courtyards. He is doubtless a leftover shade from the Second World War when part of Wollaton Park was used as a prisoner-of-war camp and some of the higher ranking officers were allowed to join their British counterparts then garrisoned in Wollaton Hall.

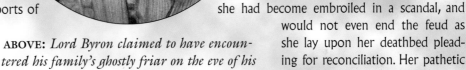

ABOVE: *Lord Byron claimed to have encountered his family's ghostly friar on the eve of his wedding, but was this just a poetic grudge?*

NEWSTEAD ABBEY
NR. RAVENSHEAD, NOTTINGHAMSHIRE
His Lordship Meets the Ghost

George Gordon Noel Byron was born in London in 1788. His mother, Catharine Gordon, was a Scottish heiress descended from James I of Scotland. His father, Captain 'Mad Jack' Byron, was a decadent spendthrift who squandered his wife's money, and then abandoned both her and their newborn son when he fled to France to escape his creditors. Catherine then took her child to the family home in Aberdeen, where they lived frugally. His father died when he was three. In 1798, his great uncle William also died and the ten-year-old boy became the 6th Baron Byron, inheriting the family's ancestral home of Newstead Abbey.

Henry II founded Newstead Abbey in the 12th century in expiation for the murder of Thomas à Becket. It was home to a community of black Augustine monks until its dissolution in 1539, when it was sold to Sir John Byron, who set about building a magnificent residence alongside the Abbey. There is an old belief that those who damage or deface a religious foundation will be thereafter plagued by bad luck. The subsequent fortunes of Sir John's descendants would seem to provide ample confirmation that there may be some truth in the theory. Poverty, scandal, family feuds and childlessness blighted successive generations. The fifth Lord, nicknamed 'Devil Byron', refused to speak to his sister after she had become embroiled in a scandal, and would not even end the feud as she lay upon her deathbed pleading for reconciliation. Her pathetic ghost is still said to wander the grounds wailing loudly: 'Speak to me my lord, do speak to me.' Many believed that 'Devil Byron' was insane and his determined efforts to run down the house and grounds in order to ruin them for his heir certainly adds weight to this belief. As a result, the estate that ten-year-old George Gordon Byron inherited was rotten throughout. Damp came up through the floors, rain poured in through the roof and the only habitable part of the house was a small corner of the kitchen.

Byron didn't actually take up residence at Newstead until after his university days. He celebrated his arrival by throwing the first of his legendary parties, at which the guests wore monks robes and chased the serving maids through the cloisters in what, some claimed, was little short of a sacrilegious orgy. A replica of the skull chalice, from which they drank their communal wine, is on display inside the building today.

Women adored Byron and his affairs became the talk of polite society. There were even whispers of an improper

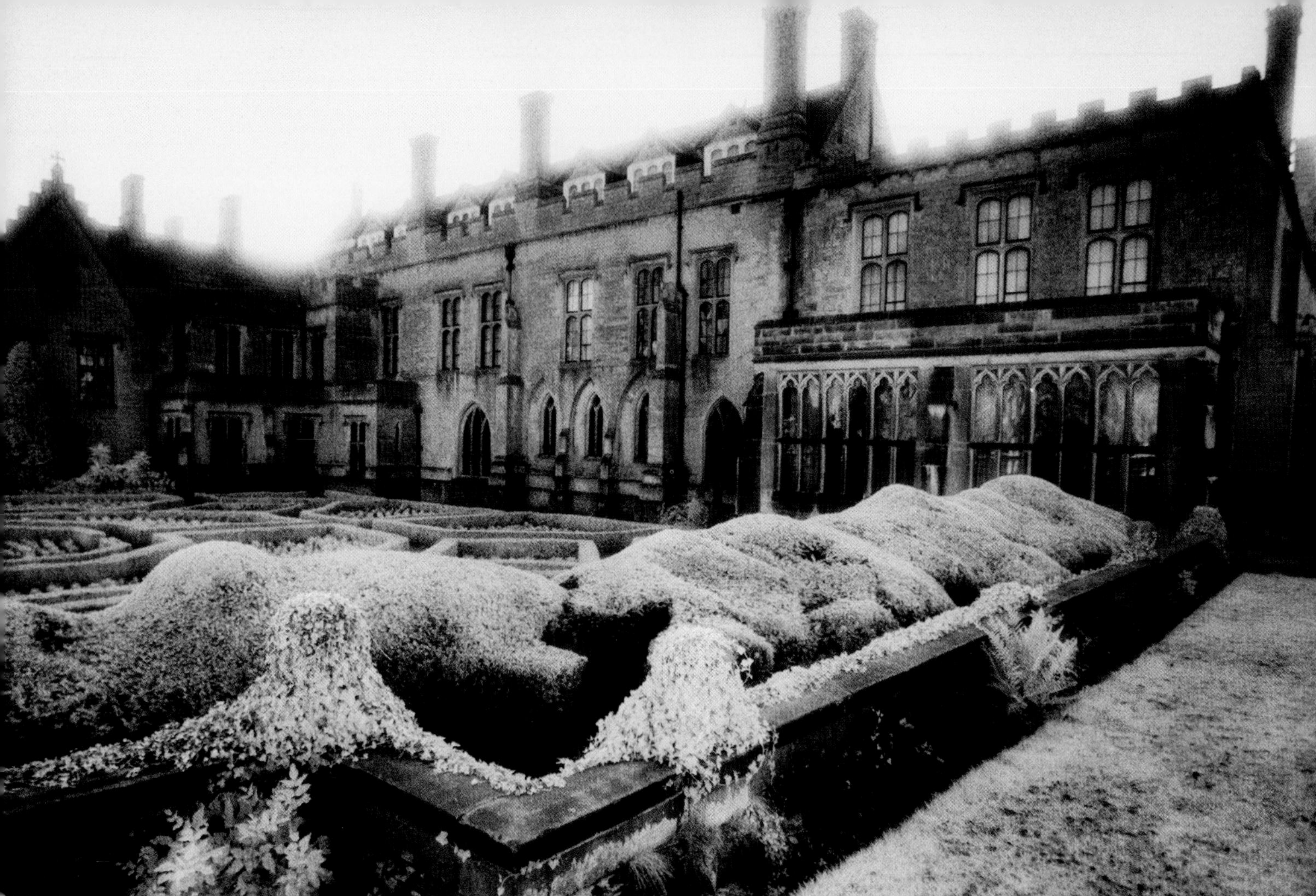

ABOVE: *Newstead Abbey is as haunted and haunting a house as you could ever wish to visit.*

relationship with his half-sister, Augusta Leigh. When her daughter Medora was born, rumour was rife that Byron was the father. His affair with the beautiful and tempestuous Lady Caroline Lamb - it was she who described him as 'Mad, bad and dangerous to know' - is perhaps the most famous of his relationships. It was his marriage to Annabella Milbanke, however, which, so he claimed, brought him into contact with Newstead's most famous ghostly inhabitant, the Black Friar.

Today, a winding stone stairway leads the visitor to a sinister and stark little room, known as the Prior's Oratory, located next door to Byron's Bedroom. Its scarred walls and wooden rafters exude an atmosphere that is nothing short of malicious, and the portrait of a friar that hangs upon the wall projects a menacing, almost threatening, aura. It is known to be a haunt of the Abbey's Black Friar whose appearance was a harbinger that tragedy was about to befall the family. Byron swore that the Black Friar had appeared to him on the night before his wedding. He later described his marriage as the unhappiest event of his career, but this may have been nothing more than poetic bitchery. The Prior's Oratory undoubtedly is one of the most chilling parts of the house, and several guides have been taken suddenly ill upon entering its ominous interior.

Mounting debt caused Byron to sell Newstead Abbey. The scandals of his personal life forced him to leave England in 1817, never to return. He died in 1824 fighting with and funding the Greek freedom fighters in their struggle against the Turks. His body was brought back to England and buried in the family vault at St Mary Magdalene's church, Hucknall.

Byron's literary, if not literal, spirit dominates Newstead Abbey and ghosts aplenty wander its wonderfully dark and atmospheric interior. The most persistent is the 'white lady', whose appearance is always presaged by a sudden drop in temperature, and who leaves in her ghostly wake the distinctive and sweet smell of rose petals.

BESTWOOD LODGE HOTEL
BESTWOOD COUNTRY PARK, NOTTINGHAMSHIRE
Who Turns The Lights Out?

In 1681 Charles II leased Bestwood Lodge for his most famous mistress, Nell Gwynn, and it became one of their love nests. In 1684 he bestowed upon their fourteen-year-old son, Charles Beauclerk, the hereditary title of Duke of St Albans and granted him Betswood Lodge. In the mid-19th century, the 10th

Duke of St Albans had the old lodge demolished and employed the eminent architect Samuel Sanders Teulon to construct the Gothic Revival fantasy which today is an atmospheric hotel, set amidst 700 acres of beautiful parkland.

Several ghosts are known to wander its cosy rooms and corridors, and chief amongst them must be the mother of the dynasty with which the Lodge's history is so inextricably linked, Nell Gwynn. Although her ghost is said to roam the premises, sightings of her are, in fact, quite rare. She is more often smelt than seen, and staff have long commented on the delicate, though distinctive, bouquet of oranges that seems to hang heavy in the air of the hotel's family room whenever families with children have stayed there.

Elsewhere people catch wraith-like glimpses of figures in medieval dress that seem to be quite solid one moment, but which vanish the next. Footsteps have been heard plodding along corridors in the dead of night, and these are occasionally accompanied by the heart-rending sound of children sobbing, even though no children are known to be on the premises when the eerie weeping occurs. Mediums visiting the hotel have detected sundry spirits lurking within its walls, and on one occasion a psychic was overcome by the choking smell of smoke followed by the disturbing sensation of flames, as though an invisible fire was raging around her. Finally, a barman at the hotel once went down into the cellar to change a barrel and was scared rigid when the lights suddenly went out and a disembodied voice enquired politely: 'Can I help you, Sir?' Letting out an almighty scream he raced upstairs demanding to know which of his colleagues had played a joke on him. When he learnt that none of them had been responsible he became decidedly unnerved, and later quit his job as a result of the terrifying encounter.

HARLAXTON MANOR
NR. GRANTHAM, LINCOLNSHIRE
This Place IS Haunted

The grandiose splendour of Harlaxton Manor is little short of breathtaking. It lies at the end of a long, straight drive, and its myriad windows and towers grow larger and larger as you approach, until the house looms over you, a vast and eccentric pile that looks every inch the traditional haunted mansion. So eerie is its appearance that its exterior was used for the 1999 remake of ***The Haunting***, starring Liam Neeson and Catherine Zeta-Jones.

The house, designed by Anthony Salvin, was built between 1832 and 1844 for Gregory Gregory (1764-1854), a wealthy

BELOW: *Bestwood Lodge was once a love nest for Nell Gwynne and Charles II; is she responsible for the ghostly aroma of oranges?*

bachelor whose family had lived at Harlaxton since the 17th century. It seems that his motivation to pull down the original house and replace it with this grandiloquent fusion of Gothic, Jacobean and Baroque styles was simply a desire to outdo his aristocratic neighbours, in particular the Duke of Rutland at Belvoir Castle. In this respect he most certainly succeeded, although he didn't enjoy the splendour of his creation, because he died in June 1854, a year or so before work on the house was fully completed. He had no direct heir and so ownership of the house fell to his elderly cousin, George Gregory. Following George's death in 1860, the house passed through the hands of distant members of the family until the death of Pearson-Gregory in 1935, when it fell derelict.

Harlaxton Manor was on the verge of demolition when it came to the attention of the immensely wealthy and eccentric businesswoman Mrs Violet Van der Elst. Having purchased the manor for £78,000, she renamed it Grantham Castle and set about an ambitious restoration project, adding numerous enhancements that included the massive chandelier in the Great Hall, which had originally been intended for a palace in Madrid (it was not delivered because of the outbreak of the Spanish Civil War).

Violet Van der Elst was strictly against field sports and decreed that her estate was to be a haven for wildlife. She would not allow rabbits to be shot in the grounds nor mice to be killed inside the house. It was during her tenure that the first signs of supernatural activity began to appear. Convinced that she was a magnet for paranormal phenomena Violet set about amassing a huge collection of almost 3,000 books on the occult in the house's library, now renamed the Van der Elst Room in her honour. It was here that she held séances in an attempt to contact the spirit of her deceased second husband, the Belgian artist Jean Van der Elst who had died in 1934.

Unfortunately, by 1948 Violet's fortune was almost spent and she was forced to sell the house to the Jesuits who used it as a seminary until 1966. Today, Harlaxton Manor is the British campus of the University of Evansville, Indiana, where up to 160 residential students at a time follow British and European studies.

The house has a long tradition of being haunted and over the years many teachers and students have spoken of ghostly encounters, particularly in the Van der Elst Room, which appears to be ground zero for the building's supernatural activity. Witnesses have spoken of seeing the hazy outline of a tall man standing in the library's doorway. He has been known to remain visible for anything up to 20 minutes before fading into thin air. Nobody knows his identity or the reason for his manifestations. Another ghost is the apparition of a man in a black cloak, who several people have seen approaching the foot of their beds.

The ghosts of Harlaxton Manor would appear to be fairly benign, and the house itself is a wonderful place to explore. It is a perfect setting for a fleeting glimpse of a shade or a ghostly encounter.

Gainsborough Old Hall
Gainsborough, Lincolnshire
Killed By The Ghost

Gainsborough Old Hall is one of the most complete medieval manor houses to survive in England today. It is a delightful fusion of ancient stone and tasteful restoration; to stand within its history-steeped interior is to be transported back in time.

The building that greets visitors today dates from between 1465 and 1485, although it stands on the site of a much older castle where, on 2nd February 1014, King Sweyn of Denmark, ruthless leader of the great Danish invasion of England, died in torment. Rumour was that he was killed by the spear-wielding

ABOVE: *A ghostly girl still pines for her lost lover at Gainsborough Old Hall.*

spectre of St Edmund, who had been martyred by the Danes 140 years earlier and whose town of Bury St Edmunds Sweyn had threatened to destroy.

It is not surprising that, with such a gruesome pedigree, Gainsborough Old Hall can boast a ghost or two. The ghostly groans and moans of King Sweyn have been known to echo eerily through the Great Hall, beneath which the foundations of the original castle are said to lie. More visual but no less enigmatic is the ghostly lady said to be that of the daughter of a former owner of the castle. In the days when the House of Lancaster fought the House of York for the throne of England during the Wars of the Roses, this girl is said to have fallen in love with a bold knight from nearby Newark Castle. Controversy arose when it was discovered that her lover's family had backed the opposition in a previous campaign and the girl's father was emphatic that the knight would not be welcome. To ensure that his daughter put all thoughts of her suitor from her mind, he locked her away in a tower of the Hall.

Whether she pined away, leapt to her death or was eventually released and found happiness in a more acceptable union is unknown. The trauma of her lonely captivity appears to have proved too much for her spirit, however, and so she haunts the darker recesses of Gainsborough Old Hall. On one occasion she even followed a caretaker along a corridor, and as the poor man tried to shake off his phantom stalker he watched her melt into a nearby wall. Tradition holds that later renovations at that very spot uncovered a doorway that had been plastered over which nobody had known was there, although whether it had any connection to the ghostly lady is unknown.

SLEEPY HAVE HORRORS

Next died the Lady who yon Hall possessed;
And here they brought her noble bones to rest.
In Town she dwelt;- forsaken stood the Hall:
Worms ate the floors, the tapestry fled the wall:
No fire the kitchens cheerless grate displayed;
No cheerful light the long-closed sash conveyed;
The crawling worm, that turns a summer-fly,
Here spun his shroud and laid him up to die
The winter-death:- upon the bed of sate,
The bat shrill-shrieking wooed his flickering mate;
To empty rooms the curious came no more,
From empty cellars turned the angry poor,
And surly beggars cursed the ever-bolted door.

From 'The Lady of the Manor'
by George Crabbe (1754-1832)

NS WHERE LURK

Shropshire, Staffordshire, Cheshire, Merseyside and Derbyshire

I must confess that I've always held a particular affection for this region since I was born and bred in Staffordshire, and when my interest in folklore and legend was first aroused it was places such as Little Moreton Hall that I first began to research. It was, therefore, a pleasure to return and pick my way through the area's haunted houses, some of which I have known since childhood. This is an area of wonderfully varied scenery, sometimes rugged and awe-inspiringly beautiful, sometimes blighted by industry. Its haunted houses are as diverse as its scenery. The peaceful solitude enjoyed by Derbyshire's Elavaston Castle, for example, contrasts sharply with the bleakly lonely setting of Shropshire's Wilderhope Hall. Likewise the town centre setting of Stafford's Ancient High House is a world away from the remote setting of Derbyshire's Highlow Hall. I was spoiled for choice as I began uncovering the stories of the ghosts that haunt these wonderful properties, and it was with great regret that I was forced to omit several that I found truly enchanting. Those that I have included belong to all ages, and present those who come seeking close encounters of a supernatural kind with a lively assortment of active spectres.

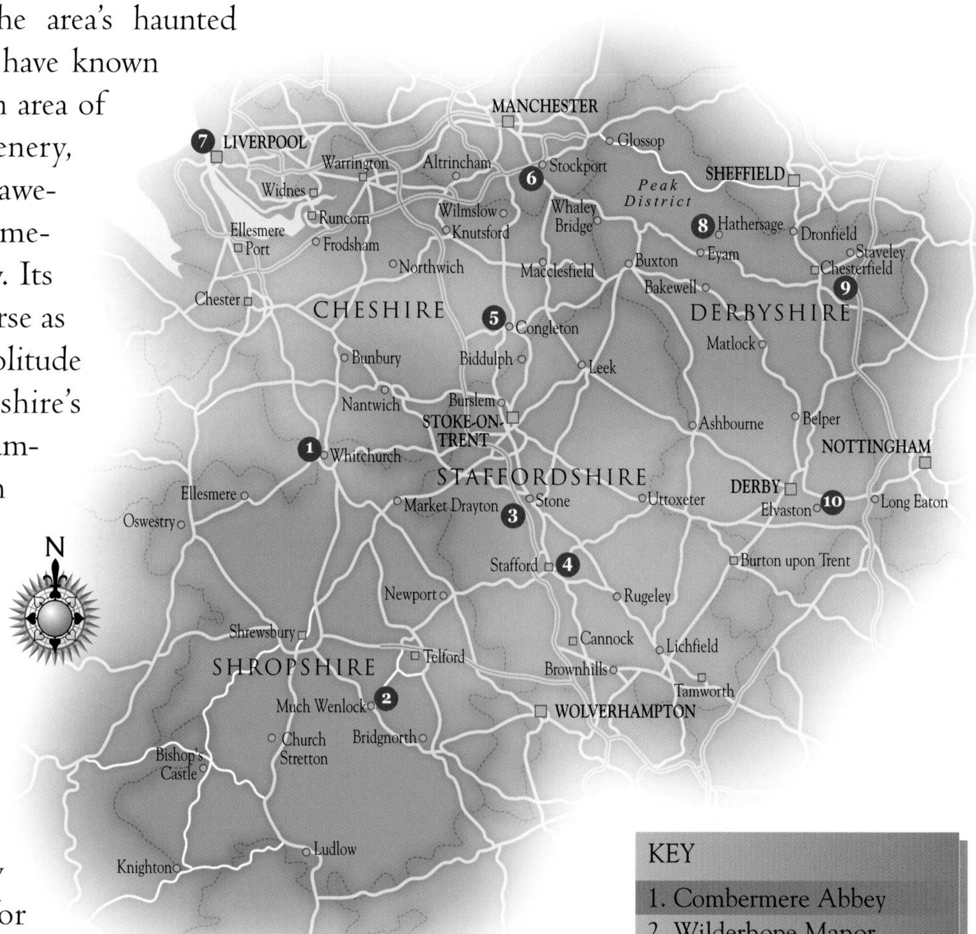

KEY

1. Combermere Abbey
2. Wilderhope Manor
3. Izaak Walton's Cottage
4. The Ancient High House
5. Little Moreton Hall
6. Bramall Hall
7. Speke Hall
8. Highlow Hall
9. Sutton Scarsdale Hall
10. Elvaston Castle

ABOVE: *Despite the fact that he was at the time being buried in the nearby church, Lord Combermere's spirit decided on one last return to his family home in 1891.*

PREVIOUS PAGES: *A forlorn aura of neglect pervades the atmosphere at Sutton Scarsdale Hall where a long ago crusader's prayers were mysteriously answered from afar.*

COMBERMERE ABBEY
WHITCHURCH, SHROPSHIRE
His Lordship Drops By

Combermere Abbey nestles amidst 1,000 acres of lush countryside on the Shropshire–Cheshire border. The Abbey was founded in 1133 by Hugh de Malbanc, Lord Nantwich. It was initially a Savignac foundation but later passed to the Cistercians before being given to Sir George Cotton during the Dissolution of the Monasteries (1536-1540) as a reward for his services to Henry VIII.

In 1814 his descendant, Sir Stapleton Cotton, was created Baron Combermere. An able soldier, he spent 73 years in military service, fought in 17 battles, and died of natural causes at the ripe old age of ninety-two. He was succeeded by his son Sir Wellington Henry Stapleton Cotton, who, in addition to following his father's military calling, served as Member of Parliament for Carrickfergus.

In 1891, Lady Combermere's sister, Sybell Corbett, was staying at the Abbey and decided to take a photograph of the large and impressive library. She noted in her photographic diary that she used an exposure of about one hour. Although the room was apparently empty throughout the exposure, the developed plate showed the faint image of a man seated in Lord Combermere's favourite chair. The figure was later identified as being Lord Combermere himself. Nothing unusual, you might think? Except Lord Combermere had been killed in an accident five days before, and at the very moment when the picture was being taken, his funeral was being held in the local church a few miles away.

The photograph caused quite a stir when it was first published in 1895 and was investigated by Sir William Fletcher Barrett, a key figure and investigator with the Society For Psychical Research. At first Barrett was incredulous about its authenticity, dismissing it as an unintentional mistake. He argued that a servant had probably entered the room, sat in the chair whilst the camera's shutter was open and then left, leaving a faint image on the photographic plate. However, he later had a change of heart when he learnt that the figure did not resemble any of the servants, and that anyway all the male servants were, at the time, at his Lordship's funeral. Sir William admitted that he was, to say the least, 'perplexed' and the photo remains a mystery to this day.

WILDERHOPE MANOR
MUCH WENLOCK, SHROPSHIRE
He Leapt into Legend

Wilderhope Manor is a lonely gabled Elizabethan house that dates back to 1586. It was built by Francis Smallman whose initials, along with those of his wife, Ellen, can still be seen in the plasterwork of the ceiling. The house, which is now a youth hostel, has hardly altered since the 16th century and boasts an impressive timbered spiral staircase, a baronial banqueting room and an atmosphere heavy with history.

During the Civil War the house was owned by Major Thomas Smallman, a staunch Royalist. One day when he was away from the house a group of Parliamentarians arrived at Wilderhope Manor and made off with some of his valuables. On his return a furious Smallman set off in pursuit, cornered the Roundheads, killed several of them and returned with his property.

Not long afterwards he was captured by another party of Roundheads whilst in possession of important Royal documents. They took him to Wilderhope Manor and locked him in an upstairs room whilst they discussed his fate. The Major managed to escape via a secret opening, however. He raced to the stables, saddled his horse and galloped away. The soldiers gave chase but were left gazing in astonishment when the fearless Smallman spurred his horse over nearby Wenlock Edge. Although the horse was killed, the gallant Major's fall was broken by a crab-apple tree and having recovered his composure he made good his escape. The spot from which he took his leap into legend is still known as Major's Leap.

BELOW: *The bleakness of its surroundings adds greatly to Wilderhope Manor's ghostly ambience.*

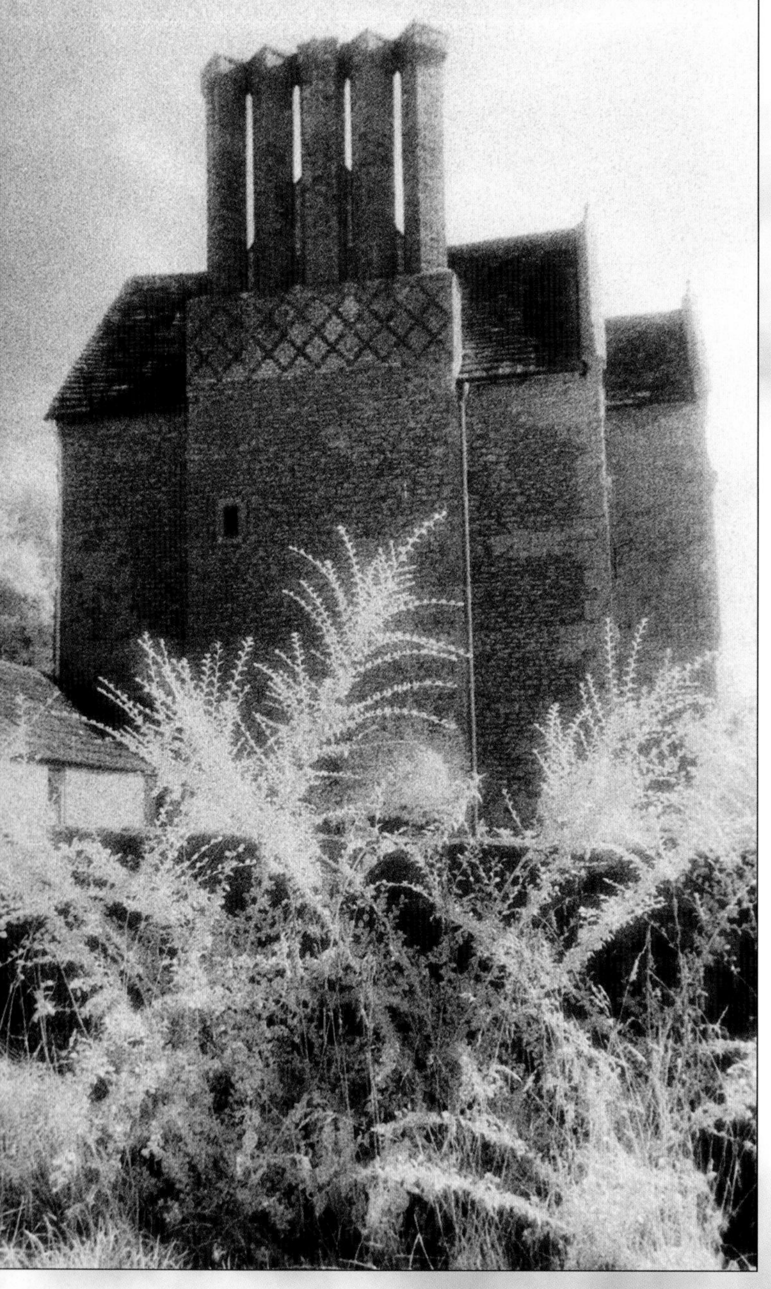

Thomas Smallman is believed to be the resident revenant at Wilderhope Manor and he has been seen at various locations around the property resplendent in full Cavalier costume. People sleeping in the small room over the house's porch have woken in the night to find him standing at the foot of their bed gazing at them.

In 1968 a Mr Crane came to stay at the property. It being a Youth Hostel, visitors were expected to help with the maintenance, and Mr Crane was given the job of painting the plaster ceiling in one of the rooms. As he went about his task he suddenly got the sensation that he was being watched, and from the corner of his eye caught a glimpse of someone standing in the doorway. Thinking it was the warden checking on his progress he turned to acknowledge him, but was astonished to find himself looking at a man in a green cloak wearing thigh-length leather boots and sporting a plumed hat. Dumbfounded, Mr Crane froze and then, overcoming his fear, bade the figure 'Good day'. The man smiled, raised his left hand, then walked towards the wall and melted into it.

Wilderhope Manor is steeped in history and mystery, and its walls drip with atmosphere. It is a true time capsule and the opportunity of a chance encounter with its ghostly Cavalier somehow seems to add to, rather than detract from its wonderful ambience.

IZAAK WALTON'S COTTAGE
NR. STONE, STAFFORDSHIRE
Fishing For Ghosts

Izaak Walton is best remembered for his book ***The Compleat Angler***, which he wrote in 1653. Its idyllic portrayal of rural life, not to mention its advice on the catching and cooking of fish, is considered both a classic of angling literature and a celebration of the English countryside. Walton was born in Stafford in 1593, and he never lost his affection for the Staffordshire countryside. The year after ***The Compleat Angler*** was published he purchased the Halfhead Estate, part of which included the timbered cottage that is now a veritable shrine to his memory and which is filled with all manner of fishing memorabilia.

ABOVE: *Visitors to Stafford's Ancient High House might possibly enjoy a guided tour from a ghostly Victorian shopkeeper.*

The identity of the 'female presence' that has taken up ghostly residence at the picturesque thatched cottage is unknown, although staff have nicknamed her 'Miriam'. She seems to be a stickler for regulation and becomes particularly active whenever the house is opened out of normal hours. Although there have been many reported sightings of her, it is more her presence that people pick up on and many are alerted to her being around by a sudden drop in temperature. She may also make her presence known in a more direct manner, because the staff are suspicious that it may well be her ghostly hand that switches on the electrical equipment which has been known to operate of its own accord.

Miriam is a typical otherworldly house guest, a memory trapped within the fabric of this ancient property who is both harmless and unassuming. Those who work in or visit the cottage are happy to accept her as the oldest resident of this archaic treasure of rustic Staffordshire.

'DUMBFOUNDED, MR CRANE FROZE AND THEN, OVERCOMING HIS FEAR, BADE THE FIGURE "GOOD DAY"'

WILDERHOPE MANOR

THE ANCIENT HIGH HOUSE

STAFFORD, STAFFORDSHIRE

Shown Round by the Ghosts

The Ancient High House, built in 1595, is considered to be one of England's finest Tudor buildings, and holds the distinction of being the largest timber-framed town house in the country. In 1642, at the start of the Civil War, the house was honoured with a royal visit by King Charles I and his nephew Prince Rupert who were en route to Shrewsbury. A year later the Parliamentarian forces took Stafford and the house became a prison for Royalist officers. The house changed ownership several times over the following centuries and by the 1890s it had been divided into shops, several of which were run by Mr William Mason. He appears to have enjoyed his tenancy here so much that he is loathe to leave. In the 1960s a group of Americans were delighted to be shown around the house by a jovial shopkeeper. So pleased were they with his hospitality that they returned shortly afterwards with several friends, hoping to enjoy a repeat visit. However, on this second occasion they were somewhat surprised to find the premises derelict. They subsequently learnt that, due to alterations in the 19th century, the structure of the building had been

ABOVE: *Little Moreton Hall is a delightful slice of old England but the disturbing sobs of a ghostly child can be unnerving.*

severely weakened and it had actually been closed for some time. It was only when they were shown a photograph of William Mason that they realized that they had been shown around by someone from the shop's Victorian past.

In 1979 Stafford Borough Council set about an extensive programme of renovation and the Ancient High House was gradually restored to its former glory and opened to the public as a museum. The restoration apparently awoke more than one former resident. In the second floor Victorian Room an old lady has frequently been seen sitting in a rocking chair. She shares her ghostly domain with a young girl in a Victorian dress who stands motionless and unblinking in the middle of the room. Disturbingly, the temperature in this room always errs towards the chilly, no matter how much additional heating is used. The heavy oak doors on the top floor have been known to open and close of their own volition. A member of staff once gazed on in amazement as this particular phenomenon occurred right in front of her eyes. As the doors opened a dark silhouette formed in the doorway, flickered for a few short moments, and then vanished. On searching the building the staff member could find no trace of anyone on the top floor, she was quite alone.

The Ancient High House is a special and atmospheric place where past and present blend harmoniously. Should you be standing in one of the rooms and happen to glance a former resident stepping across whatever line or threshold separates our age from their's, just bid them 'good day' and continue about your business. For, as the jovial shade of Mr Mason proved to that bemused group of American visitors, the ghosts might be dead, but that doesn't stop them from being accommodating.

LITTLE MORETON HALL

CONGLETON, CHESHIRE

A Moated Manor with an Unknown Phantom

Little Moreton Hall is widely regarded as Britain's finest timber-framed, moated manor house, with its reeling walls leaning at drunken angles, its tiny mullioned windows, picturesque moat and inner cobbled courtyard. To walk its sloping corridors, or gaze in awestruck wonder at its magnificent long gallery is to feel the 21st century fall away and find yourself slipping back into the past. So little has changed in this lovely old place that it has been used as a film location for several historic romps, including *Lady Jane* and *Moll Flanders*.

Little Moreton Hall can offer several ethereal residents to complement the history that surrounds you. In the spectacular Long Gallery, a mysterious 'grey lady' has been known to drift slowly past astonished witnesses before slowly fading into nothingness. More disturbing are the sobs of an invisible child that have been heard around the chapel. Nobody knows the living identity of either of the ghostly residents, nor what long ago act of infamy or fate has left their spirits earthbound. They just remain two of the secrets that a house of this age is inevitably going to harbour.

BRAMALL HALL
STOCKPORT, CHESHIRE
A Stranger Came a-Calling

One storm-tossed New Year's Eve in the 1630s a mysterious traveller wearing a billowing red cape came galloping into the courtyard of Bramall Hall and asked for shelter. William Davenport, Bramall Hall's then owner, invited the stranger inside and offered him food and drink. Gratefully the man accepted his host's hospitality and offer of a night's lodging.

The next morning William Davenport was found dead on the floor of the medieval Great Hall, and the red-caped stranger had vanished without trace. This event has, inevitably, left its mark on the building, and the ghost of the red rider has become the most famous of several spectres that have remained earthbound at this magnificent old property. It is on the anniversary of William Davenport's death, New Year's Eve, that you are most likely to see him, a handsome phantom in a billowing red cloak that comes galloping into the courtyard astride his trusty steed. Sadly, his manifestations are not particularly noteworthy, since no sooner has he approached the hall than he simply melts away into thin air.

Bramall Hall is a superb black and white, half-timbered house that nestles amidst 64 acres of beautiful parks and gardens. The core of the house dates back to the 14th century, although succeeding ages have left their marks upon it with the result that the overall impression one gets is of a mélange of differing architectural styles. For over 500 years it was home to the Davenport family and, the red rider excepted, it is their kith and kin who are believed to inhabit the house in spirit form.

In October 1997 a woman visitor was exploring the hall alone and went into Neville's Room, which is situated on the first floor. Suddenly a feeling of dreadful unease overcame her. She moved on to the Plaster Room where the feeling seemed to intensify. Moments later a misty female form proceeded to glide across the room, her feet apparently cut off at the ankles. The visitor gazed on agog as the figure vanished into the wall. Panic-stricken, the woman rushed into the nearby Withdrawing Room but was met by the same apparition materializing out of the wall. Hurrying downstairs she breathlessly blurted out her story to the house guides. Having calmed her down, they informed her that the house was indeed haunted and that a new floor had been laid in the Plaster Room, and this may have been why the figure appeared to have no feet. There is a long tradition of strange happenings within the Plaster Room. Dogs have been known to suddenly freeze in terror as they approach it, and no matter how much they are coaxed, nothing will entice them to enter

BELOW: *New Year's Eve is the day to make the acquaintance of Bramall Hall's resident spectre in the billowing red cape.*

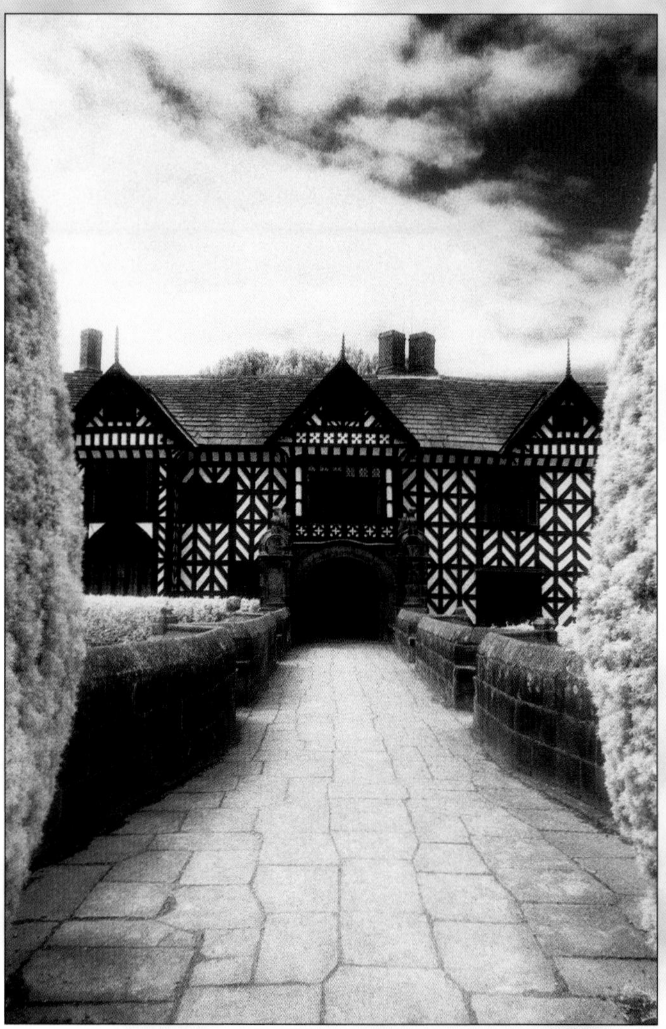

ABOVE: *A ghostly something of regular habits returns to the Tapestry Room at Speke Hall and chills the blood of witnesses.*

the room. A carpenter, who was once constructing a display case in the room, suffered the unnerving experience of having a jar of nails snatched from his hand and flung to the floor as he stood on the top rung of his ladder.

Bramall Hall is true a gem of bygone England and to walk through its doors is to enter a timeless interior where past and present merge and where residents from the past seem happy to return, often with alarming results.

SPEKE HALL
SPEKE, LIVERPOOL
He Lost Their Money

Speke Hall nestles amidst tranquil gardens and peaceful woodland on the banks of the River Mersey and is one of England's finest half-timbered mansions. Its walls date from 1530, although the Hall is mentioned as far back as the Domesday Survey of 1086. The house is a joy to explore and boasts numerous priest holes that bear testimony to the Catholic sympathies of the Norris family who lived here for several generations.

In the late 17th century the house passed to a granddaughter of the family who had married Lord Sidney Beauclerk, a grandson of King Charles II and Nell Gwynn. Three generations of their family would own it, although none of them took any actual interest in living there and the house was allowed to fall into ruin. In 1795 it was acquired by the Watt family and about a century later much restoration work was undertaken by Adelaide Watt. She bequeathed the house to the National Trust which became its owner in 1943.

At least one former inhabitant has chosen to remain as a ghostly occupant of regular habits, but unknown origin. This female phantom appears in the Tapestry Bedroom and confines her activity to gliding across the room and disappearing into the wall. On one occasion a guest sleeping in the room was startled by a sudden drop in temperature followed by a full-blown ghostly manifestation. A later examination of the location where the figure had appeared uncovered a secret passageway, the purpose of which remains a mystery, although it may have been used for sheltering priests during the Catholic persecutions. As to the identity of the ghostly form nobody is certain. There is a tradition that she was the young wife of either Lord Sidney Beauclerk or his son Topham. On being told that her husband had lost all his money and the family were now penniless, she is said to have thrown her child from the window of the Tapestry Room, and then committed suicide in the house's Great Hall. Detractors are quick to point out that although the Beauclerks certainly owned the property they never actually bothered to live in it. Thus she remains a mysterious inhabitant of a house whose wonderful atmosphere will reward even the most diehard cynic.

HIGHLOW HALL
HATHERSAGE, DERBYSHIRE
She Thought He Loved Her

Highlow Hall once held the dubious distinction of being 'Reputedly the most haunted house in Derbyshire,' although it must be said that in recent years supernatural activity has declined somewhat. The 16th-century house appears to have settled into a peaceful dotage and now operates as an atmospheric and delightfully unique bed and breakfast.

The most famous ghost at Highlow Hall is that of a jilted lover whose origins date back to the 14th century, when Sir Nicholas Eyre set about wooing two sisters of the last male heir in a devious attempt to claim their inheritance. Both sisters were enamoured with their suitor, although the younger sibling was particularly smitten. It therefore came as a particu-

ABOVE: *A long-ago act of betrayal brought about the curse that blighted fourteen generations of the residents at Highlow Hall.*

lar shock to her when Sir Nicholas announced his intention to marry her older sister. With a scream of anguished despair, the poor girl fled the house and was never seen alive again.

The wedding went ahead and Sir Nicholas and his bride settled into married life. A few years later he was walking by the staircase of Highlow Hall when the ghost of his jilted lover appeared before him. She proceeded to curse the male line of his family, vowing that although his descendants would rank alongside the greatest landowners in Derbyshire and marry into influential families, their good fortunes would last but 14 generations. Events would occur to leave them 'without rood and soil', and they would be forced to leave Highlow Hall. So saying, the prophetic phantom vanished.

Over the succeeding centuries, all that the spectre predicted came to pass and in time the Eyres became lords of over 20 manors. In the 19th century, however, their fortunes took a turn for the worse and in 1842, all but bankrupted, they were forced to leave Highlow Hall – just as the revenant of the jilted lover had predicted.

Sutton Scarsdale Hall

Derbyshire

A Forlorn Aura of Bygone Splendour

A forlorn aura of neglect and decay hangs heavy over the desolate ruin of Sutton Scarsdale Hall. Although dating from the 18th century, it stands on the site of an older house and much of the stonework from that original property was incorporated into the design of the present building.

For ten generations the old hall was owned by the Leke family, one of whom features in a well-known Derbyshire legend that dates back to the Crusades. Sir Nicholas Leke was a bold knight who one day set off to fight in the Holy Land. Before he left, however, he broke his wedding band in two, gave half to his wife as a token of his love and fidelity, and took the other half with him. Unfortunately, Sir Nicholas was captured by the Saracens, who perceiving him to be a very wealthy man, held him prisoner for many years believing he would fetch a fair ransom. One night, as he lay in his dungeon, Sir Nicholas prayed that God would allow him to see his beloved Sutton Hall once more, vowing that if his wish were granted, and he should one day return to his home, he would make provision for the poor for evermore.

When he awoke next morning he was amazed to find himself in the porch of Sutton church. Hurrying back to the Hall he banged on the door. His years of incarceration, however, had taken such toll on his once handsome features that the servants failed to recognize him, and thinking him a poor beggar, refused him entrance. Dejected, he turned to leave, but then remembered the wedding band that he had broken in two, which he had kept hidden on his person throughout his imprisonment. Presenting his half of the band to the servants he begged them to show it to their mistress, and soon he and his wife were enjoying a tearful reunion. Remembering his promise he ordered that from that day forth eight bushels of wheat were to be baked into loaves and distributed amongst the poor of the area every St Nicholas' day 'as a testimony of his gratitude for his marvellous escape'. An heir of Sir Nicholas once neglected to comply with the provisions of his will and on the 'morrow of Saint Nicholas' day' a deep well situated between the hall and the church overflowed and did a considerable amount of damage. The conscience-stricken heir immediately ordered the bread ovens to be lit for the bread to be baked, and the water in the well subsided.

BELOW: *Legends and ghosts swirl through the history of Sutton Scarsdale Hall in equal measure.*

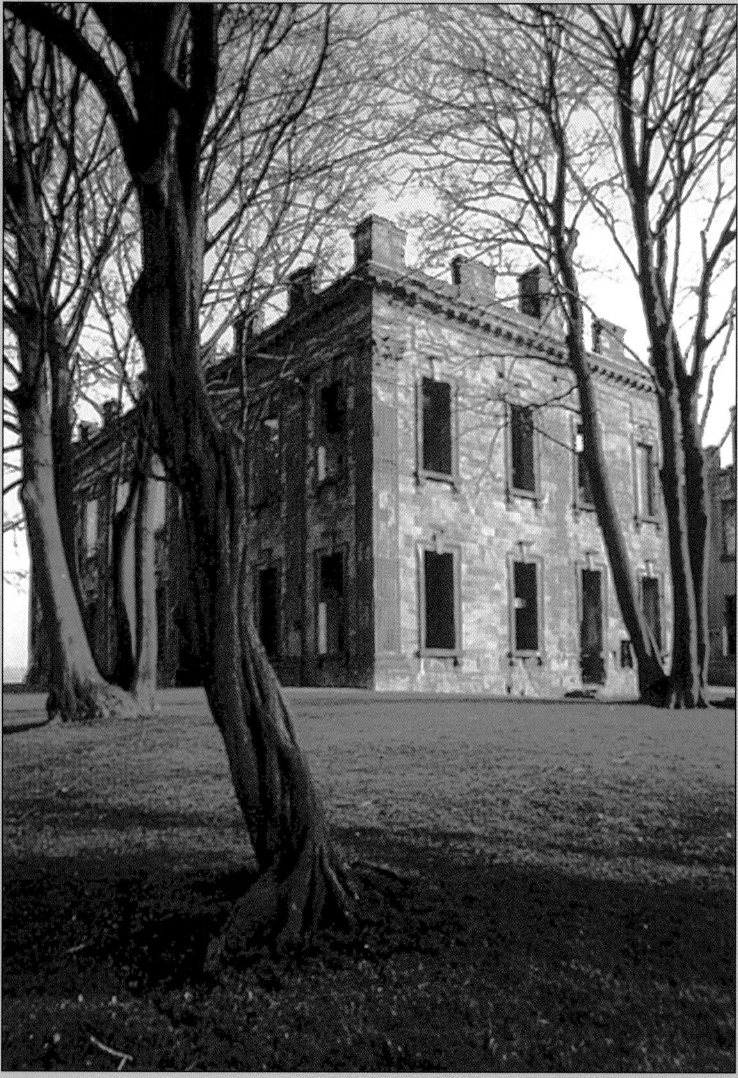

The Lekes were always faithful to the Crown and their loyalty was rewarded in 1624 when Sir Francis Leke was created Lord Deincourt. He remained a steadfast Royalist during the Civil War and was forced to defend his property against a force of some 500 Parliamentarians who eventually succeeded in battering down his defences and taking him prisoner. Following the execution of Charles I in 1649, Lord Deincourt became somewhat disillusioned and had his grave dug in the nearby churchyard. Each Friday evening he would don sackcloth, and lie in the grave to pray.

The present hall was built by the fourth and last Earl Scarsdale, Nicholas Leke, in 1720. The cost of rebuilding left him heavily in debt and following his death the family sold the Hall. By the early 20th century the building had fallen into disrepair and in 1920 it was purchased by a firm of builders who began stripping it of its fixtures and fittings. So deteriorated had it become by 1946 that instructions were given to pull it down, but fortunately three days before demolition was to begin Sir Osbert Sitwell purchased it, and the future of what remained was at last secured. It is owned by English Heritage today and visitors can stroll around the hollow shell of a building that is justifiably acclaimed as 'the finest of its type and era in the Midlands' and inside which various ghosts are known to lurk.

In the 1960s two men who were walking in the vicinity of the hall in the early hours were startled by the appearance of a female apparition that had no legs and wore a white hood with slits for the eyes. They watched dumbfounded as the ghostly, sobbing figure glided between the church of St Mary's and the moonlit shell of the old hall. Quite who the spectre was is unknown, but no doubt she would have felt right at home on arrival at Sutton Scarsdale Hall with its decent complement of spectral occupants. The smell of tobacco drifts around different sections of the building and can be quite overwhelming. There are phantom footsteps that pad their way around the property. Occasionally, strange lights of differing colours have been seen hovering in mid-air. Suddenly they dart into dark corners where they disappear. If none of these are sufficient to inspire cold shudders, then it's worth keeping a keen eye peeled for the disembodied arm that appears to beckon people to the cellar area, where it has been suggested that a long ago act of forgotten infamy left the livid limb earthbound for evermore.

ELVASTON CASTLE
ELVASTON CASTLE COUNTRY PARK, DERBYSHIRE
Love Amongst the Ruins

ABOVE: *Elvaston Castle is a secluded ruin where two white ladies vie for the attention of intrepid ghost hunters.*

A long, winding road twists its way through the sylvan landscape of Elvaston Castle Country Park and eventually arrives in the courtyard of Elvaston Castle itself. This early 19th-century Gothic-style house was once the home of the Stanhope family, the earls of Harrington. In the 1930s they upped sticks and moved to Limerick, leaving their castle to fall into decay. Most of the house may today be in a melancholic and decrepit state, but the Gothic Hall through which you enter, is absolutely breathtaking in its grandeur. It even achieved a semblance of immortality when it was used as the location for the controversial nude wrestling scene between Oliver Reed and Alan Bates in Ken Russell's film of D. H. Lawrence's ***Women in Love***.

The house as it stands today was built in the early 19th century by the 3rd Earl of Harrington. It is, however, during the time of the 4th Earl, Charles Stanhope, that the origins of its ghosts and legends belong. Charles was a beau, a dandy and a society trendsetter. He was addicted to snuff and was the proud owner of 365 snuff boxes, one for each day of the year. In the 1820s he met and fell in love with the Covent Garden actress Maria Foote. Their affair became the talk of London Society. The 3rd Earl disapproved immensely of his wayward son's involvement with a mere actress and made his displeasure known.

Charles seems to have been genuinely in love and when, following his father's death in 1829, he became the 4th Earl of Harrington he wasted no time in marrying his mistress. This proved too much for the delicate sensibilities of the upper classes and the couple found themselves shunned. Charles therefore took his new bride to Elvaston Castle, where he commissioned gardener William Barron to create a magnificent garden that would both flaunt and celebrate his love for his wife. Here the two remained, totally absorbed in each other. When their only son died, aged just four, the Earl forbade his wife to leave the grounds, and refused to allow anyone else to enter. The ban remained in place right up until his own death in 1851. The loneliness of her enforced reclusiveness appears to have affected Maria deeply and eternally, for it is she who is believed to be the 'white lady' whose sombre shade has been seen either sitting in a chair by a window in the Gothic Hall or else walking between the house and its nearby church.

Just outside the churchyard there stands the solitary grave of Kathleen Emily, wife of the 9th Earl. Not only does she lie in unconsecrated ground, but her grave also faces the wrong way, and no satisfactory explanation for either fact has been discovered. She is, however, believed to be the other 'white lady' that has been sighted gliding effortlessly around the grounds. A harmless spectre who is sometimes accompanied by an equally harmless ghostly white dog.

Elvaston Castle is certainly a slumbering gem and its 200 acres of parkland are a joy to wander through. Its future at the time of writing is uncertain, but the ghosts of those to whom this place has been home seem unconcerned and are happy to roam the house and grounds just as they have in the past, and doubtless will continue to do so in the future.

Brooding Mount

AINS AND SECRET ABODES

Thy soul shall find itself alone
'Mid dark thoughts of the gray tombstone -
Not one, of all the crowd, to pry
Into thine hour of secrecy.

Be silent in that solitude
Which is not loneliness, for then
The spirits of the dead who stood
In life before thee are again
In death around thee, and their will
Shall overshadow thee: be still.

From 'Spirits of the Dead'
by Edgar Allan Poe

WALES

The haunted houses of Wales present a diverse contrast. Some are almost lost amidst lush grounds, hidden away from the eyes of all but the most intrepid ghost hunter. Others are well-known tourist haunts and yet their stories are only ever whispered in hushed tones for fear of offending the spirits. The Welsh landscape, with its soaring mountain wildernesses, lush green valleys and sea-swept cliff tops makes a dramatic backcloth for tales of feckless lovers, family curses and wandering spectres. It is a land of history and mystery, whose bards and storytellers have ensured that the past is not forgotten. To find yourself standing alone in a haunted house on a windswept winter's day is to feel centuries removed from the modern age.

KEY

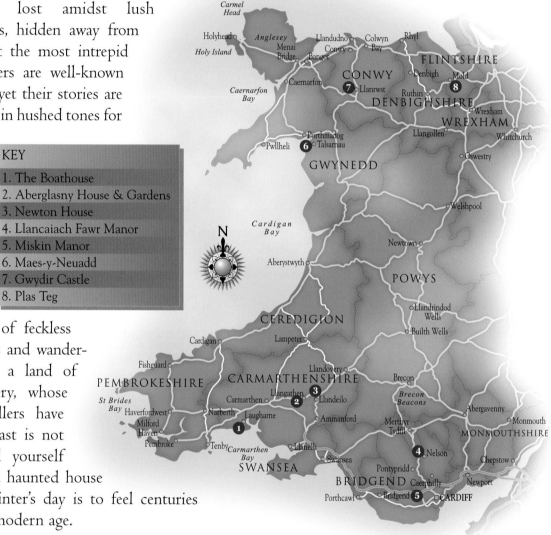

1. The Boathouse
2. Aberglasny House & Gardens
3. Newton House
4. Llancaiach Fawr Manor
5. Miskin Manor
6. Maes-y-Neuadd
7. Gwydir Castle
8. Plas Teg

THE BOATHOUSE
LAUGHARNE, CARMARTHENSHIRE
He Did Not Go Gentle

On Tuesday 3rd November 1953, Dylan Thomas returned to his room at the Chelsea Hotel in New York and uttered the legendary words, 'I've had eighteen straight whiskies I think that's a record.' Six days later, having slipped in and out of consciousness, he was dead, killed by what was poetically described as an 'insult to the brain', but which most would call acute alcohol poisoning.

His body was returned to the town of Laugharne and his coffin placed on public display at his mother's house 'The Pelican'. Mourners who came to pay their last respects, and raise the odd glass to his memory, were allowed to lift the lid and view his body. On 24th November, he was buried in the

'SIX DAYS LATER, HAVING SLIPPED IN AND OUT OF CONSCIOUSNESS, HE WAS DEAD, KILLED BY WHAT WAS POETICALLY DESCRIBED AS AN "INSULT TO THE BRAIN"'

THE BOATHOUSE

local graveyard beneath a simple white cross. The tiny Welsh town soon became a place of pilgrimage as admirers from all over the world came to pay their respects and visit the 'seashaken house on a breakneck of rocks' that had been his home for the last four years of his life.

He and his wife Caitlin had moved into the boathouse in the spring of 1949. It was a ramshackle, primitive building. Damp stained the ceilings and made the woodwork spongy. The rats that scurried around the outside toilet often found their way into the house itself. Money, or the characteristic lack of it, was a constant worry, causing him to observe wryly that he found himself 'forever at debt's door'. In the tiny workshed, which still perches precariously over the edge of the cliff, he gazed out across the tidal flats and sandbanks of the Taf estuary, and composed what is perhaps his best-known poem, 'Do Not Go Gentle Into That Good Night'. He also completed his 'play for voices', ***Under Milk Wood***, resurrecting a joke Welsh place name, Llareggub, that he had first used in 'The Orchard'. The BBC, who had commissioned the piece as a radio play, never thought to spell the name backwards and thus it successfully evaded the censors.

Following his death, Caitlin would not stay at the boathouse, and so his mother Mrs Florence Thomas became the tenant. It is her ghost that is thought to haunt the building. She is never seen, but rather makes her presence known in various other ways. Several staff have been surprised, on opening the premises, to hear the sound of a chair scraping over the floor upstairs, as though someone has risen briskly from the table to avoid them. Lights switched off at the end of the day have been found on again the next morning. On several occasions paintings have been removed from the walls overnight, and placed carefully on the opposite side of the room. The psychically inclined have detected cold spots, most notably around the staircase of the house, and several mediums have sensed Florence's presence in the parlour where she died in 1958.

BELOW: *Dylan Thomas might have drunk himself into an early grave but it is his mother, Florence, who now haunts his former home in Laugharne.*

PREVIOUS PAGES: *Llancaiach Fawr Manor is a house in a time-warp where the ghosts of former residents mingle with costumed guides who still think it's 1645.*

ABOVE: *Aberglasney is a garden lost in time that was recently awoken from a long slumber.*

ABERGLASNEY HOUSE AND GARDENS
LLANGATHEN, CARMARTHENSHIRE
The Ghosts Stir

One day in the 1630s, a housekeeper saw five candles floating around the house's newly plastered 'blue room'. The next morning, five maidservants were found dead in their beds there. A charcoal stove, left burning to speed the drying of the plaster, had asphyxiated them as they slept. Over the following centuries, the 'corpse candles' became one of Aberglasney's most abiding legends. Their fearsome flicker became renowned as a dreadful omen of approaching death, and one could be forgiven for thinking that the tragedy of the five maids had brought about a curse that has blighted the house ever since.

It was Anthony Rudd, Bishop of St David's, who built Aberglasney House in the 17th century. He intended it to be a family home for successive generations, but within a hundred years mounting debts forced his descendants to put the estate on the market. Succeeding owners found that their family fortunes seldom fared better as, within two or three generations, they too would be forced to sell up.

However, the renovations and extensions, carried out by various owners greatly enhanced the property. The Dyer family, owners between 1710 and 1798, added the magnificent Queen Anne façade. A later owner, John Walters-Phillips, graced this with an aggrandized portico. The beautiful gardens were justly famous, and the row of yew trees, planted in the Middle Ages, and which were later bent over to form an extended arch, is still wondered at today just as it was by visitors throughout the 19th century.

At least one owner from the 19th century haunts the house. In 1803 Thomas Phillips, a wealthy surgeon with the East India Company, purchased Aberglasney. Following his death in 1824, his amiable phantom was soon seen flitting about the house and grounds. Over the years he has appeared to gardeners, servants and tradesmen, whilst more recently guides at the property have heard his ghostly footsteps.

Following Thomas Phillips's death, successive owners found their lives blighted by ill luck. Children would die in infancy. Couples with dynastic ambitions would remain childless. Old and young alike would die suddenly or find their fortunes, both monetary and spiritual, brought to the brink of ruin. An aura of melancholic decay descended upon the property and

ABOVE: *Tucked away in glorious parkland Newton House has a fascinating history and one or two ghosts to complement it.*

by the end of the 1960s it had been abandoned. Weeds crept over the magnificent gardens, whilst damp and rot chewed through the fabric of the house. Whatever nature left untouched vandals were quick to destroy. By the 1990s the place lay forgotten and derelict.

And then a miracle occurred. A small band of enthusiasts had kept a concerned eye on Aberglasney's decline. They formed a trust and, thanks to a wealthy American benefactor, were able to purchase the property. They rescued the gardens and halted the decay. But the spirits of the past were also reawakened. The builders, who set to work on the hollow shell of the old house, often saw the wraith of a young girl standing in a corner of the basement, apparently cooking. Guides, absorbing the atmosphere of the peaceful cloisters, would often be disturbed by the sound of footsteps behind them, only to find themselves quite alone when they turned round.

It is, however, in Pigeon House Wood at the rear of the property that the most disturbing phenomenon is experienced. There is a certain spot where many visitors sense a feeling of dreadful unease. It intensifies as they descend the earthen path until, at the edge of the wood, it is replaced by sudden fear, followed by an eerie coldness. A medium who visited the property in 1999 said that she sensed someone trying to evade capture in the wood. Where people begin to feel uneasy, she explained, was where his pursuers had spotted the fugitive. He made a desperate run for freedom, but was felled by a single bullet, at the spot where the sudden fear and coldness is most often felt.

Aberglasney is a gem, nestling amidst some of the most stunning scenery imaginable. The sad aura that still hangs heavy over the house is a sharp contrast to the sheer beauty of its gardens. It is a tranquil place that has been restored to enjoy its ripe old age and its sobriquet of 'a garden lost in time' is both deserved and accurate.

NEWTON HOUSE
DINEFWR PARK, LLANDEILO, CARMARTHENSHIRE
Thee Wronged Miss Cavendish

Newton House huddles at the heart of a glorious landscape and has a story which stretches back over 1,000 years of Welsh history. Originally, it was the site of the Rhys family's castle, the ruins of which still loom large over Dinefwr Park. They were descendants of the ancient princes of Wales and in the early 16th century they Anglicized their name to Rice as the Welsh aristocracy was absorbed into the English with the coming of the Tudors under Henry VII. The house as it stands today was built in the 1660s by Edward Rice, although its present façade was added in Victorian times. It is a strange-looking house of solid grey stone, its corners crowned by four tall towers each capped by a sloping slate roof. As you approach it you just know that the place must have a ghost story or two to tell.

It is haunted by a 'white lady', who is thought to be the wronged wraith of Elinir Cavendish, first cousin of the lady of the house in the 1720s, although some versions of the story say she was her sister. Tradition maintains that she was being forced to marry a man that she didn't love, and in order to escape his clutches she sought sanctuary with her family in Dinefwr Park. Incensed by the rejection, her spurned suitor gave chase and having caught up with her at Newton House, murdered her in cold blood.

The ghost of Elinir Cavendish has walked the building ever since and appears to have been particularly active in the 1980s, when the premises were occupied by a television facilities company. There was much talk of the house possessing a very strange atmosphere and during their tenure a number of television editors fell ill one after the other. This may have been completely coincidental, but all the same it gives some pause for thought. On another occasion a director and an editor were both working in an edit suite when suddenly a young and very beautiful girl appeared, seemingly out of nowhere, and proceeded to glide across the room before vanishing into a cupboard. They searched the area where she had disappeared but there was no sign of their mysterious visitor. They were left to contemplate the fact that they had been honoured by a visit from the spectral White Lady of Newton House.

ABOVE: *Walk up the grand staircase at Llancaiach Fawr Manor and you may well encounter the house's spectral children.*

LLANCAIACH FAWR MANOR

NELSON, CAERPHILLY

It's Forever 1645

Admittedly, the name of this historic manor house doesn't exactly trip off the tongue, but on virtually every other count it is truly an impressive place. It is as though the calendar has frozen in 1645 (though the manor was built in 1530 on the site of an earlier medieval house), which was the year when the then house's owner, Colonel Edward Pritchard, switched his allegiance from the Royalist to the Parliamentarian cause. 'Servants' in period costume greet and escort you around their 'master's' house, and chat amiably away about the events and gossip of 1645, doing so in their interpretation of the language of the day.

By contrast, when the dark winter nights drape themselves across the time-scarred walls, and the wild winds murmur around the windows and doors, the house echoes to the steady tramp of nervous footsteps as bands of visitors set off by candlelight to seek the ghosts that wander what is widely acknowledged as the most haunted house in South Wales. 'Llancaiach Fawr Manor is one of the spookiest and most atmospheric places I've ever been to,' paranormal investigator Phil Wyman told me, 'and when the lights go out and it's pitch black, there is an overwhelming sense of desolation.'

The grand staircase, which is situated to the left as you enter, is haunted by two spectral children who sometimes

those circumstances were. Her bedroom, situated on the upper floor, is acknowledged to be the building's most haunted room. A feeling of crushing sadness seems to hang in the air and many visitors – tough Australian rugby players and case-hardened senior police officers included – have been overcome by emotion on entering her room and have been forced to leave with tears streaming down their faces. The house's custodians and guides sensibly have chosen not to attempt to come up with a story to explain away this strange phenomenon, but are content to let the room's melancholic feel speak for itself. They will only add by way of explanation that whatever the fate that befell Mattie, it must have been 'something awful'.

The most bizarre of the regular inexplicable occurrences are the disembodied voices that always seem to be chatting one room ahead of people. They are very distinct, but when those who hear them actually enter the room, they appear to have

appear and then disappear, but who are mostly heard rather than seen as they enjoy a ghostly game. Their phantom whoops and giggles are clearly audible to bemused witnesses. Several ghostly children are apparently loose inside the house and seem to delight in playing childish pranks on staff and visitors alike. The costumed female guides have long grown used to their aprons falling to the ground at the most inopportune moments when their bows have been untied by invisible impish hands. A steward who was once descending the house's green spiral staircase placed his hand on the railing and suddenly jumped back in surprise when beneath it he felt a cold childish hand.

The manor's kitchen is haunted by a lady in a white blouse who appears to be baking bread. She is generally believed to be the ghost of Mattie, a former housekeeper who died under tragic circumstances, although nobody knows exactly what

moved in to the next room or even gone upstairs, where their chatter is still clearly perceptible. On one occasion a film crew spent an entire day filming inside the house for what was apparently going to be a long television piece, and naturally the staff were excited at the prospect of such exposure. When the programme was aired, however, they were puzzled by the shortness of the segment. They duly contacted the television company and were told that much of the film's soundtrack had been spoilt by 'foreign' voices talking very loudly and drowning out the presenters and interviewees. No one at the time of filming had heard these voices. The reference to 'foreign' was probably the London production company's interpretation of the native Welsh language that the mysteriously vociferous intruders appeared to be speaking.

A man in what has been described as Tudor/Stuart costume who has been seen sitting on a window ledge in the

ABOVE: *Llancaiach Fawr is home to the ghost of Colonel Pritchard, an anti-social ghost who doesn't like visitors.*

Great Hall is thought to be the ghost of Colonel Pritchard. It is presumed that his are the ghostly footsteps sometimes heard pacing back and forth across the room's dais. During the house's refurbishment in the 1980s, the ceiling in the kitchen directly beneath the Great Hall was plastered using traditional methods and materials. No sooner had the task been completed than a portion of the plaster came loose and fell down. The section was replastered but again it came away. It fell down several more times before experts were called in to investigate. They concluded that there was no fault in the workmanship, nor in the quality of the materials being used. The only possible explanation they could think of was that vibrations from the Great Hall above must be responsible. Interestingly, it was just one portion of the ceiling that was affected and that section was the one directly beneath the dais where the ghostly footsteps were known to walk.

Reports of ghostly activity at Llancaiach Fawr Manor continue to come in from staff and visitors. It is without doubt one of Britain's most supernaturally active buildings. Although the ghosts might sometimes prove annoying they are not in the least bit malevolent and those who work at the house seldom find them frightening. Aside from a ghostly voice that once screamed 'Out! Out!' to an astonished visitor, the overall spirit of the place is convivial and few people fail to fall beneath its spell. Perhaps the final word should go to custodian Marianne Anderson who perfectly summed up the Manor's ambience when she told me,'as you walk into the house you can feel the energy buzzing through the soles of your feet.'

MISKIN MANOR HOTEL
MISKIN, NR. CARDIFF
It's Time To See The Ghost

Despite its proximity to the M4 the lovely and atmospheric Miskin Manor Hotel is a world removed from the hustle and bustle of the 21st century. The Manor itself has enjoyed an eventful and chequered history that dates back to the 10th century, although the current house was constructed in 1857 when the estate was purchased by David Williams, a well-known Welsh bard and philanthropist. The house has survived two major fires, one in 1922 which destroyed all but the external walls and a similarly devastating conflagration in 1952, shortly after its conversion from wartime hospital to flats.

Restored, it remained as flats until 1985 when it was transformed into a luxury hotel. The current owners are the Rosenberg family. Lost amidst a tranquil profusion of stunning greenery, Miskin Manor is blessed with a timeless atmosphere which makes it a delightful rural retreat in which to while away a peaceful and relaxing few days – or for the whole of eternity, as in the case of its ghosts.

The most active ghost to roam the interior of Miskin Manor is that of a ghostly lady who appears regularly in the bar area. She is a harmless revenant who can be counted on to put in an appearance most nights between midnight and 1 a.m. The hotel porter has long grown used to her appearances interrupting his well-earned cup of tea at around 1.40 a.m. He simply watches as her hazy figure drifts from the drawing room over to the bar opposite and slowly disappears. Ben Rosenberg believes that she was a former resident of the house who is simply following a regular path that she once walked in life. 'There used to be a staircase where the bar stands today,' he told me,'so she is evidently coming from the drawing room and going up the stairs just as she did when she lived here.' Psychic medium Norie Miles brought a team of researchers to the hotel in June 2004 to see if they could uncover any clues as to the identity of the mysterious figure. Although nothing actually appeared to those present, everyone noticed a sudden change in atmosphere at the time when the mysterious visitation is known to occur. An hour or so later she and Ben Rosenberg were walking along a back corridor when they happened to comment on the lack of activity

ABOVE: *Guests at Maes-y-Neuadd can look forward to the prospect of being lulled to sleep by a ghostly nanny.*

that night. No sooner had they done so, than a heavy picture was lifted off the wall and thrown onto the floor in front of them. It was as if one of the ghostly residents was desperate to make the point that, just because they couldn't be seen, it didn't mean that they weren't about.

MAES-Y-NEUADD
TALSARNAU, GWYNEDD
Rock - a -Bye Nanny

Maes-y-Neuadd is a sturdy manor of solid Welsh granite and slate which dates back to the 14th century. Its name literally means 'mansion in the meadow' and the house certainly occupies a tranquil location, perched on a wooded hillside, high above the waters of Tremadog Bay and affording stunning views across the Snowdonia National Park. It now operates as a lovely country house hotel and boasts one haunted bedroom, the Morfa suite. Guests in this suite can look forward to the enchanting possibility of being lulled to sleep by a female phantom of goodly intentions. She is thought to be the ghost of a former children's nursemaid, and her attire of long gown and mobcap certainly suggests that she was of the serving rather than the owning classes. Nobody who has seen her has found her to be in the least bit frightening or troublesome. Indeed, witnesses say that she has a very calming presence and emits an aura that helps them drift into a deep and restful sleep.

GWYDIR CASTLE
LLANRWST, CONWY
Shaded Ladies

This impressive and beautiful place is not a castle in the strict sense of the word as it has more of the appearance of a sturdy manor house, resplendent with soaring chimneys, turrets and tower. During its fascinating and intriguing history, it has been visited by numerous royals, including Charles I in 1645 and the Duke and Duchess of York in 1898 (the future George V and Queen Mary).

Tales of supernatural occurrences at the house date back at least to the 19th century. The most frequently encountered ghost is that of the 'white' or 'grey lady' who walks the North Wing and the panelled corridor between the Hall of Meredith (a magnificent room with a vaulted ceiling and inglenook) and the Great Chamber. In the 19th century the room behind the panelling was actually called the Ghost Room and it was here that the female revenant was most frequently seen. The worst aspect of her manifestations was a dreadful, putrid stench.

ABOVE: *The lingering smell of death is just one of the phenomena to afflict Gwydir Castle*

Although her spirit has not been seen for some time, visitors continue to sense her presence and there are reports of people being touched on the shoulder by an unseen hand, whilst experiencing a sudden and inexplicable drop in temperature.

The mysterious woman's identity is unknown, but there is a tradition that Sir John Wynne, a member of the family that formerly owned the building, once seduced a serving wench. Having had his wicked way with her, he murdered her and walled up her body inside a niche in a chimney breast. The smell of her rotting cadaver is said to have lingered for months and vestiges of it evidently remained to accompany the poor girl's spectre whenever she set out on a ghostly wander. Interestingly, in the early 20th century a hidden recess was uncovered in the chimney breast that backs onto the Ghost Room, and although no mortal remains were discovered, it was always around this area that the foul odour was often strongest.

PLAS TEG

PONTBLYDDN, MOLD, FLINTSHIRE

He Rode Into the Supernatural

Standing back from the main Mold to Wrexham road, Plas Teg, the 'fair mansion', is a sturdy 17th-century Jacobean property that has a decidedly eerie atmosphere and a reputation as one of the most haunted houses in Wales. It was built in 1610 by Sir John Trevor and over the years has acquired a number of illustrious connections, not to mention one or two decidedly infamous ones. The most notorious of the latter is 'Hanging' Judge Jeffries, whom tradition maintains held court in the house where, true to his nickname, he sentenced many a felon to death, some it is suggested even being dispatched on a makeshift gallows that would be erected in Plas Teg's downstairs dining room.

It is inevitable that, with such a sinister heritage, several of those who have resided at the house are moved to return in spirit form. In the Twin Poster Bedroom guests have been disturbed by the sound of heavy breathing echoing around them. Strange glowing white lights have also been seen passing by a window of this room, even when the house was known to be empty. Elsewhere, the Blue Bedroom is haunted by a little girl said to be aged between six and nine, who is harmless enough and just stays around for a few short minutes before disappearing.

Undoubtedly, the house's most haunted room is the Regency Room, and a rather gruesome tale lies behind its supernatural occurrences. Sir John Trevor, the fifth squire of the Hall, was the last of the male line of the Trevors. He married in 1742, but a year later he made the devastating discovery that his wife was embroiled in a passionate affair. Soon afterwards she was found dead under mysterious circumstances and Sir John, beside himself with the combined effects of grief and rage, reacted to the news of her death by riding his horse and trap around the grounds at breakneck speed

Rounding a bend, he lost control and suddenly the carriage flipped over and was dragged for some distance by the horse. When it finally came to a halt Sir John was pulled from the wreckage and carried to the Regency Room, where he lingered in agony for a month before dying. His ghost has remained earthbound ever since and several visitors have encountered him. Many have reported catching ethereal glimpses of a shadowy figure standing by the foot of the bed as they pass the open door. One lady suddenly jumped up and ran out of the room when someone suddenly 'got hold' of her. Others have felt something, or someone, push past them on their way out of the door. The current owners' two Great Danes have been known to run barking and yelping from the room, apparently terrified by something.

The Cheshire Paranormal Society has conducted several overnight vigils at Plas Teg and has obtained some very interesting results. Its files are full of photographs showing hazy mists and floating orbs. On one visit in 2004 a picture taken of a female member of the group showed what appeared to be the apparition of a young girl on her right as she walked across the top-floor landing. Members of the public have also come away from Plas Teg with unexplained objects and forms on their photographs.

ABOVE: *Paranormal researchers have discovered a plethora of ghosts behind the ancient façade of Plas Teg.*

On the A541 outside the hall many drivers have been forced to swerve suddenly to avoid a misty white shape that has appeared without warning on the road in front of them. Both witnesses to and victims of numerous accidents on this stretch of road have cited the unexpected appearance of a mysterious white figure as the cause.

Plas Teg is a wonderful old house that is now owned by antique dealer and interior designer Cornelia Bayley. Since purchasing it as a virtual ruin over 20 years ago, she has set about lovingly restoring it and the house is very much imbued with the dedicated spirit of this remarkable lady. The ghosts with whom she shares her lovely home are an integral part of its ambience, and to roam its corridors and rooms is to join them on a soul-inspiring journey through haunted history.

MIDNIGHT BAN
RESTLESS RUINS

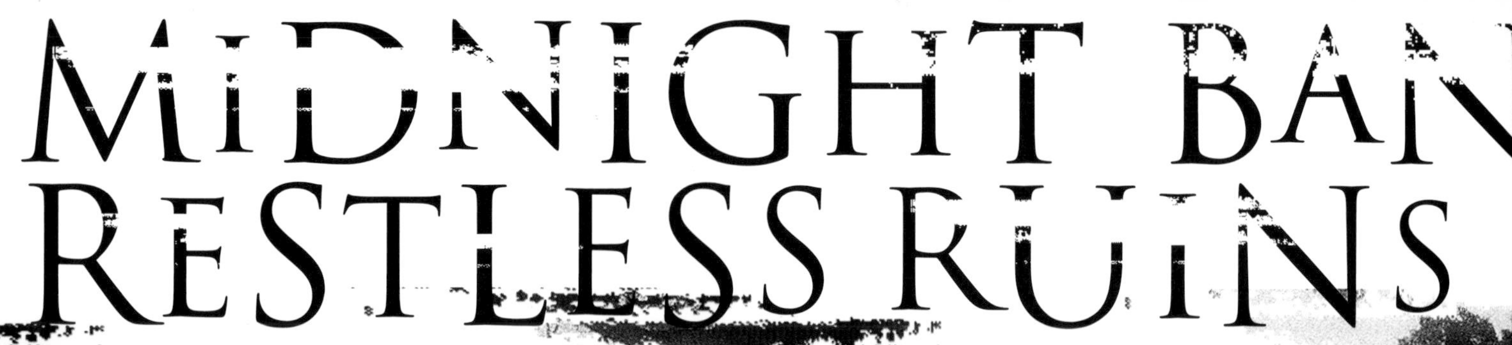

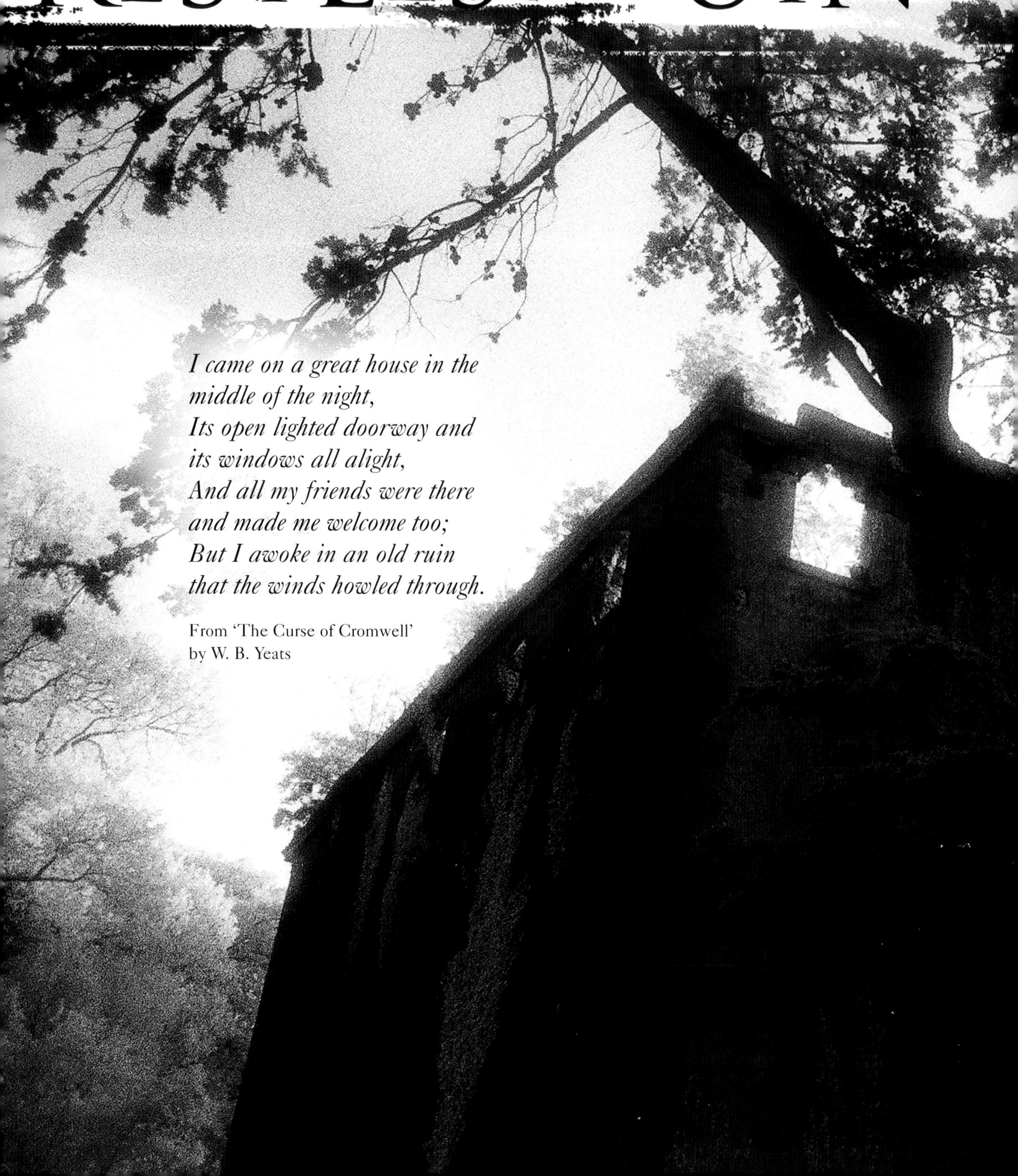

I came on a great house in the
middle of the night,
Its open lighted doorway and
its windows all alight,
And all my friends were there
and made me welcome too;
But I awoke in an old ruin
that the winds howled through.

From 'The Curse of Cromwell'
by W. B. Yeats

SHEES AND

IRELAND

Ireland is a magical country and its landscape is both mysterious and melancholic. Its great houses were not designed or built for the benefit of the indigenous population, but rather for the all-powerful Anglo-Irish aristocracy. These families employed the finest craftsmen and architects to create stately piles that reflected their fortunes and belief in their own importance. Over the centuries these houses came to be seen as symbols of subjugation. The rising tide of Irish nationalism that swept the country in the early 20th century meant that they became prime targets for the republican forces. Consequently, many of Ireland's once great houses are now little more than hollow shells. They lie forgotten in peaceful abandoned seclusion. Enigmatic ruins whose crumbling walls reflect bygone ages of grandeur and glory. Yet to discover them is a wonderful and awesome experience, and to stand within their tottering walls and contemplate their ghosts can elicit the coldest of shivers even on the brightest of summer's days.

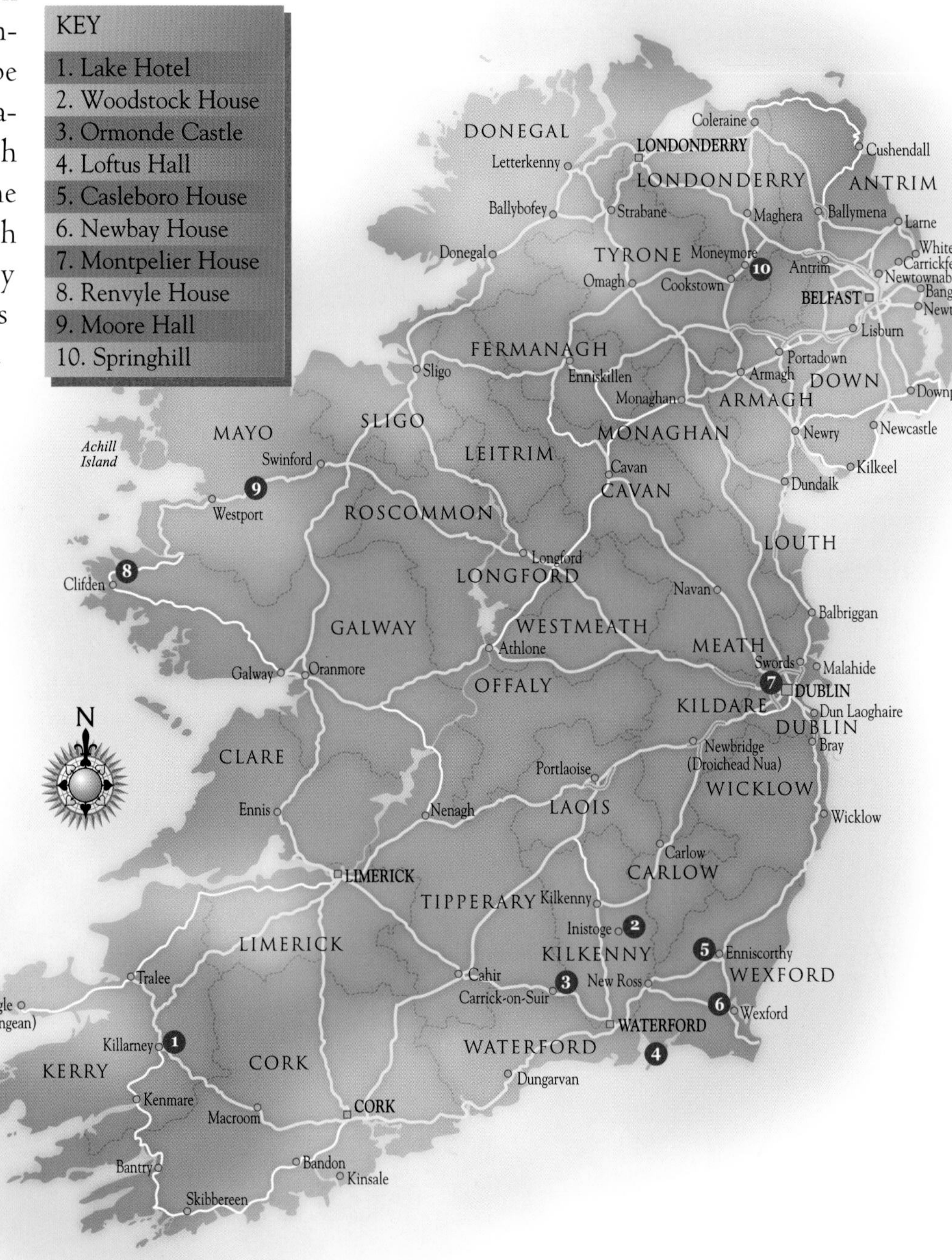

ABOVE AND PREVIOUS PAGES: *There is no rhyme nor reason why poet Mary Tighe should still wheeze her ghostly way along the drive of Woodstock House.*

LAKE HOTEL

KILLARNEY, COUNTY KERRY

Dan of the Feathers Makes a Stand

The Lake Hotel sits in tranquil isolation on the shores of Lough Leane, the lower of Killarney's beautiful and justifiably renowned lakes. It is a long and modern-looking building with creamy yellow walls. But once inside enough of the 19th-century manor house has survived to give a strong impression of that bygone age. Its darkwood staircase ascends to a veritable labyrinth of long shadowy corridors where the darker recesses – of which there are many – have a truly haunting ambience. In the hotel grounds, and on the very edge of the Lough itself, stand the overgrown ruins of Castlelough Castle. Built in about 1220 and once home to the McCarthy Mórs, the castle's lakeside location made it virtually impregnable and the McCarthys came to enjoy a fearsome reputation as hard fighters and harder drinkers.

During the reign of Elizabeth I, one of their number, Donal McCarthy, acquired the nickname of 'Dan of the Feathers' due to his fondness for collecting as trophies of war the plumed helmets of vanquished English troops. It is said that he even employed a retinue of women to make mattresses and cushions from these collected feathers. His ghost still drifts in a spectral boat across the glassy surface of the Lough in the dead of night. He has even been seen in the hotel's Devil's Punchbowl Bar looking sadly across at the ruined castle, no doubt remembering long-ago days of glory and bloodshed – although the pint of Guinness that he reputedly holds in his hand should perhaps be taken with a large pinch of salt.

When Cromwell's troops invaded Ireland, the castle was severely battered and eventually its defenders, having put up a fierce resistance, were forced to submit. This and nearby Ross Castle were the last in Ireland to surrender and it was here on the tranquil shores of Lough Leane that the Cromwellian Wars in both Ireland and England came to an end.

Over the years, many guests have reported close encounters with the hotel's other resident ghost, a girl aged between twelve and fourteen, who has been seen flitting about the building's darker corners and who has a fondness for wandering at leisure across the front of the building that faces onto the Lough. Her appearances are always accompanied by what has been described as 'a body-chilling feeling' coupled with a sense of 'total calm'. No one knows for certain who she is, nor what long-ago event caused her wraith to walk the corridors. A medium once succeeded in making contact with her spirit, but since the ghost insisted on speaking in 'some form of Irish' not a great deal could be learnt of her reason for haunting the hotel.

Woodstock House
Inistioge, Kilkenny
The Poetess's Ghostly Ramblings

The hollow shell of Woodstock House is surrounded by a garden that was once considered one of the glories of Ireland. The house itself was built between 1745 and 1747 and designed by Francis Bindon for Sir William Fownes. It was, however, the acquisition of the property by the Tighe family towards the end of the 18th century that saw the estate bloom into magnificence. They also gave it the ghost that is said to still wander the shattered remnants of its once majestic interior.

In 1793 Henry Tighe, a second son and lawyer, married his first cousin Mary Blanchford. She was a talented poet who became known as 'Psyche' Tighe after her most famous work ***Psyche: or the Legend of Love.*** Unfortunately, she contracted tuberculosis and came to spend her declining years at Woodstock House in the hope that the fresh air and relaxed pace of life would help her battle against the disease.

On the morning of 24th May 1810 Mary went for a walk from Woodstock House to the village of Inistioge. The stroll back, however, proved too much for her delicate constitution and having lain down on a sofa to rest, she suddenly let out a gasp and died. The sculptor John Flaxman was summoned from London to make a cast of her reclining form. During the three days it took him to reach Woodstock, her lifeless form was left where she had gasped her last, so Flaxman was able to cast her just as she had died. His sculpture shows her graceful figure reclining upon a couch and now reposes in the mausoleum at Inistioge graveyard where she is buried. Her ghost, however, has been known to make periodic returns to Woodstock House where she has been seen repeating her last fateful journey, a melancholic shade picking her way wearily along the driveway that leads to this ruinous though enchanting house of memories.

Ormonde Castle
Carrick-on-Suir, County Tipperary
Black Tom's Tribute

Thomas Butler, or 'Black Tom' as he was nicknamed, 10th Earl of Ormonde, was a cousin to Queen Elizabeth I. The two met as children in London and they remained close throughout their lives. Suggestion was rife that the man whom Elizabeth liked to call her 'black husband' was more than just a friend, and there were even rumours that one of his sons, Piers

BELOW: *A long-ago ball is still re-enacted by ghostly participants behind the history-draped walls of Ormonde Castle.*

ABOVE: *Amongst the many guests who have visited Wexford's Loftus Hall the Devil must take pride of place.*

Fitzthomas Butler, was the result of Thomas's fondness for the Virgin Queen.

In the 1560s, anxious to ensure that the Queen had a suitable palace at which to stay whenever she visited Ireland, Black Tom set about adding a fine Tudor mansion onto the family castle at Carrick-on-Suir. Once it was completed he awaited the honour of a royal visit. Sadly it was never to be, for Elizabeth never set foot on Irish soil, and with Tom's death in 1614, Ormonde Castle's days of glory were over. During the next 400 years, what is now considered to be the best example of an Elizabethan manor house in Ireland was allowed to sink into a sorry decline.

Today, thanks largely to the efforts of Heritage Ireland, the old house is gradually assuming something of its former glory, and visitors can admire its atmospheric huddle of rooms, including a Long Gallery that stretches for an impressive 100 feet, and which is unique in Ireland. As you cross the threshold and enter the house's first short passageway, two frescoes – both long faded – are situated high on the wall on either side. They show the outlines of the heads of Black Tom and Elizabeth I together with their initials and the date 1565.

To the left is a room that leads to what are now the kitchen and toilets. On its wall the marks of the original staircase are clearly visible. It is here that ghostly activity has been experienced. Michael Wallace, a sprightly guide who looked far younger than his 80 years when I met him, used to live in the house. There were nights when as he sat close to the bottom of the staircase, he would hear the distinct sound of a ball apparently being held in the Long Gallery above. He would hear the swish of the ladies' skirts, the echoing sound of their footfall and from time to time the voice of a lone minstrel that would burst into song and entertain the assembled phantom throng with a mournful rendition of 'Greensleeves'.

LOFTUS HALL, THE HOOK PENINSULA, COUNTY WEXFORD
The Devil Stops By

Standing amidst the bleakly desolate, though eerily beautiful, terrain of Wexford's wild and sea-swept Hook Peninsula, Loftus Hall appears centuries removed from the modern age. It rises like a mirage from the wind-rattled grasses that surround it, a sprawling mass of grey stone walls, tall chimneys and a seemingly endless number of dark windows in whose panes are reflected bygone ages of grandeur and glory.

The Redmond family built the first hall on the site some time in the 13th century. In 1666 the Loftuses acquired it and changed its name to reflect their ownership of the estate. The present hall dates from the 1870s and although it is not open to the public, it is clearly visible from the road that twists its torturous way around the Hook Peninsula. A plaque on one of its gateposts provides the tantalizing information that 'the

ABOVE: *The ivied ruins of Castleboro House are steeped in melancholic neglect, but the ghost doesn't seem to mind.*

ghost story ... recalls strange events which happened here in the 18th century', and so the Hall certainly deserves at least a cursory, if distant, glance from those who come in search of things spectral and ethereal.

According to local tradition, in the 18th century one Charles Tottenham and his family came to live in the hall that previously stood on this site. One night, soon after they had moved in, a dreadful storm blew up over the Hook Peninsula. Great gusts of wind hurled themselves with demented fury at the walls of the old hall, rattling its windows and howling like banshees around the chimneys. The family closed the shutters against the night and drew closer to the fire. Charles Tottenham suggested that they pass the time playing cards and a deck was duly produced.

No sooner had the first hand been dealt than a loud and agitated knocking sounded upon the hall's heavy front door. When the servants unlatched it they found a tall stranger standing in the rain-lashed darkness his cloak billowing around him. He explained that his horse had thrown a hoof on the road outside and wondered if he might warm himself by their fireside before continuing to the local blacksmith. Tottenham informed the man that this was no night to be outdoors, and invited the stranger to change into some dry clothes and spend the night as their guest. Gratefully the stranger accepted and was soon seated by the fire enjoying the game of cards with the family.

A little way into the game, however, he accidentally dropped a card and one of the Tottenham's daughters obligingly stooped down to retrieve it. She was horrified to discover that the stranger had a cloven foot. With a scream of terror she leapt up and denounced their guest as the Devil. The stranger stood and fixed his accuser with a menacing stare and made as though to attack. But as he did so Charles Tottenham leapt to his feet, made the sign of the cross and, in the name of Jesus and all the saints, commanded that the Devil depart. With a howl of indignation, the Devil dissolved into a plume of white smoke and vanished into the ceiling.

Thereafter the Hall was long troubled by demons and evil spirits and eventually the family called upon their local priest Fr. Thomas Broaders to perform an exorcism. His powers appear to have been more than a match for Satan, and soon the great adversary, together with his devilish cohorts, had been banished from the hall. Thomas Broaders died in 1773 and was buried in Horetown Cemetery, where his epitaph reads:

Here lies the body of Thomas Broaders,
who did good and prayed for all.
And banished the devil from Loftus Hall.

'HERE LIES THE BODY OF THOMAS BROADERS,
WHO DID GOOD AND PRAYED FOR ALL.
AND BANISHED THE DEVIL FROM LOFTUS HALL.'

LOFTUS HALL

Castleboro House
Enniscorthy, County Wexford
A Ghostly Stitch in Time

Castleboro House is a haunting and melancholic place that is both emotionally and historically impressive. Ivy clings to the crumbling red brick of its sprawling walls. Hollow windows gaze in upon a fire-scarred interior, the floors of which have long since collapsed and left fireplaces and stairways tottering precariously in mid-air. In its heyday it must have been a truly grand and impressive stately pile, but it now lies forgotten at the end of a rutted farm track, a sleeping colossus left alone with its memories.

The present building was built in 1840 and replaced an earlier mansion that had been destroyed by fire. The architect was Daniel Robertson, a colourful character who suffered from gout, and who supervised the construction from a wheelbarrow in which he was pushed around the site – his plans in one hand and a bottle of fine wine in the other. The completed building was a Venetian Palace, resplendent with Corinthian columns and elegant fountains that basked amidst lush countryside, its image reflected in the rippling waters of a magnificent artificial lake.

But its days of glory were short-lived. After the 1850s the family spent less and less time at the house, although they occasionally held lavish parties there for their English friends and acquaintances. During one such party on the night of Monday 5th February 1923, a group of local Republican Army sympathizers arrived at Castleboro and ordered the guests to leave. Standing at the foot of the great steps that lead to the house, the guests looked on as the building was torched. Suddenly a scream sounded out and the guests watched in horror as Lady Carew rushed back up the steps and entered the building's blazing west wing in a fruitless endeavour to retrieve her favourite heraldic needlework cushions. Her efforts proved in vain, for the roof collapsed. Ever since that fateful night her screaming wraith is said to haunt the burnt-out shell, as a trapped spirit condemned to repeat her futile dash over and over again.

Newbay House
Nr. Wexford, County Wexford
Piked To Death On The Step

Newbay House is a house of memories, imbued with the spirits of past residents and its soothing aura envelopes you the moment you enter. One of its more unusual features is a visitors' book in which faded sepia photographs of long-departed house guests can be viewed. Some of them wear fancy dress, others are more formally attired, but all are enjoying the hospitality of a house that exudes a timeless appeal and which evokes a poignant nostalgia for a more genteel age.

The present building dates from 1822, but its most famous ghost story belongs to the previous building that stood on the site. In 1798 a man named George Middleton, who according to some accounts was the owner of the house, was piked to death on the doorstep by an insurrectionist. His ghost is said to wander the nearby woods, no doubt keeping a concerned eye on his silver, which he reputedly buried there before his death. Dick Bishop, a steward at the house, was

BELOW: *Newbay House is a truly magical place where guests can search for ghosts and buried treasure!*

ABOVE: *The spooky ruins of Montpelier House once echoed to the sounds of acts of infamy and debauchery.*

adamant that he had encountered George Middleton's restless wraith wandering the woodlands one day in the late 19th century. Today, such is the allure of the peaceful woods that the current owners are happy to provide would-be ghost or treasure hunters with a picnic hamper to keep hunger pangs at bay whilst seeking similar encounters.

Inside the house, guests have experienced other supernatural happenings. There is a place on the upstairs landing where the ghostly rustling of spectral skirts has been heard. A child has been heard crying in rooms that are known to be empty, whilst dark shadows have been seen flitting across mirrors and windows. All who witness these happenings agree that the spirits are not in the least bit frightening or malevolent, and are happy to accept them as nothing more than the memories and shadows that a house of this age naturally harbours within its fabric.

Montpelier House
Montpelier Hill, Dublin
A Place of Wicked Repute

On the summit of Montpelier Hill stands a gaunt, grim ruin, the walls of which ooze malevolence. As you approach its forlorn shell, its empty windows appear to watch you warily. Once inside its foreboding interior, the sickly odour of damp and decay fills your nostrils and a feeling of extreme unease engulfs you.

Montpelier House dates from 1725 when the Right Honourable William Conolly, Speaker of the Irish House of Commons, built it as a hunting lodge on the lonely summit of Montpelier Hill. Conolly broke up a sizeable megalithic stone circle, traces of which are still visible behind the lodge, and used its slabs in the construction of his building. This desecration of an ancient monument to the pagan gods of Ireland did not go unnoticed by the locals. They began to whisper amongst themselves that Conolly was trifling with forces that were best left alone. Their fears seemed well founded, for shortly after its construction a terrible storm erupted one night and the lodge's slate roof was blown off. Some said it was the work of the devil, others that it was the old deities showing their displeasure. Conolly was undeterred and he ordered the construction of a huge arched roof, its stones keyed together like a bridge. It was a tremendous feat of engineering which, according to Weston St John Joyce in his ***The Neighbourhood of Dublin*** published in 1912, is '... of such impregnable strength that it has effectually withstood the efforts of wind or devil from that day to this.'

Following Conolly's death, the hunting lodge passed into the hands of a group of hedonistic aristocrats led by Richard Parsons, 1st Earl of Rosse, who is said to have been a 'sorcerer, dabbler in black magic ... and a man of humour and frolic'. He and a group of fellow bucks used the lodge as a meeting place for their infamous Hell Fire Club. Its lonely setting made it the perfect venue to celebrate their black masses at which defrocked priests would conduct parodies of the Catholic service, and black cats would either be sacrificed to the devil or worshiped. On one occasion a legitimate priest is said to have interrupted one such mass. He seized the cat that they were worshipping and uttered an exorcism which tore the creature apart. Suddenly a demon shot from its corpse and hurtled through the roof, causing plaster from the ceiling to crash down on the startled assembly.

For at least 20 years Montpelier House flourished as a den of iniquity as its members competed to out-drink, out-debauch and out-blaspheme each other. No one knows for certain when it fell into ruin, but it is generally agreed that it happened around 1740 when the club's 'Principle' was Richard Chappell Whaley, a man who was feared and detested by the native Irish in equal measure. A descendant of the hated Oliver Cromwell, he was a vicious tyrant who earned himself the nickname 'Burn-Chapel' Whaley, due to his love of riding around the countryside on Sunday mornings setting fire to the thatched roofs of Catholic chapels. Fittingly, legend holds that it was his pyromania that brought about the downfall of Montpelier House.

The story goes that one night a defrocked priest had just finished a black mass in one of the house's upstairs rooms. The congregation had, as usual, sunk into a bout of orgiastic drunken revelry. A servant was picking his way with difficulty through the sprawling, writhing bodies when he tripped and spilt drink all over Whaley's coat. Whaley leapt to his feet, doused the unfortunate servant in brandy and set fire to him. The blazing man raced screaming down the stairs and clutched at a tapestry hanging by the hall door. Within moments the house was engulfed in flames and many of its occupants were so drunk that they were incapable of escaping. Whaley and a few of his more sober companions leapt from the windows, but the rest were consumed by the flames. The people of Dublin watched the blazing pyre which they were convinced was God's revenge against the members of the Hell Fire Club.

Today, the gaunt ruins stand aloof and sinister on their bleak summit and several ghosts have been seen by those who have endured the struggle up the steep slope of Montpelier Hill. There is a strange and unnerving atmosphere and even on the calmest of days a brisk wind whistles around the granite walls. Come twilight and you get the sense that, despite the stunning views over Dublin below, this is a place where evil lurks and where the memories of long-ago acts of infamy are seared into the very fabric of a truly haunting ruin.

ABOVE: *W.B Yeats is just one of the many people who have sought the ghosts at Connemara's Renvyle House.*

Renvyle House
Renvyle, Connemara, County Galway
Yeats's Psychic Hunt

Renvyle House once belonged to the Blakes, an old Galway family whose fortunes took a severe downturn in the 1840s during the Irish Famine. Forty or so years later one of their number, a strong woman of independent mind, turned the family home into an hotel and in September 1883 the first paying guests trundled their way along the rutted Connemara roads, up the pitted, twisting drive and stepped inside a place that is situated so far in the west of Europe that, as one guest put it, 'the next village is America'.

The hotel prospered for a time, but then it had to be sold. In 1917 it was acquired by Oliver St John Gogarty, an athlete, poet, raconteur, aviator and, almost incidentally, an ear, nose and throat surgeon. 'My house ... stands on a lake' he wrote in ***As I was going down Sackville Street***, 'but it stands also on the sea - water-lilies meet the Golden seaweed. It is as if in the faery land of Connemara at the extreme end of Europe, the incongruous flowed together at last, and the sweet and the bitter blended.' Here he entertained many luminaries of his age such as W. B. Yeats and his wife. Winston Churchill and Augustus John also visited. John had the distinction of being about the only man able to stop Gogarty in full conversational flow by using the simple, though effective, device of throwing a bowl of nuts in his face.

Along with the deeds of the property Gogarty also acquired a resident ghost. There was a north-facing upstairs room with heavy bars across its windows where no maidservant would dare sleep for fear of the 'presence'. One night this lurking spirit moved a heavy linen chest across the door, barring access. Only when a workman had sawed through the bars on the window could the room be entered again. On another occasion Gogarty was sleeping when he was woken by ponderous, limping footsteps approaching along the corridor. Lighting a candle, he went to investigate but the moment he left his room, the flame was extinguished and he found himself alone in the dark. Suddenly his limbs became very heavy, 'as if I were exercising with rubber ropes'. Moments later the feeling lifted and he was able to return to bed where nothing further happened that night.

Although the ghosts were fairly active most of the time, whenever the Yeats's came to stay the supernatural activity increased dramatically. One night as Yeats sat in the oak-panelled library, reciting his latest poems to an attentive group

ABOVE AND OPPOSITE: *Moore Hall is a crumbling ruin and is one of Ireland's most chilling places, even on a summer's day.*

of companions, the door began to creak open. The other occupants of the room were terrified, but Yeats raised his hand and shouted: 'Leave it alone, it will go away, as it came.' Not willing to cross swords with the imposing figure of the poet, whatever spirit was responsible for the intrusion politely closed the door and left.

Evan Morgan (later Lord Tredgar) showed himself to be less in command of the revenants. He had recently embraced Catholicism, and on learning that one particular room was haunted he attempted an exorcism. But no sooner had he lit three candles and begun reciting some prayers than a thick mist filled the room and he was flung to the ground. Luckily, his friends were able to drag him to safety and, on recovering his senses, he revealed that he had seen the ghost of a pale-faced boy with large luminous eyes, who appeared to be clasping his hand to his own throat as if strangling himself. This led Morgan to conclude that he had committed suicide in that very room.

Determined to get to the bottom of the disturbing manifestations, Yeats held a séance and proceeded to make contact with the ghost. Using automatic writing it revealed that it objected to the presence of strangers in the house. It did, however, agree that it would appear before Yeats's wife, Georgie, and reveal its true identity. Georgie Yeats was a talented and well-known medium and she felt no compunction at entering the haunted room alone. As she stood by the fireside a vapoury mist began to swirl in front of her and assumed the form of a red-haired, pale-faced boy, aged around 14. 'He had the solemn pallor of a tragedy beyond the endurance of a child,' Georgie later told her husband. The boy informed her that he was a member of the Blake family, the original owners of the house, and that he resented the presence of strangers in the home of his ancestors. 'He is to be placated with flowers and incense,' Yeats told his fellow guests.

However, these were troubled times for Ireland, and in February 1923 Renvyle House was burnt to the ground by anti-treaty forces. 'Memories, nothing left now but memories', lamented Gogarty, '... and ten tall square towers, chimneys, stand bare on Europe's extreme verge'. The house was rebuilt in the 1930s and Gogarty ran it as a hotel before relinquishing ownership in the 1950s.

Today it is still a luxury hotel that sits in quiet seclusion amidst the wilds of Connemara. Ghosts still wander its snug, though in parts eerie, interior but these tend to be of the vague 'sensing a presience' variety and although the house is, here and there, quite spooky, the ghosts are described as 'very friendly'. So perhaps the final words on this mystery-steeped building should be those of Oliver St John Gogarty who described how, '... There is something else, something indescribable, but as real as dim colour or soft sound. The countryside was magical, even in the rain ... and the soft atmosphere made you feel that you were in a region that was your proper home, a home where there was neither time nor tide, nor any change at all ... And you did not want to speak ...'

MOORE HALL
COUNTY MAYO
A Face Carved from a Turnip

In 2002 I received a letter from an American reader of my book ***Haunted Britain and Ireland***, in which he suggested that if I was planning a follow-up book I might like to consider

including Moore Hall in County Mayo. He and his wife had visited the property on their recent vacation in Ireland and both had heard footsteps from inside the house, followed by the sound of a door slamming and excited chatter as though two people were involved in a very animated conversation. I must confess that I had never heard of Moore Hall, but following a little research I was delighted to find that, ghosts aside, the building had been the childhood home of the novelist George Moore, a man who nobody seems to have liked very much. W. B. Yeats described Moore's face as looking like it had been carved out of a turnip. Henry Arthur Jones said that he resembled 'a boiled ghost'. To Oliver St John Gogarty he was simply 'that egregious ass', whilst James Stephens labelled him 'the famous novelist that everybody talks about and nobody reads'. However, what none of them could deny was that, for all his faults, George Moore was a talented and original writer. In ***The Lake,*** his greatest novel, his description of Lough Carra is as enticing as it is exquisite.

Lough Carra is one of Ireland's loveliest lakes and also one of the least visited. On a hill above the Lough Carra, lost amidst dark and gloomy woodland, stand the ruins of Moore Hall. It is a gaunt shell of broken walls, toppled brick and fallen masonry. The gnarled branches of skeletal trees poke from its empty windows, whilst its basement is a sinister labyrinth of arched corridors and dark rooms, their floors carpeted by a mulch of decaying leaves and squelching mud.

On the day I visited a grey pall hung heavy over its roofless bulk. I found it to be a truly chilling and eerie place. Although entrance is now forbidden, due to its tragically precarious state, enough of its interior was visible from the outside to give the impression of what a glorious house it must have been in its heyday. At the rear of the building I discovered an arched, dark tunnel that led to a wooden gate through which I could see the basement rooms, all of them exuding a gloom-laden and ominous air. Maybe it was the effect of the surroundings at work on my imagination, but as I gazed into the cavernous rooms before me I suddenly heard the distinct sound of childish laughter echoing from the upper floors. I looked up quickly but could see nobody. I walked around the whole property and wherever possible peered in through the windows, but the house seemed quite empty. I took a little more time to look around and to take my photographs before heading back to the car along the tree-lined avenue that leads to the hall. As I did so, I became convinced that someone was watching me from the dark shell of the old house. A few times I felt compelled to look back, just to ensure that I was alone. It was only when I arrived back at the car park, and the rippling dark waters of the lough stretched before me, that the feeling of foreboding that had been with me since hearing the laughter began to lift and I felt at ease once more.

SPRINGHILL
NR. MONEYMORE, COUNTY LONDONDERRY
If Only She could Have Saved Him

On every count Springhill is a truly attractive house. Its brilliant white walls, dark, narrow windows and grey slate roof, capped by chimney stacks of dull red brick, blend harmoniously into the rural landscape. No one who ventures here can help but fall beneath its spell. Its interior has a lived-in and welcoming feel, and you can just sense that little has changed in centuries. Those to whom this place was once home would have little trouble recognizing it today, no matter from which period of its 300-year history they may have come.

Although the exact date of its construction is uncertain, its origins go back to 1680 when 'Good-Will' Conyngham married sixteen-year-old Ann Upton. Her father was anxious to ensure that she and any offspring should be kept in the manner to which he thought they should become accustomed, and so he drew up a marriage contract requiring Good-Will to build 'a convenient dwelling house of lime and stone, two stories high with the necessary office houses, gardens and orchards'. Rising to the challenge, Will erected a handsome tall-roofed house which was added to and lived in by ten generations of his family, until in 1957 Captain William Lenox-Conyngham bequeathed Springhill and its contents to the National Trust. Today, visitors to the house can admire its period furnishings and the renowned oak staircase, whilst enjoying the eerie sensation of having their every footstep watched by long-dead members of the family whose portraits gaze down from the walls.

Without doubt, Springhill's spookiest place is the Blue Room. The moment you step into it the temperature drops alarmingly and it remains cold throughout all the time you spend there - a fact that the guides who lead the tours put down to the 'presence' which is known to haunt the room. In 1814 George Lenox-Conyngham, a man prone to bouts of melancholy, was away on his duties in the army when he received news that his children had gone down with smallpox. Out of his mind with worry he awaited news of their conditions, and when none came he abandoned his post early one night and headed for Springhill. On the way he met his commanding officer, Robert Stewart, but since they were good friends, and given that he had similarly covered for Stewart on similar occasions, he felt sure that he would understand the urgency and necessity of his quest. Stewart raised no objections and Lenox-Conyngham made it back to Springhill where he found that his wife, Olivia, had nursed all the children back to health. His relief, though, was soon tempered by the news that he was to be court martialled for abandoning his post. His so-called 'friend' had betrayed him. This, coupled with the

ABOVE: *Springhill's Blue Room is always icy cold and many visitors have encountered its ghostly resident who wanders in eternal remorse.*

sudden death shortly thereafter of one of his daughters, brought on a fit depression that lasted two years.

Eventually, one night he went downstairs to the gun room, took a pistol from the wall, returned to the Blue Room, sat on the bed and shot himself. Olivia, realizing what he was about to do, rushed to prevent his suicide but had just reached the bedroom door when she heard the gunshot. Later Olivia would write in the family Bible: 'George Lenox-Conyngham being in a very melancholy state of mind for many months prior, put an end to his existence by a pistol shot. He lingered from the 20th November 1816 to the 22nd, and died, thanks to almighty God, a truly penitent Christian...'

Olivia's ghost is still said to repeat her desperate dash to prevent her husband's death and has been seen on several occasions standing at the door of the Blue Room, her hands raised in horror. She was seen in the latter part of the 19th century by a house guest named Miss Wilson, who had sat up late one night chatting with the daughter of the house, Milly Conyngham. When Milly finally retired to bed Miss Wilson noticed that she had left her diary behind. Leaving the room to return it, she was startled by the sudden appearance of a tall woman at the top of the stairs. The apparition moved to the door of a bedroom, proceeded to raise her arms, apparently in despair, and then slowly faded away.

Years later another guest of the house, a Miss Hamilton, had gone to bed one night in the Blue Room when, just as she was starting to fall asleep, the room appeared to fill with agitated servants who were 'pushing and wrangling in whispers'. As she lay there terrified she heard a clicking noise from the wall behind her bed. She turned and saw a door open and a light shine from it. She later recalled how 'someone seemed to come out through this light and stilled the commotion, so that all fear left me, and after a while I fell asleep.' On waking the next morning she was startled to find that no door existed anywhere behind her bed. However, when she reported her experience to Charlotte Lenox-Conyngham, she was told that there was in fact a door behind the bed but that it had been long since been papered over. Interestingly, years later the Blue Room's wallpaper was stripped off and the secret door uncovered. It opened into a powder closet, on the floor of which lay an ancient pair of gloves and a small pouch containing bullets.

In the early years of the 20th century the last generation of Lenox-Conyngham children to live at the house were sleeping one night when their nursemaid suddenly awoke to find Olivia's phantom standing over her charges gazing intently at them, as though checking the well-being of each one of them in turn. The nursemaid felt no fear at all. She was moved by the concern that the apparition appeared to show towards the children. Within a few moments, evidently satisfied that all was well, the ghost simply faded away and was gone.

Springhill is a lovely and atmospheric place and the custodians are at pains to point out that there is nothing malevolent about its otherworldly residents. It is a genuinely tranquil and fascinating place to visit, and should the ghost choose to honour you with an appearance you can leave this tranquil piece of old Ireland knowing that you have been welcomed to the house by its oldest and most illustrious resident

GHOSTS, GHOULS MOONLIT

I hear a cry of spirits faint and blind,
That, parting thus, my chiefest part I part.
Part of my life, the loathéd part to me,
Lives to impart my weary clay some breath;
But that good part, wherein all comforts be,
Now dead, doth show departure is a death -
Yea, worse than death; death parts both woe and joy.
From joy I part, still living in annoy.

From 'Farewell'
by Sir Philip Sidney (1554-1586)

AND
MEANDERING

LANCASHIRE, YORKSHIRE, CUMBRIA, DURHAM & NORTHUMBERLAND

You cannot fail to be moved by the scenic variety of these northern counties, and the haunted houses that stud the landscape are reflective of this ever-changing panorama. From the awesome majesty of the Lake District in the northwest, where many ancient properties have evolved into delightful country house hotels; through the gentle pastures of Yorkshire and County Durham; and on to the wild and untamed splendour of Northumbria, where many of the older houses reflect an age when this was a dangerous place to live and the residents had to be constantly on their guard against outlaws and raiders coming across the Scottish border. Add to this heady brew the mansion houses of Lancashire, several of whose ghosts reflect the county's former strong Catholic leanings, and the stage is set for an eventful journey through a truly haunted and haunting land.

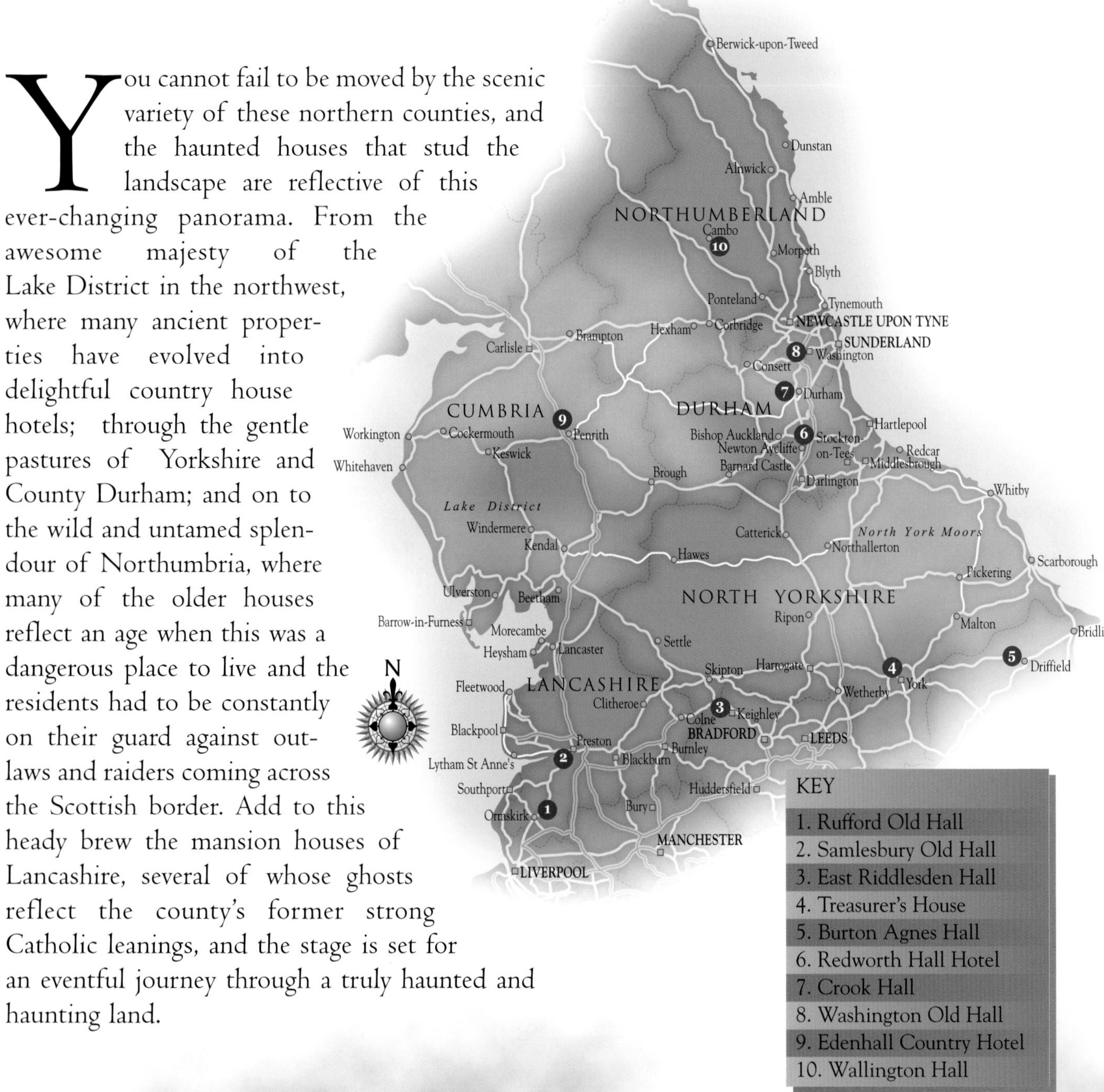

RUFFORD OLD HALL
ORMSKIRK, LANCASHIRE
And Still She Waits

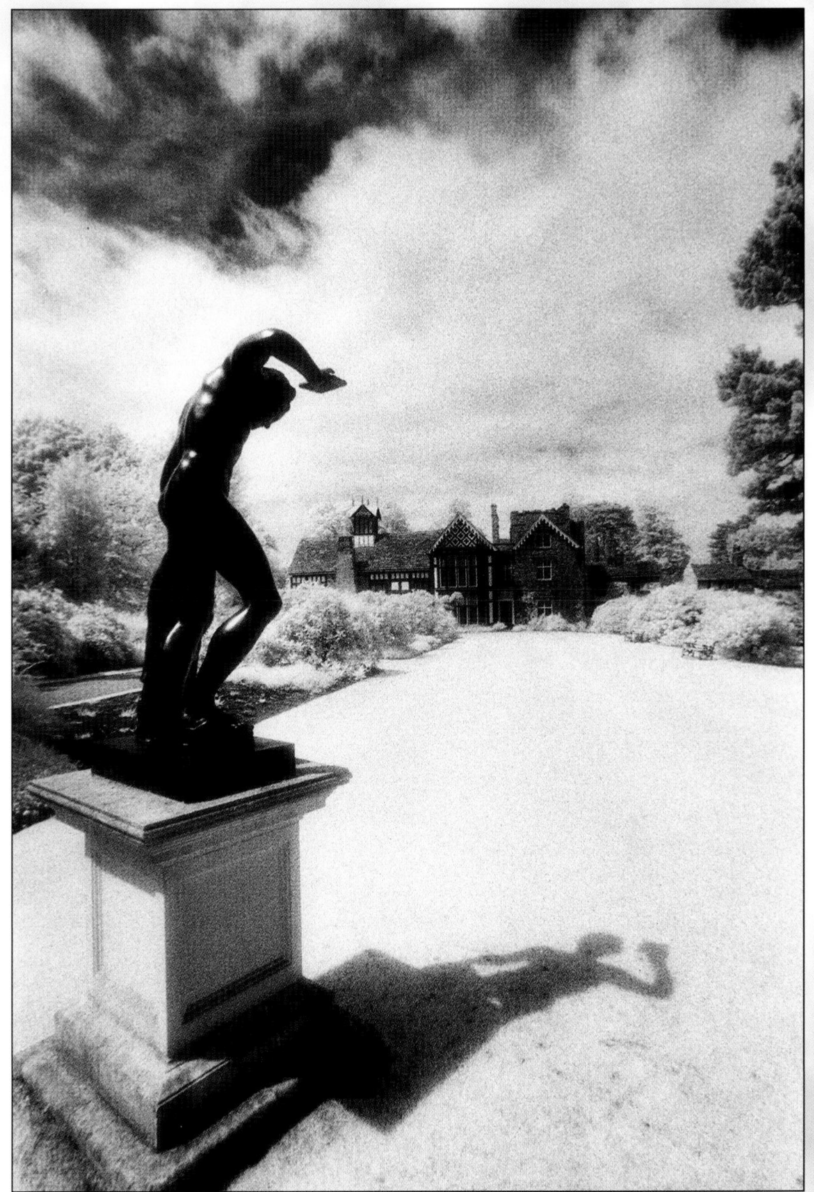

Rufford Old Hall with its splendid black-and-white timbered exterior and spectacular Great Hall, resplendent with magnificent hammer-beam roof, has long been considered one of Lancashire's finest 16th-century buildings. The first mention of a hall on the site dates from the 1450s when it was home to the Hesketh. In the 16th century Robert Hesketh, an illegitimate son of the family, inherited the estate and, determined to establish his rightful place in the family hierarchy, set about building the elaborately decorative Great Hall. There is a local tradition that a young William Shakespeare – or Shakeshafte as the Hall records refer to him – was employed at the Hall in the 1580s, although the evidence for this is somewhat tenuous. What is generally agreed upon, however, is that at some stage in the 16th century the Hall managed to acquire its resident wraith the 'off-white lady'.

Tradition has it that a daughter of the family, whom some maintain was named Elizabeth Heskith, agreed to marry a local soldier. But no sooner had their engagement party begun than he was called away to quell an uprising by a gang of insurgents who were raiding to the north. Patiently, Elizabeth awaited his return and after a few days her patience was rewarded with the news that the campaign had been successful and her fiancé would soon be home.

The family commenced the preparations for the wedding, and the bride-to-be put on her white wedding dress and looked forward to plighting her troth. Then a second messenger arrived and informed her that the earlier reports of her lover's survival had been somewhat premature and that he had in fact been killed in the skirmish. The shock proved too much for poor Elizabeth. She refused to accept that her lover was dead and insisted that the wedding would be going ahead no matter what. Day in and day out, she sat at the window watching for her fiancé's return. Her white dress gradually dulled and her health began to give way until, all hope gone, she pined to death.

Her ghost still wanders the hall searching for her dead lover, her faded white dress and grey countenance chilling the marrow of all who encounter her. Although in recent years her manifestations have become rarer, many visitors report sensing a 'presence' in certain rooms and complain of the sudden drop in temperature that means that the 'off-white lady' of Rufford Old Hall is continuing with her sad, pointless search.

ABOVE: *When Elizabeth Heskith's soldier love rode away to war she never realised that she would still be awaiting his return five hundred years later.*

PREVIOUS PAGES: *Although several ghosts roam the night hours at Burton Agness Hall, it is the skull of 'Awd Nance' that is the house's best-known ethereal fixture.*

SAMLESBURY OLD HALL
PRESTON, LANCASHIRE
The Sobbing Woman's Rambles

In 1948 a bus driver stopped to pick up a passenger on the road that runs past Samlesbury Old Hall. His conductor was somewhat bemused by the fact that there was no one stand-

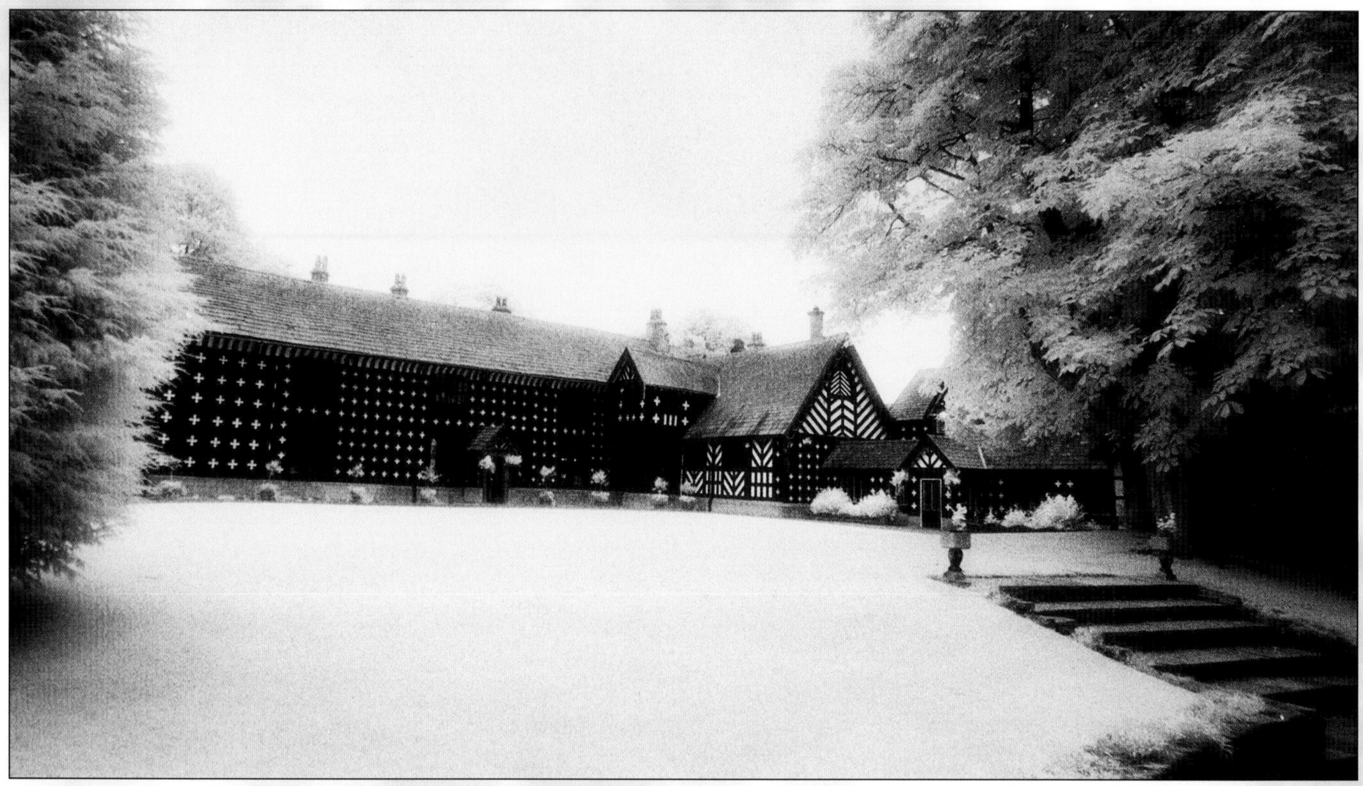

ABOVE: *The white lady who roams the shadows of Samlesbury Old Hall has been offered a lift by many drivers on the road outside.*

ing at the spot where the driver swore blind he had seen a lady in a white coat apparently waiting for the bus. Following a quick search of the vicinity, the two men continued on their way, unaware that they were just two of a long line of eyewitnesses to the ghostly roaming of the enigmatic 'white lady' of Samlesbury. Tales of her nocturnal rambles are legion in the vicinity and several motorists have, over the years, stopped to offer her a lift only to have her fade away in front of them. One couple even drove into her and felt the bump as their car apparently went over her body. But on searching for almost an hour they could find no trace of her on the road.

The 'white lady' also haunts the interior of the hall, where she drifts aimlessly along corridors, and melts into walls. In 1878, during the Lancashire cotton riots, a young subaltern was garrisoned with his company at the hall. In the early hours of one morning he was awakened by the disturbing sound of a woman sobbing in the corridor outside his bedroom. He climbed out of bed to investigate but found no trace of anyone. Next morning he reported his experience to his host and hostess, who exchanged concerned glances and proceeded to tell him the tragic tale that lies behind the 'white lady'.

In the latter half of the 16th century the staunchly Catholic Southwood family owned the hall. Given the risks that adherence to their faith entailed they were obviously a little nonplussed when a daughter of the family, Dorothy Southwood, fell in love with a son of the fanatically Protestant Hoghton family, who lived at nearby Hoghton Tower. When their families forbade them to see each other, the young couple began meeting in secret in the grounds of the hall and eventually hatched a plan to elope. What they hadn't realized was that Dorothy's brother, Christopher, had overheard them, and when the young Hoghton arrived to carry his lover off her sibling was waiting for him. Dorothy's joy at her lover's approach was short lived, for no sooner had she opened her window in welcome than her brother leapt from the shadows and killed both the lover and his attendant. There are two versions as to what happened next. One states that Dorothy was so overwrought that she flung herself from her window and fell to her death. The other version has it that she was sent to a convent where she died of sorrow soon afterwards.

Whatever her sad fate, her spirit still wanders through the night lamenting the wicked act that has left her pining for a lost love that was never consummated.

EAST RIDDLESDEN HALL
KEIGHLEY, WEST YORKSHIRE
Whose Hand Rocks the Cradle?

East Riddlesden Hall, a mid-17th-century gentry house that possesses one of the finest medieval barns in Yorkshire, seems to ooze mystery and intrigue from every pore, and ghosts galore are said to swirl both around and within its rustic brown walls.

There is the ubiquitous 'white lady', who is reputedly the bedraggled spectre of a former lady of the manor, who drowned in the fish pond after being thrown into it from her horse. There is also an equally traditional 'grey lady', whose sadistic husband once locked her away in her bedroom and left her to starve to death after he found her ***in flagrante*** with her lover. Inevitably, the anguish of her final weeks has proved eternal and she has remained at the place of her incarceration, a doomed spirit condemned to linger for as long as the old hall shall stand. It could be argued, however, that she fared somewhat better than her lover, who suffered the ignominy of being bricked up alive by the cuckolded husband. The lover is said to appear from time to time as a disembodied head floating in front of a window in the wall behind which he was incarcerated.

Another irregular phantom to have made his spectral home at East Riddlesden Hall is the ghostly Scotsman. In life he was reputedly a commercial traveller engaged in the wool trade. One night in 1790 he sought shelter at the house during a ferocious blizzard. The steward had come to hear of the small fortune that the man was carrying and duly informed his master. Together they killed their guest as he slept, and having disposed of his body, settled down to enjoy the rewards of their infamy. But the crime was discovered and the murderous steward was hanged at York. His master, however, was acquitted of any involvement. It is perhaps this blatant miscarriage of justice that brings the ghostly Scotsman back to East Riddlesden Hall, where he appears near the window over the front porch.

The final haunting occurs only on New Year's Eve and focuses on an antique wooden cradle that has been seen rocking back and forth. It is moved by an unseen hand as an invisible revenant marks the passing of the old year in a harmless fashion.

ABOVE: *A white lady who drowned in the fishpond and an ethereal Scotsman who was murdered in his sleep are just two of the ghosts that roam East Riddlesden Hall.*

TREASURER'S HOUSE
YORK, NORTH YORKSHIRE
Have You Seen The Romans?

Treasurer's House was originally home to the treasurers of York Minster. The holders of this office occupied successive buildings on the site from the 12th century until the Dissolution of the Monasteries (1536-1540), when Henry VIII's officers stripped York Minster of its assets in 1539. Although the last treasurer, William Clyffe, managed to cling to office for seven more years, he finally resigned his post in 1546, observing famously, abrepto omni thesauro, desuit thesaurarii munus ('there being no treasure left, there would seem to be no need for a treasurer'). The property then passed into private ownership and was largely rebuilt in the 17th century, although sections of the older building still survive in the cellar of the house.

It was here in 1953 that a young apprentice plumber named Harry Martindale was working one day when he heard the sound of a distant trumpet. His puzzlement intensified when this was followed by a second blast, this time much closer and, apparently, behind him. Turning round he was astonished when a horse's head suddenly emerged from the cellar wall. The rest of the horse's body together with a ghostly rider dressed in the regalia of a Roman soldier followed. The shock of the apparition sent the petrified apprentice tumbling from his

ABOVE: *Ghostly Roman soldiers have been seen to march nonchalantly through the cellar of York's magnificent Treasurer's House.*

ladder. Looking up, he saw other similarly attired figures following behind the horse and rider. Harry Martindale gazed in disbelief at the ragged detachment of around 16 soldiers, all of whom were cut off at the knees. Their heads were downcast, giving them a gloomy aura of utter dejection, and their appearance was grubby and dishevelled. They carried spears or swords, wore plumed helmets and kilt-like skirts. They shuffled across to the opposite wall where they melted slowly into the stone and were gone. Racing from the cellar, Harry chanced upon the curator of the building who took one look at his terrified face and said, 'You've seen the Roman's haven't you?'

It transpired that Harry Martindale was just one of a long line of people who had encountered the ghostly patrol in the cellar of the Treasurer's House. Later excavations unearthed a section of Roman road some 30 centimetres (12 inches) beneath the floor of the cellar. The ghostly soldiers would have been marching on this road and this would give them the appearance of being cut off at the knees.

BURTON AGNES HALL

DRIFFIELD, EAST YORKSHIRE

Alas Poor Anne

Burton Agnes Hall is a splendid example of late-Elizabethan architecture and is crowded with an eclectic mix of carvings, paintings and period furnishings. As befits a house of such antiquity it has a few ghosts roaming its palatial interior. There is the lady in the long gown who has been known to glide gracefully into one of the bedrooms and settle herself in a chair by the fireplace. There is the headless woman who was once sighted in the Norman undercroft. There is the delicate fragrance of ghostly perfume that has been known to hang in the air for a few moments after certain rooms have been unlocked by staff on some mornings. However, none of this ghostly activity comes close to matching the most famous relic at the hall, the skull of 'Awd Nance'.

When Sir Henry Griffith began building his splendid manor house his enthusiasm for the project knew no bounds. His three daughters, Margeret, Frances and Anne, shared his keenness, and following his death saw to it that the property was completed in accordance with their father's wishes. The most dedicated of them was Anne who went about extending and perfecting the house with a gusto that exceeded even that shown by her father. Sadly, she was not to enjoy the completed property for long.

In 1620, with the building finally completed, she set off to visit Lady St Quentin at nearby Harpham Hall. On her way back she was attacked and robbed by a gang of footpads who left her battered, bleeding and barely alive. She was carried back to Burton Agnes Hall where she languished for several days before dying from her injuries. But before she died, she made her sisters promise that they would keep her head at the hall, so that part of her at least would remain in residence forever in the house she loved so much.

No sooner was Anne dead than her sisters forgot all about the morbid pledge and she was buried, head and all, in the nearby churchyard. Her sisters soon had cause to regret their actions, for a wave of poltergeist activity swept through the family home. Crashes and bangs echoed throughout the hours of darkness. Doors opened and closed of their own accord. Agitated footsteps stomped back and forth over floorboards. But worse of all was the moaning, wailing and howling that echoed from supposedly empty rooms. Eventually, the two terrified sisters consulted the local

ABOVE: *Mayhem usually ensues when anyone attempts to remove the skull of 'Awd Nance' from Yorkshire's Burton Agnes Hall.*

vicar and told him of the promise they had made. He advised them that if they were to have any peace, their sister's body must be exhumed and her skull returned to Burton Agnes in compliance with her final wishes.

It was with some trepidation that Anne's coffin was raised from her grave and the lid removed. There inside lay the shrouded body of Anne Griffith, perfectly preserved except for the head. This had somehow become detached from the cadaver and was little more than a fleshless, gleaming skull. Overcoming their revulsion, the onlookers lifted the grisly relic from the coffin and carried it back to Burton Agnes Hall where it has remained ever since.

The poltergeist activity ceased and successive generations of the Griffith family were able to enjoy their home without further ghostly interference. The skull has supposedly only ever been removed twice since then. On one occasion it was buried in the garden, but this resulted in a return to the bad old days of wailing and moaning, and so it was once more dug up and taken back inside. Another time a maidservant, who was new to the hall, came across it and threw it out of a window in disgust. It landed in a passing cart, whereupon the donkey that was pulling the vehicle became suddenly transfixed and stood rooted to the spot, unable to move. However, the girl soon told the family what she had done and they were able to retrieve their heirloom and bring it back indoors. The moment they did so the donkey shuddered and was once more able to move as if a spell had been broken.

Today the skull is no longer on show at Burton Agnes Hall, because it has long been bricked up behind one of the walls to ensure that it will always remain in the house, according to Anne's wishes. Visitors can admire a portrait of Anne looking decidedly uncomfortable in a large ruff collar and standing alongside her two sisters. Every so often, her ghost is said to wander the corridors and rooms of the house she helped to build, and from which part of her at least will never depart.

REDWORTH HALL HOTEL
NEWTON AYCLIFFE, COUNTY DURHAM
A Ghostly Challenge

Redworth Hall Hotel is a beautiful Georgian building that dates from 1744 and which stands in 25 acres of gorgeous grounds. It retains a few ghosts that have chosen to remain within its mellowed walls. In the 1980s the hotel became something of a magnet to ghost hunters and many of them went away convinced that the house was very haunted indeed. Reported ghostly activity included a number of cold spots around the building, the sound of a baby coughing and crying in an empty room, a phantom piper and a mysterious ghostly figure seen sitting in front of the fire in the lounge.

In 1990, the management decided to throw caution to the wind and offered a reward of £5,000 to anyone who could prove beyond a shadow of a doubt that supernatural activity did indeed occur at the hall. The challenge was accepted by a team made up of a medium, two paranormal investigators and a journalist. Straight away the medium picked up on a man who had apparently committed suicide in the tower. The team later learnt that the hall had once been a home for disturbed children and that a member of staff had indeed hanged himself there. In the course of a subsequent séance phantom footsteps were heard crossing the floor of a room that was known to be empty. The medium made contact with the spirit of a Lady Catherine who claimed to have committed suicide over two centuries ago. Interestingly, local legend maintains that the hall is haunted by a 'Grey Lady' who flung herself from the clock tower in despair after finding herself betrothed to a man she didn't love.

All in all the team appear to have come up with a reasonably impressive amount of information regarding the ghosts of the hall, although none of it proved impressive enough for the hotel's management who decided that the data was insufficient to warrant the £5,000 reward.

BELOW: *Did a long-ago resident's suicide spark off the haunting that once afflicted Redworth Hall Hotel?*

CROOK HALL
FRANKLAND LANE, DURHAM
Ghost on Tour

This beautiful medieval manor house dates from the 13th century. It boasts a splendid banqueting hall, has Jacobean and Georgian extensions and is the ghostly abode of that traditional mainstay of all haunted houses, a 'white lady'. In the Hall's Jacobean room there is an old flight of ancient wooden steps, which go up to the ceiling and abruptly stop. It is on this staircase that the mysterious lady is most frequently seen. It is believed, though by no means proven, that she is the earthbound spirit of the niece of a former owner of Crook Hall, Cuthbert Billingham. He was an irascible character who inherited the Hall in 1615. His niece is said to have been very beautiful and very pale, a description which tallies with witness descriptions of the 'white lady'. Nobody, however, seems to know her name, or what long ago act, infamous or otherwise, has caused her to wander the hall. In 2002 Keith and Maggie Bell, owners of Crook Hall, launched a ghost tour of their house. On one tour Maggie was standing up in the gallery talking to her audience in the hall below and began telling them the story of the 'white lady'. No sooner had she done so than she felt a brisk tap on her shoulder. 'I literally jumped,' she later told the ***Northern Echo***. 'I assumed it was someone from the tour messing around and having a bit of fun to give me a fright. But I turned round and there was no one there. Not wishing to frighten the party I just carried on with my talk. Later on though a woman in the party approached me and said. "that was the White Lady, wasn't it?"'

ABOVE: *A tap on the shoulder gave Crook Hall's owner, Maggie Bell, a bit of a shock during a ghost tour in 2002.*

WASHINGTON OLD HALL
WASHINGTON VILLAGE, COUNTY DURHAM
I Cannot Tell a Lie: It's The Ghost.

This lovely old manor house dates largely from the 17th century. The structure does incorporate parts of a previous building, however, that was built in 1183 by William de Hertburne, who upon acquiring lands at what was then called Wessington, became William de Wessington. Over succeeding centuries Wessington became Washington and the Wessingtons became the Washingtons (their most famous descendant being George Washington).

In 1613 the hall was purchased by William James, the Bishop of Durham, and it was he who pulled down much of the old fabric and replaced it with the medium-sized dwelling that greets visitors today. The centuries that followed did not deal kindly with the fortunes of the good Bishop's house, and by 1891 it had been partitioned into family units. The census of that year records 35 people living at the hall. Evidently pride in the heritage of their home was not high on the list of the tenants' priorities, and by 1936 the building was declared unfit for human habitation and its future seemed uncertain. But then a dedicated band of enthusiasts took up the cause to raise awareness of its importance and with funding from both America and Britain, it was restored to its former glory.

'THAT WAS THE WHITE LADY, WASN'T IT?'

CROOK HALL

Now run under the auspices of the National Trust, visitors can immerse themselves in the ambience of a bygone era, mull over the house's American connections and keep keen eyes peeled for the ethereal ramblings of the resident phantom - the ghostly 'grey lady'. This unassuming revenant roams the upper floors of the house clothed in a long, grey dress and is occasionally seen weeping, although the cause of her grief is not known. The building's Great Hall is sometimes used as a wedding venue, and there have been occasions when the 'grey lady' has appeared as an uninvited guest at ceremonies, although it should be stressed that she is in no way malevolent and not in the least bit frightening.

Edenhall Country Hotel

Edenhall, Penrith, Cumbria

The Ghostly Revenant Resident

Edenhall Hotel was originally known as Woodbine Cottage and its oldest parts may well date back to the mid-17th century. Its interior presents an intriguing mishmash of fixtures and fittings. The overall impression is that the building has been simply cobbled together whenever its owners have been moved by the whim to extend. The hotel is haunted by several ghosts, one of which, a female phantom, appears to have a great fondness for what was formerly Room 25. It is held in such high esteem that people actually request that particular bedroom in the hope of making her acquaintance. Some guests have spoken of witnessing her materializing from out of the mirror as they have been relaxing in the bath, whilst others have reported waking in the dead of night to find her sitting on the bottom of their bed.

Mirrors seem to play an important part in the ghostly activity at Edenhall Hotel. Several members of staff working in the bar area often used to see the reflection of someone walking past them in the mirror on the opposite wall from the bar. So frequent were these sightings that the owner had the mirror taken down. Although it put an end to the ghostly reflections, it did little to deter the spectral appearances and several staff reported seeing an old woman sitting in a chair in the corner of the room. Having acknowledged her, they would go about their business, only to be taken aback when a few minutes later they looked up to find that the old woman had vanished.

In 2004 the hotel underwent a major refurbishment and many of its furnishings were replaced, including the mirror from which the ghost of Room 25 liked to emerge. In the process the room numbers were also changed and thus those who might arrive in search of a decent night's unrest should be sure to request the haunted hospitality of Room 4. Sweet dreams!

Wallington Hall

Morpeth, Northumberland

The Ghostly Fluttering

Wallington Hall was constructed in 1688 over the cellars of an earlier medieval property. Much of its interior dates from the 18th century, although the central hall is a 19th-century addition and was decorated by John Ruskin and William Bell

Scott. From 1777 to 1942 it was owned by the Trevelyan family and is now run by the National Trust. In 1697 Sir John Fenwick was executed for plotting to assassinate William III. His horse, Sorrel, was confiscated and used by the King, who was one day riding it in Richmond Park when it stumbled on a mole hill and threw him. William later died of his injuries.

Whether the haunting of Wallington has anything to do with the executed Sir John Fenwick is uncertain, but there have been reports over the years of a sound 'like invisible birds' wings' being heard beating against the windows of the house. From time to time people have also reported the disturbing sound of heavy breathing behind them, but when they turn to investigate there is never anybody there.

ABOVE: *Washington Old Hall was once owned by the ancestors of George Washington, although the ghostly lady that haunts it appears to belong to another era.*

HOLLOW WALLS AND

Go! Crown with thorns thy gold-crowned head,
Change thy glad song to song of pain;
Wind and wild wave have got thy dead,
And will not yield them back again.

What profit now that we have bound
The whole round world with nets of gold,
If hidden in our heart is found
The care that groweth never old.

From 'Ave Imperatrix'
by Oscar Wilde (1854-1900)

Lurking Terrors

SCOTLAND

The ghosts that inhabit Scotland's haunted houses can be ethereal reminders of the days when this was a divided nation and the animosity between Highlanders and Lowlanders led to many a bloody conflict. They can be star-crossed lovers left earth-bound by long ago acts of betrayal. They can be battle-hardened warriors who made one last valiant attempt to restore the Stuarts to the throne of England, only to see their hopes and aspirations dashed in the mud of Culloden (1746) with the defeat of Bonnie Prince Charlie. All of them inhabit a land where the past has never really died and where the memories of a turbulent history can be both poignant and fascinating. One of my favourite discoveries on this part of my journey was the wonderful Spynie Palace. It has an atmosphere that is both terrifying and enthralling. I would urge all who seek an encounter with the otherworldly spirit so lacking in many of our everyday lives to visit this magical place.

KEY

1. Traquair House
2. Dalzell House
3. Balinakill Country House Hotel
4. Falkland Place
5. The Prince's House Hotel
6. Ravenswood House
7. Meldrum House
8. Leith Hall
9. Spynie Palace

TRAQUAIR HOUSE

NR. INNERLEITHAN, BORDERS

Where the Infant James VI Slept

The dazzling white walls of Traquair House rise majestically from the rolling countryside. To cross its threshold is to find yourself wandering through passages and corridors where time stands still. Ancestral portraits gaze down from time-worn walls. Stone stairwells spiral upwards to meandering corridors, where with each step you find yourself falling under the spell of a house that has enjoyed continuous habitation for longer than any other in Scotland, and which claims to have played host to no fewer than 27 Scottish monarchs. Mary Queen of Scots came here with Lord Darnley in 1566, and the cradle in which their infant (later King James VI of Scotland and I of England) slept is still on show in the room that they occupied.

Bonnie Prince Charlie arrived during his 1745 campaign to reclaim the English throne. At the time hopes of success were running high, and as the Prince left the house through the Bear Gates (so-called because of the two stone bears that surmount the sturdy gateposts) the 5th Earl of Traquair locked them behind him and vowed that they would not be opened until a Stuart once more sat upon the throne. When hopes for a Stuart restoration were dashed in the blood-spattered carnage of Culloden (1746) the gates remained locked, and today's visitors approach the house via a driveway that bypasses the Bear Gates.

Given its tumultuous and emotional past, ghosts are conspicuous by their absence in the house. However, the solemn wraith of at least one former resident has been seen wandering the grounds. A portrait of Lady Louisa Stewart, sister of the 9th Earl of Traquair, and the last Stewart lady to live there, can be seen inside the house. She died in 1896 a few months short of her 100th birthday. Perhaps it was the disappointment at not reaching her centenary that brought her ghost back in the early years of the 20th century? One day a groundsman was ploughing in the fields when he saw a lady in old-fashioned clothing come drifting towards him. He watched in astonishment as she walked by him, passed effortlessly through a closed gate into the wood beyond and disappeared. He was later able to identify the fabric of the dress that his ghostly visitor was wearing from a book of fabrics shown to him by a woman who had been Lady Louisa's dressmaker.

DALZELL HOUSE

NR. MOTHERWELL, LANARKSHIRE

Was She Walled Up Alive?

Nestling in a well-wooded park, Dalzell House is one of the finest mansions of the Scottish Lowlands and boasts an impressive pedigree that stretches far back into the foggy mists of time. The present structure is an eclectic mix of buildings that cluster around a largely complete 15th-century fortified tower house. Originally, the home of the Dalzell earls of Carnforth who owned the estate from the 13th to the 17th century, when the then earl, Robert, was found guilty of treason and sentenced to death. The sentence,

PREVIOUS PAGES: *A long-ago duelist is just one of the ghosts that haunts the timeless corridors of Scotland's Leith Hall.*

BELOW: *Bonnie Prince Charlie and Mary, Queen of Scots are just two illustrious visitors who have enjoyed the hospitality on offer at Traquair House.*

RIGHT: *Green and White Ladies are known to wander the corridors at Dalzell House, one of the finest mansion houses in the Scottish Lowlands.*

however, was commuted and instead he was stripped of rank, titles and lands and fined 100,000 Scots merks. The earldom and estates passed to his son, Gavin, who in 1649 sold the house to the Hamiltons of Boggs, to pay his father's fine.

In 1886 John Glencairn Carter Hamilton was created the first Baron Hamilton of Dalzell and the house hosted many royal visits, with at least five of Queen Victoria's children dropping by to enjoy its hospitality. William Ewart Gladstone was also a visitor and in the grounds there is still a small round building known as 'Gladstone's Tearoom'.

Although the house itself is private, the grounds that surround it are open to the public and from there you can gaze upon its sturdy walls and ponder the ghosts of the 'green', 'grey' and 'white' ladies that are said to wander through the house. The 'green lady' is a spectral fixture of the house's South Wing and her ghostly wanderings are often accompanied by the distinct scent of sweet perfume. The 'grey lady' favours the North Wing and may well be the ghost of a nurse from the days when it was used as a hospital during the First World War. The 'white lady' is apparently of no fixed abode and can suddenly appear unannounced at sundry locations around the property. One tradition holds that she is the shade of a former maidservant, who having become pregnant was so overcome by despair that she threw herself to her death from the upper storeys. Another story maintains that she was bricked up somewhere in the house as punishment for some long-forgotten indiscretion, and it is this that has caused her spirit to roam the night hours. People walking in the park at dusk have reported the unnerving sensation of being watched and some have even caught glimpses of a forlorn female gazing at them from the windows of the house, although her form is not distinctive enough for them to be sure of the hue of their phantom observer.

Balinakill Country House Hotel

Nr. Tarber, Argyll

The Shipping Magnate's Sumptuous Haunted Home

Balinakill House was built by Sir William Mackinnon. Born in nearby Campletown he began his working life in the grocery trade before setting off at the age of twenty-four to seek his fortune in India. In 1856 he founded the British India Steam Navigation Company. Beginning with just one steamer that sailed between Calcutta and Rangoon, Mackinnon forged it

grand baronial house, Balinakill. Here he entertained the likes of the explorer David Livingstone, whom he had met in Africa, and here too came Leopold II, King of the Belgians. In 1895 it was announced that Queen Victoria herself was to honour him with a visit, but before she could do so Sir William Mackinnon died during a visit to London.

Today, his baronial country house operates as a sumptuous hotel and the whole building is charged with an atmosphere that is as spiritual as it is historic. The long, dark corridors are lined with Victorian furnishings and antiques, but the rooms to which they lead are light and airy, thanks to the high ceilings and huge windows. It has its ghosts, though they are harmless and not in the least malevolent. They are content to occupy their time in mischievous pursuits such as moving or hiding objects. The fact that in one bedroom guests can sometimes enjoy the soothing sensation of being tucked in at night by an unseen 'someone' seems perfectly in keeping with the overall ambience of a house where the past and present appear to merge so completely and comfortably.

into one of the greatest shipping companies in the world and in the process made his fortune. He would later turn his attention and business skills to East Africa and become friends with the Sultan of Zanzibar, and go on to found the Imperial East Africa Company. Although he became the very embodiment of Victorian entrepreneurial zeal he never forgot his Scottish roots and only Campletown Malt Whisky was ever served on his ships. Many a Kintyre youngster began his working life with the British India Line. He also took a warm interest in the language and literature of the Highlands, to which end he provided bursaries for local boys with a knowledge of Gaelic.

In 1889 he was created a baronet and over the next few years settled down to enjoy the ample fruits of his labour, living in sumptuous style and entertaining lavishly at his

FALKLAND PALACE

FALKLAND, FIFE

He Died With A Sigh

Falkland, with its picturesque old houses and cobbled streets, sits at the foot of the Lomond Hills and is one of the loveliest towns in Scotland. Its chief glory is the graceful and beautiful Falkland Palace, once a favoured residence of Scottish kings. It soars majestically over the main street and behind its walls many an intrigue of Scottish politics has unfolded. David, Duke of Rothesay, son of Robert III was imprisoned there in 1402 by his uncle Robert, Duke of Albany, who proceeded to starve his unfortunate nephew to death.

It was at Falkland Palace that James V lay ill when news was brought to him that his wife, Mary of Guise, had given birth to a daughter - the future and ill-fated Mary, Queen of Scots. The disappointment of having a daughter rather than a son is said to have hastened his demise, but before he died he observed wearily of the Stuart dynasty, which had started with Marjorie, the daughter of Robert the Bruce, that 'it began with a lass and will end with a lass'.

Mary, Queen of Scots was a frequent visitor and loved its country air and relaxed pace of life. However, when her son, James VI, took his court to London, Falkland's days of glory were over and its fortunes went into a steady decline until its was burnt by Cromwell's troops in the mid-17th century. Restored in 1887 it is now open to visitors and offers an eclectic mix of art treasures and curiosities, not least of which is the original royal tennis court, the oldest still in use in Britain, which dates back to 1539.

Unusually for a building that was associated with her, Falkland Palace is not haunted by the ghost of Mary, Queen of Scots but by another female resident from its distant past, although her identity is unknown. She has a propensity for visiting the tapestry gallery and her most notable feature is the greyish light which she exudes as she drifts her weary path in front of incredulous witnesses. There is a tradition that she was once the lover of a soldier who went off to fight in a battle from which he never returned. Ever since, her solemn shade has roamed the palace in search of her lover, and only when the two are reunited will she be able to find rest. As with many ghost stories the identities of the protagonists are now long forgotten and the only solace for the poor wretch is that there can be few finer places than the beautiful corridors of Falkland Palace to be condemned to wander for evermore.

ABOVE AND OPPOSITE: *Falkland Palace is a Glorious Pile of Ancient Stone, it is also haunted by a long ago lady who seeks her soldier lover.*

THE PRINCE'S HOUSE HOTEL

FORT WILLIAM, INVERNESS-SHIRE

The Giant and The Ghost

Set against a stunning backcloth of moody hills, the Prince's House dates back to 1658 when it started life as a 'change house', providing shelter and fresh horses for travellers travelling 'The Road to the Isles'. It stands close to the spot where Bonnie Prince Charlie raised his standard in 1745, an act that signalled the start of the Jacobite uprising. Although there are no records of the Prince ever staying here, there are suggestions that he may well have dropped in for a 'wee dram'.

By the 1840s the 'Stage House', as the building was then known, had become a notable coaching halt for Victorian travellers. Its keeper had even achieved a modicum of fame as the tallest man in Scotland, although there is some debate as to his exact stature - six feet seven according to one account, seven feet six according to another.

It is, of course, inevitable that some of those who have crossed the threshold of this delightful white-walled house have chosen not to leave, and at least two ghosts are known to haunt it. One is a 'grey lady' who in the past appears to have been sighted regularly on the stairs, although the current proprietors, Kieron and Ina Kelly, have yet to make her acquaintance. The other is the ghost of a bearded Highlander who occasionally wanders the building, bothering nobody as he keeps to a routine that he no doubt established in life and is loathe to give up in death.

RAVENSWOOD HOUSE

BALLATER, ABERDEENSHIRE

An Apparition in An Arran Sweater

Wandering around the cosy interior of Ravenswood House, you might chance upon a bearded figure, wearing an Arran sweater, the arms of which are rolled up to the elbows to reveal an old-fashioned long-sleeved vest. You might bid him 'good day' and might even be tempted to exchange a few pleasantries. What you might not realize is that you have met one of the two resident ghosts that wander the cosy and little-changed interior of this delightful hotel.

It is presumed that he is the ghost of the house's builder and original owner, a seafaring man who erected the property in 1820. Strangely, since his cargoes consisted largely of tea and alcohol, for some reason a clause was inserted into the lease

ABOVE: *Many people who encounter the spectral seafarer at Ravenswood House remain convinced he is flesh and blood until told they have met with the ghost.*

that forbade the house to sell either alcohol or tea. Such a ban presented few problems whilst the building remained a family home. But in 1970, the house became a hotel and the new proprietors set about overturning the restrictive clause. The ban on the sale of alcohol was lifted, but the one on tea was not. Thus the current owners, Scott and Cathy Fyfe, will happily sell their guests the cup, spoon, water and milk, but the accompanying tea bag is on the house!

The roving, sea-faring shade has been encountered by many guests and all have commented on how solid and real he looks. Many of them have not even realized his true nature until they have asked Scott or Cathy who he is and are told that they have been honoured with a sighting of the house's ghost.

Ravenswood's other ghostly inhabitant is a spectral nanny who only becomes active when small children come to stay. She has never actually been seen, but babies sleeping in cots have been heard over the monitoring intercoms gurgling and calling 'nanny' to some unseen presence. When adults go to investigate they often find the child staring at someone that it can apparently see but which adults cannot. On some occasions laughing babies have even pointed to their feet as if their ghostly supervisor is tickling them. No one finds her antics in the least bit frightening and all who have encountered her have commented that it feels as though her sole intention is to watch over children who come to stay and to ensure that no harm befalls them.

MELDRUM HOUSE

OLD MELDRUM, GRAMPIAN

Her Ladyship is Still At Home

The history-steeped walls of Meldrum House sit peaceably amidst glorious woodland and parkland. Reached via a long drive that winds past an 18-hole golf course, the house itself is a sprawling baronial mansion with impressive round towers and exquisite chimney stacks. Its origins date back to the 13th century, although considerable additions and renovations were carried out in the 17th, 19th and 20th centuries.

The house's oldest resident is the mysterious 'white lady'. She is believed to be the ghost of Isabella Douglas, whose portrait hangs above the fireplace in the hotel's cosy reception area. Women in particular are susceptible to her spectral attentions and several housekeepers have reported feeling their apron strings being tugged by her invisible hand. Her shade has frequently been seen around the hotel and she often appears when the air is heavy with thunder. In 1985, during a raging thunderstorm she gave a male guest quite a shock when she suddenly appeared from nowhere and planted a cold kiss upon his cheek. At other times staff can actually tell whether she is happy or agitated by the way in which her phantom moves around. If she is content, she walks slowly but should she be discontented she will glide around the premises, chilling the blood of any who encounter her. She seems to have settled down considerably since her portrait was moved from elsewhere in the hotel to its current position over the fire. Maybe it's because she is now able to greet guests as they enter her house, but as one member of staff told me, 'she's been a lot happier since the move'.

Finally, should a male guest who is even remotely descended from either the Meldrum, Seton or Urquhart families (the three dynasties with whom the house's history is most inextricably linked) be placed in Room 3, he can look forward to being woken in the night by the alarming sensation of an invisible female scratching his chest. The staff confess that they are at a loss as to whether or not the ghost of Isabella Douglas is actually responsible for this.

BELOW: *Leith Hall basks in its own glorious grounds and is a stunning slice of haunted Scotland.*

LEITH HALL, HUNTLY, ABERDEENSHIRE

A Shot in the Night

Leith Hall enjoys a lovely location amidst peaceful and rolling countryside. It is a squat, grey building resplendent with round towers and an abundance of chimneys. Although owned by the National Trust for Scotland it possesses the intimate feel of a family home, due largely to the fact that for over 300 years, from its construction in the mid-17th century to its handing over to the Trust in 1945, it was owned and lived in by successive generations of the Leith family. Following the tragic death of the last laird in a motorcycle accident in 1939, his mother set about researching the lives and histories of the Leith ancestors. Although stating that

'SOME OF [THE FAMILY] COME OUT OF THE SHADOWS INTO CLEAR LIGHT AND LIVE AND SPEAK.'

LEITH HALL

'There is no haunting', she did acknowledge that 'some of [the family] come out of the shadows into clear light and live and speak.'

One former family member who most certainly does haunt the house is John Leith, the 3rd Laird. At the age of twenty-five he married Hariott Steuart of Auchlunchart, and set about turning Leith Hall into a suitable family home. She bore him three sons and was pregnant with a fourth when, just before Christmas 1763, John rode to Aberdeen to dine with friends. Copious amounts of alcohol flowed at the meal and John reacted angrily when one of the diners accused him of adulterating the grain sold from Leith Hall. There is confusion as to what happened next. Either John challenged his detractor to a duel or else his accuser simply shot him in cold blood. Whichever, on Christmas Day 1736 John Leith died from the head wound he received, and his widow was left to run the estate as best she could.

The tragedy appears to have left an indelible stain on the psychic fabric of Leith Hall, and his ghost has been both sensed and seen at several locations. In 1968, guests who were sleeping in the Master Bedroom reported that they found its atmosphere somewhat unsettling. Their discomfort was not helped by the fact that in the early hours of one morning, the wife awoke to find a man in Highland dress, his head swathed in bloody bandages, standing at the foot of the bed. She later commented that he bore an uncanny resemblance to the portrait of John Leith that hangs elsewhere in the house. A female ghost of unknown identity, but dressed in the garb of the 18th century, has also been seen about the property, whilst ghostly footsteps and slamming doors have been known to shatter the silence of the night hours.

It would seem that the ghosts of those to whom this lovely old house has been home are still active about the property, and there are certainly parts of it where you can sense them gazing at you across the centuries, telling you in no uncertain terms that this is their house, and though you are welcome to visit, it is strictly on their terms.

SPYNIE PALACE

NR. ELGIN, MORAY

Ghostly Skulls and Phantom Photos

For over 500 years Spynie Palace was the seat of the bishops of Moray, and its hollow shell looks back at past ages of grandeur and glory, whilst the march of history is etched into its time-scarred walls. It nestles in quiet seclusion, almost lost amidst tranquil countryside, and to discover its rambling ruins is to walk in the footsteps of kings and queens, not to mention a rich array of historical and legendary figures from Scotland's past.

One of the more infamous of its residents was Alexander Stewart, Earl of Buchan, whose mob of 'wyld wykkd Heland-men' torched the town of Elgin in 1390 and burnt its cathedral. Whether Spynie Palace suffered damage at this time is not known, but Alexander Stewart - known to history as the 'Wolf of Badenoch' - was later appointed Keeper of the Palace by King Robert III, following the death of the then bishop in 1397. Although his tenure was no more than a year, he appears to have found its allure irresistible, and his sinister spectre has been seen many times leaning on a railing on the first-floor landing of David's Tower, gazing down at people with seemingly wicked intent.

It is within and around the unyielding bulk of David's Tower (named for Bishop David Stewart who began its construction in the 15th century) that much of Spynie Palace's paranormal activity is centred. Visitors approaching it have caught glimpses of a hazy face gazing at them from its upper storeys. Once inside you find yourself almost overwhelmed by the vastness of the stone walls that soar six storeys above you. The inner walls and vaults have long since collapsed leaving a shell to whose sides a tenacious covering of dull plaster clings defiantly. Mysterious rooms and dark recesses are set into the tower's east wall and here a veritable cornucopia of phantoms and presences are known to lurk.

Many visitors have reported sighting a ghostly woman sitting in an arched niche to the tower's right side as they enter. Trudging up to the next floor and traipsing along the narrow stone corridor, some people have been overcome by a nauseous feeling accompanied by a headache. However, all they have to do is politely say 'excuse me', step to one side and the feeling quickly passes, as the unseen entity responsible simply moves on by. More disturbing is the column of white mist, human in size, that has been known to materialize in mid-air and drift briskly towards astonished witnesses. On one occasion this unnerving phenomenon succeeded in knocking a startled sceptic to the ground as it swept over him. A mysterious phantom skull often appears on photographs taken inside the tower, as does the indistinct form of a ghostly lion, said to be the revenant of a pet once owned by one of the bishops.

Spynie Palace is one of Scotland's eeriest and most haunted buildings, yet it possesses an atmosphere that both captivates and engrosses. Its history is fascinating, its location enchanting and its ambience is greatly enhanced by the chance of an encounter with a resident wraith.

OPPOSITE: *Now a hollow shell, Spynie Palace was once a grand Bishop's residence. Today it is home to a ghostly woman, and, stranger still, a ghostly lion.*

FURTHER READING

Abbott, Geoffrey *Ghosts of the Tower of London*, Heinemann, 1980

Adams, Norman *Haunted Scotland,* Mainstream, 1998

Alexander, Marc *Phantom Britain*, Muller, 1975

Baldwin, Gay *Ghost Island. Books One to Five*, Gay Baldwin, 2004

Brooks, J.A. *Ghosts and Witches of the Cotswolds*, Jarrold, 1981

Brooks, J.A. *Ghosts and Legends of the Lake District*, Jarrold, 1988

Byrne, Thomas *Tales From The Past*, Ironmarket,1977

Clarke, David *Ghosts and Legends of the Peak District*, Jarrold, 1991

Coventry, Martin *Haunted Places of Scotland*, Goblinshead, 1999

Coxe, Anthony D. Hippisley *Haunted Britain,* Pan, 1975

Dunne, John J. *Irish Ghosts*, Appletree Press, 1977

Forman, Joan *Haunted East Anglia*, Jarrrold, 1993

Green, Andrew *Our Haunted Kingdom,* Fontana/Collins, 1973

Hallam, Jack *The Haunted Inns of England*, Wolfe, 1972

Harper, Charles *Haunted Houses*, Bracken, Reprint, 1993

Jeffery, P.H. *Ghosts, Legends and Lore of Wales*, Orchard

Jones, Richard *Walking Haunted London*, New Holland, 1999

Jones, Richard *Haunted Britain and Ireland*, New Holland, 2001

Jones, Richard *Haunted Castles of Britain and Ireland*, New Holland, 2003

Jones, Richard *Haunted Inns of Britain and Ireland*, New Holland, 2004

Jones, Richard *Haunted London*, New Holland, 2004

Maddox, Brenda *George's Ghosts. A New Life Of W. B. Yeats*, Picador, 1999

Marsden, Simon *The Haunted Realm*, Little, Brown, 1986

Mason, John *Haunted Heritage*, Collins and Brown, 1999

Munthe, Malcolm *Hellens. The Story of a Herefordshire Manor*, Gerald Duckworth and Co Ltd, 1991

Puttick, Betty *Ghosts of Hertfordshire*, Countryside, 1994

Puttick, Betty *Ghosts of Essex*, Countryside, 1997

Puttick, Betty *Oxfordshire Stories of the Supernatural*, Countryside Books, 2003

Seafield, Lily *Scottish Ghosts*, Lomond, 1999

Turner, Mark *Folklore and Mysteries of the Cotswolds*, Hale, 1993

Underwood, Peter *This Haunted Isle*, Javelin, 1986

INDEX

Page numbers in **bold** refer to illustrations.

ACKNOWLEDGEMENTS

So many people helped with the researching and writing of this book. There were the staff at the numerous historic properties who answered my questions and graciously furnished me with updates on their hauntings. Ian Addicoat of the Paranormal Research Organisation; John Millington at the Cheshire Paranormal Society and Judy Farncombe of the online e-zine *www.psychic-tymes.com* were all particularly generous in sharing their information and experiences with me. Paul Keene and his team's investigations at Grace Dieu also proved invaluable. At Spynie Palace Lynda Dean was a treasure trove of historical information. Librarians all over Britain and Ireland were always willing to look up pieces of information. To all of you, and to those I haven't mentioned, I owe a very big thank you.

I'd like to thank Karl Beattie and Yvette Fielding of Living TV's *Most Haunted* for permission to report on things that have happened on their programme. Also, Richard Felix and Phil Wyman for providing me with usable quotes. At New Holland I'd like to thank Jo Hemmings, Charlotte Judet and Alan Marshall for their faith in the project and for their patience and assistance, and John Mason for his photography. I'd also like to pay tribute to Andrew Green, whose book *Our Haunted Kingdom* was instrumental in my initial interest in ghost stories and whose death in May 2004 was a great loss to the world of Paranormal Investigation.

On a personal note I'd like to thank my sister Geraldine Hennigan for her assistance and for being ever willing to lend an ear and proffer useful opinions. I'd like to thank my wife Joanne for being there for me and for the support she has always given so willingly and generously. A big thank you to my sons Thomas and William who accompanied me to several of the sites and who, not at all troubled by being just four and six, were happy to listen to my stories and offer critical appraisal. Finally, to those who have gone before and whose stories have made this book possible, as always, long may you wander but may it always be at peace.

Richard Jones

PHOTOGRAPHIC ACKNOWLEDGEMENTS

All photographs by John Mason except: p30 © Longleat House, Wiltshire www.longleat.co.uk, pp39, 43 (background), 51 (background), 53 (bottom), 58-59 (background), 80-81 (background), 109 (background) and 126-127 (background) New Holland/Alan Marshall, pp56 and 66 New Holland/Illustrated London News, p89 New Holland/The Outline of Literature, p97 © Mary Evans Picture Library, p114 © Llancaiach Fawr.